Ama Adhe

THE VOICE THAT REMEMBERS

AMA ADHE

THE VOICE THAT REMEMBERS

THE HEROIC STORY OF A WOMAN'S FIGHT TO FREE TIBET

BY

Adhe Tapontsang

AS TOLD TO JOY BLAKESLEE

Wisdom Publications • Boston

WISDOM PUBLICATIONS
199 ELM STREET
SOMERVILLE, MASSACHUSETTS 02144

Library of Congress Cataloging-in-Publication Data

Tapontsang, Adhe, 1932–
    Ama Adhe, the voice that remembers : the heroic story of a woman's fight to free Tibet / Adhe Tapontsang, as told to Joy Blakeslee.
      p.   cm.
    Includes bibliographical references.
    ISBN 0-86171-130-0 (alk. paper)
    1. Tapontsang, Adhe, 1932– . 2. Political prisoners—China—Biography.
3. Women in politics—China—Tibet—Biography. 4. Tibet (China)—Politics and government. I. Blakeslee, Joy. II. Title.
DS786.T37 1997
951'.505'092—dc21   97–18579
[B]

ISBN 0-86171-130-0

02 01 00 99 98
6 5 4 3 2

Front Cover Photo: HUGH SMITH
Design: LJ·SAWLit

Wisdom Publications' books are printed on acid-free paper and meet the guidelines for the permanence and durability of the Committee on Production Guidelines for Book Longevity of the Council on Library Resources.

Printed in the United States of America.

TABLE OF CONTENTS

PUBLISHER'S ACKNOWLEDGMENT

The publisher gratefully acknowledges the generous help of the Hershey Family Foundation in sponsoring the printing of this book.

FOREWORD

This book is a moving testimony of both the suffering and the heroism of the Tibetan people. It mostly concerns Ama Adhe, who spent twenty-seven years of her life in Chinese prisons. She and the members of her family were imprisoned because they participated in the Tibetan resistance movement that started in the early 1950s. It is people like them who have given the Tibetan struggle its impetus and endurance.

I am happy not only that people will be able to read Ama Adhe's story, but also that she survived to tell it. Hers is the story of all Tibetans who have suffered under the Chinese Communist occupation. It is also a story of how Tibetan women have equally sacrificed and participated in the Tibetan struggle for justice and freedom. As she herself says, hers is the "voice that remembers the many who did not survive."

I am convinced that people who read this book will come to understand the true extent of the suffering of the Tibetan people and the attempts that have been made to eliminate their culture and identity. I hope that as a result some may also be inspired to lend their support to the just cause of the Tibetan people.

Tenzin Gyatso
His Holiness the Dalai Lama

PREFACE

There are few stories that can be told that match the one you are about to read. It is the heroic story of one woman who sustained her human dignity, integrity, and compassion in the face of immense degradation and suffering. Imprisoned for twenty-seven years for her resistance to the Chinese occupation of Tibet, this extraordinary woman, Adhe Tapontsang, bears witness to the ongoing tragedy of the Tibetan people through the lens of her own experience. Unfortunately, the conditions described within this book have not disappeared; the hardships that Adhe tells of continue to prevail for the millions of Tibetans still living in Tibet.

My involvement with this story began in the summer of 1988. My friend Joan sat on the steps of her garden in upstate New York, showing me photographs of herself with her Tibetan friends in Dharamsala, India—the Himalayan village that became the headquarters of the Tibetan Government-In-Exile shortly after His Holiness the Dalai Lama's flight from Tibet in 1959. It was in Joan's garden, among the roses and daylilies, that I first heard of the terrible struggle and betrayal of a brave people overwhelmed by the calculated Communist invasion of their previously independent land.

Joan, knowing that she would soon die of cancer, had decided to spend her last days in Dharamsala, among the people she had come to love. As we said good-bye to each other, standing by her garden wall that summer day, I realized I would never see her again. She passed away in India the following winter.

The next spring, I visited Dharamsala for the first time, partly to meet the friends of whom she'd spoken so highly and partly to offer whatever help I could to the Tibetans. During that visit, I had the opportunity to meet with Tenzin Geyche, the personal secretary of the Dalai Lama, and to explore how I might be of service. When I returned to Dharamsala in the spring of 1990, the human rights officer of the Tibetan Government-in-Exile, Ngawang Drakmargyapon, introduced me to one of the most remarkable human beings I have ever met: Adhe Tapontsang.

At our first encounter, both Adhe and I immediately felt a deep affection and an inexplicable bond, which has deepened over the years. Adhe now considers me her adopted daughter. Likewise, I address her with the respectful and affectionate term "Ama," or mother, as she is known throughout the Tibetan community. She requested at that first meeting that I take the time to write down her story with special attention to the details that she wanted to relate; this included describing not only the wounds of her besieged land, but the precious memories of an ancient culture she had known before her arrest. Moved by her chilling story and her inspiring strength and integrity, I agreed to set down her tale, beginning with her idyllic childhood, through her long imprisonment, torture, and eventual release.

During our early interviews, Ama Adhe and I sat on two beds in a stark room in the refugee reception center in Dharamsala, accompanied by the human rights officer, Ngawang, who served as our translator. I listened with amazement as her story unfolded. When speaking of her youth, she closed her eyes, and her face was transformed into that of a laughing, lighthearted child. In contrast, reminiscences of her own incredible suffering were told with hardly any emotion. I struggled to maintain a similar degree of equanimity when, for example, she showed me a finger disfigured by the insertion of bamboo shoots beneath the nail. Throughout all of our interviews, the only times Ama Adhe cried were when she recalled the misery of others—the many family members, friends, and strangers whose tortures and terrible deaths she had witnessed.

The matter-of-fact tone with which Ama Adhe recounts her horrifying experiences is at times almost unsettling. However, the reader should understand that this tone is a reflection of the Tibetan language and culture itself. It has often been noticed by foreigners that Tibetans are disinclined to speak of their own lives in dramatic or tragic terms. This may be because dwelling on one's personal misfortunes implies self-centeredness—an undesirable trait from the Buddhist perspective that pervades Tibetan society. The selflessness implied by Ama Adhe's strikingly straightforward tone may be what enabled her to survive the horrible events she relates in this book.

Like many Tibetans, Ama Adhe had no formal education. Her story, therefore, reads like a richly woven oral narrative rather than a carefully wrought literary work. Wherever possible, I have left her stark narrative style and use of terminology intact. The Tibetan and Chinese terms, proper names, and locations that appear throughout the text are rendered phonetically as Ama Adhe pronounced them in her regional Kham dialect. Although this approach may not fully satisfy scholars of Tibet, I hope that it allows Ama Adhe's story to be encountered just as she told it to me in Dharamsala. Tibetan and Chinese terms are italicized at their first usage, and readers may refer to the glossary for further details and technical definitions. A summary of the main historical events in eastern Tibet during Ama Adhe's lifetime may help you to better appreciate the historical context of her story. Interested readers should refer to the appendix and bibliography at the back of the book.

Many people have been of tremendous assistance in the completion of this book. First, I must thank the many who shared their own experiences or family history with me: Ama Adhe's husband, Rinchen Samdup, provided indispensable information. Lodi Gyari, Executive Director of the International Campaign for Tibet in Washington, D.C., and his father, the Nyarong chieftain Gyari Nyima, provided much useful background regarding the Gyaritsang and Shivatsang families and life in Nyarong under Chinese rule. Mr. Kunga Gyaltsen, a member of the Shivatsang family, and his son, Chemey Tashi, provided information on Karze. For information on the 1959 uprising, I must thank Jughuma Tapontsang for his recollections, and Lobsang Tenpa for his written statement. Mr. Tenzing Atisha of the Department of Information and International Relations accompanied Adhe to the 1989 international hearing in Denmark and supplied useful information regarding her visit to that country.

Turning to written sources, I am indebted to His Holiness the Dalai Lama for information regarding his life as recounted in his autobiography, *My Land and My People*. For additional details describing the situation in eastern Tibet prior to the Communist occupation, I have referred to *Travels of a British Consular Officer in Eastern Tibet* by Eric Teichmann, and *Tibet and Its History* by Hugh Richardson. Jamyang Norbu's book, *Warriors of Tibet*, helped me verify certain events in Nyarong and Communist policies in eastern Kham. Prayers mentioned in Chapter 10 are quoted from Yeshe Tsondru's *The Essence of Nectar*, a poetic supplement to the Great Exposition of the Graded Path by the great thirteenth-century Buddhist scholar Tsongkhapa (with permission from the Library of Tibetan Works and Archives). Chapter 15's description of the Bonn Hearing draws upon transcripts of the hearing itself.

I must also thank the many who, in as many ways, helped with my research and the preparation of this manuscript. I would like to thank Sonam Topgyal of the Political Affairs Committee of the Kashag in Dharamsala, who, aside from Adhe herself, was my greatest source of inspiration and encouragement. Thanks to Tenzin Tethong for his encouragement and belief in the importance of this project. I would especially like to thank Ngawang Drakmargyapon, now of the Tibet Bureau in Geneva, who initiated this project and aided Adhe and me with translation. Thanks to all those whose names I do not know who aided Ama Adhe and me in our correspondence. Tashi Tsering, Tibetologist of the Tibetan Library and Archives in Dharamsala, provided many helpful suggestions regarding Tibetan culture and checked the text for accuracy. Mr. Adrian Moon, an independent researcher of Tibetan history, suggested invaluable source material. Pema Namgyal's son kindly translated many rare and useful documents. Tsetan Wangchuk, a Tibetan historian with Voice of America,j was tremendously helpful in translating Chinese texts and clarifying certain dates and statements. He and Jigme Ngapo of the International Campaign for Tibet helped me check the transliteration of Chinese words. Any remaining errors are my own oversight. Professor Eliot Sperling of Indiana University,

Bloomington, Indiana, aided us in suggesting sources. Tsetan Samdup of the London Office of Tibet kindly aided me in finding sources. Warren Smith, a historian of Tibet, was also an indispensable resource. Thanks to Meg Lundstrum and Garry Dorfman for proof-reading early versions of the manuscript, and to Robyn Bem, Sara Shneiderman, and the staff at Wisdom Publications, whose efforts brought this book into its final form. Finally, I would like to thank Alan Blakeslee, for all of his help and patience.

Ama Adhe and I hope that this book will serve as a voice for the Tibetan people in the remembrance of the many who have not survived and who continue to be threatened by the ongoing Chinese occupation of Tibet.

Although the circumstances of her life are tragic, the wisdom, strength, and courage that Ama Adhe sustained through those many torturous years place her among those rare human beings who would not turn their backs on those in need or repeat a doctrine they did not believe in. To Tibetans, Adhe is a symbol of courage and determination; to me, she speaks for a people who against great odds valiantly maintain their culture, their religion, and their inner freedom.

Joy Blakeslee
Oneonta, NY
June 1997

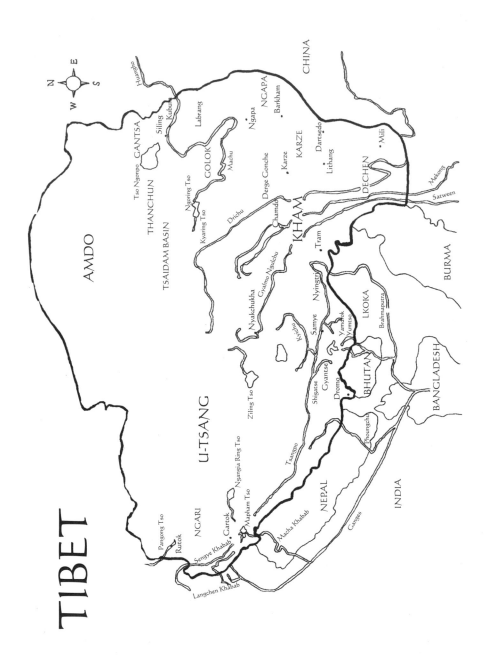

TIBET

AMDO

NGARI

U-TSANG

KHAM

NGAPA

KARZE

DECHEN

GOLOK

GANTSA

THANCHUN

TSAIDAM BASIN

LKOKA

BHUTAN

NEPAL

INDIA

BURMA

BANGLADESH

CHINA

N
E
W
S

Pangong Tso
Rutok
Sengye Khabab
Cartok
Mapham Tso
Ngangla Ring Tso
Langchen Khabab
Macha Khabab
Ganges
Tsangpo
Brahmaputra
Phoungchu
Dromo
Gyantse
Shigatse
Samye
Kyichu
Nyingtri
Yamdok
Yumtso
Tram
Ziling Tso
Nyakchukha
Gyalmo Ngulchu
Drichu
Chamdo
Derge Gonche
Karze
Lithang
Dartsedo
Mili
Machu
Ngapa
Barkham
Labrang
Siling
Kubun
Huangho
Tso Ngompo
Ngoring Tso
Kyaring Tso
Mekong
Satween

PART ONE

BEFORE
THE YEARS OF
SORROW

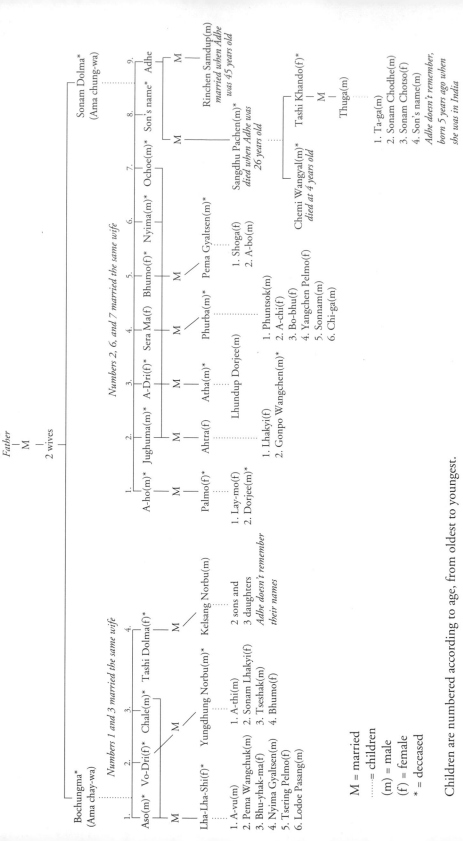

Children are numbered according to age, from oldest to youngest.

PROLOGUE

I have traveled a long distance from the land of my youth, from the dreams and innocence of childhood, and have come to see a world that many of my fellow Tibetans could never have dreamed of.

There was no choice but for me to make this journey. Somehow, I have survived, a witness to the voices of my dying compatriots, my family and friends. Those I once knew are gone, and I have given them my solemn promise that somehow their lives will not be wiped out, forgotten, and confused within a web of history that has been rewritten by those who find it useful to destroy the memory of many I have known and loved. Fulfilling this promise is the only purpose remaining in my life.

As a witness, I have prepared long and carefully. I do not understand the reason that this has come to be my part to play; but I understand very well the purpose of what must be said. Although the world is a bigger place than I had dreamed, it is not so large that all its inhabitants are not somehow connected. Sooner or later, actions make their way in a chain of effects from one person to another, from one country to another, until a circle is completed. I speak not only of the past that lives in me, but of the waves that spring from the rock thrown into the water, moving farther and farther until they reach the shore.

I am free now. There are no guards outside my door. There is enough to eat. Yet an exile can never forget the severed roots of beginnings, the precious fragments of the past carried always within the heart. My greatest desire is to return to the land of my birth. That will not be possible until Tibet is once again the land of her own people. At this time, I am considered an outlaw by the Chinese administration because I have chosen not to lower my head and try to forget the years of slavery that so many of my people have endured.

But I can remember back beyond the years of sorrow...looking outside the window of my present home in Dharamsala, I can see a mountain illumined by the evening moon. Though it is beautiful, it reminds me of another, greater mountain below which my early life unfolded.

I grew up in freedom and happiness. Now those memories seem to belong to another time, to a place far away. As I pass through the hours of each day, my heart remains with the memories of my family and friends whose bones have become part of a land now tread by strangers.

In 1987 the time came for me to leave my native land. In order to do this, it was necessary to convince the authorities that I would soon return and would speak to no one of my life's experiences: of the destruction of so many lives through torture, starvation, and the degradation of slave-labor; of so many monasteries, the ancient treasures of which were desecrated and stolen for the value of the gold they contained; of the countless thousands of monks, nuns, and lamas who died in the labor camps; of my own family, most of whom perished as a direct result of the occupation of our land.

As I prepared for my journey they told me, "It is not good to die in a foreign land. One's bones should rest in the land of one's birth." My heart agrees, and it saddens me to live with my people in a community of refugees. Yet, the heart of a culture lives in its people. Its preservation resides in their willingness and freedom to carry on its traditions. It is only in exile that I am free to speak of my life's joys and sorrows. Until my land is free, it is in exile that I must remain.

Within my heart lies the memory of a land known as Kham, one of Tibet's eastern regions. In voicing my experiences, I hope that the culture of my homeland as well as the horrendous suffering and destruction imposed on its people will not continue to be easily dismissed as a casualty of what has often been termed progress.

1

CHILDHOOD IN THE LAND OF FLOWERS

Even now as I close my eyes, I can recall my first memory—laughing, spinning, and falling in fields of flowers beneath an endless open sky. Playing among the flowers was our favorite summer pastime. My childhood friends and I would take off our boots and chase each other. Then we looked to see if a specific type of flower had gotten caught between our toes. To us this meant that we must run again through the part of the meadow where that flower grew. We loved to roll about on the hills, breathing deeply the fragrance of fresh earth and blossoms. We looked closely at the many different forms and colors of the flowers: so delicate, yet they had claimed this region as their own. In summer, such a vast variety of every color and shade inhabited the meadows that it was difficult for us to identify them all. In fact, our land was known as *Metog Yul*, or Land of Flowers.

The Tibetans in our region of Kham were nomads and semi-nomadic farmers. In summer, most farming families like mine took their herds to graze in the mountains. When this season arrived, the people of my village and various family members from outlying areas packed all our necessary belongings on yaks and mules, and journeyed to the nomadic mountain regions to graze our animals. There, we would stay from late June to October, camping in the grasslands and high alpine meadows of the Kawalori Massif.

Sometimes we children asked our parents to provide us with utensils, tea, and food, which we took to wherever we were playing and used to prepare our own refreshments. First we collected dry wood and built a fire, and then we made the tea. As it began boiling, we felt as if we had really accomplished something. I always remember the food we children shared together in the meadows as being more delicious than what we ate at home with our parents and elders.

My friends and I discussed things we had overheard from our parents' conversations. We recalled pilgrimages our families had taken with us, describing to each other the various sights we'd seen on the way. Another favorite topic was the apparel and jewelry of our older sisters. All of us eagerly awaited the day when we could wear our own jewelry of silver, gold, and semiprecious stones. At mealtime our parents called us, but we pretended not to hear and continued playing, teasing each other, and sharing our dreams.

My father often sat with his friends discussing their various interests and enjoying *chang*, a popular barley ale. In the late afternoons, having grown tired of play, I loved to sit at his feet. He often gazed in the direction of the Kawalori peaks. Just the sight of those mountains often inspired him to raise his cup in a toast and sing:

Upon the snowy peaks the lion cub is born.
O mountain treat gently that which is your own.
May the white mountain be mantled always with eternal snow,
And may the mane of the snow lion grow long.

I would listen to my father and ask him to sing those words again and again. He explained to me that Kawalori, or "Eternal Snow," is the name of a great Himalayan deity who resides within the mountains, and that the land on which we stood was his domain. Memories of my father have become intertwined with the recollection of that mountain's snowy peaks. He taught me to love them as he did, illumined as they were with ever-changing sunlight, or silhouetted by the moon, surrounded by clean, ice-laden winter winds and the swirling mists of autumn and spring.

We had many friends among the region's nomads, who were known to us as *drogpa*. They were a simple and very hardy people, suspicious of strangers, but true friends once their confidence was won. The nomads were very independent, preferring the open grasslands to the protection and confinement of towns. They were comfortable in even the harshest weather, residing their entire lives in large tents woven of yak hair. At seasonal intervals the nomads packed up their sturdy tents and moved their herds to new pastures. They relied almost solely on their herds for sustenance, for they did not farm and never saw the value of eating vegetables. They felt the growing of "such grass" for human consumption to be a foolish waste of time, and they found it humorous that people would give up the freedom of the open spaces to grow something that should rightly be eaten by yaks.

The only time the nomads came down from the mountains was when they wanted to trade, to pay yearly taxes in animal products, or for the purpose of pilgrimage. The tribes had their own hereditary chieftains and lived according to their own tribal laws. Though they spoke a dialect somewhat different than our own, we could understand each other.

During our summer stay in the nomads' region, we camped in comfortable yak-hair tents like theirs. It was a very peaceful time. Aside from tending the herds, there were not many responsibilities, and we spent the season enjoying the company of family and friends. During the summer the whole mountain was full of animals—cattle, horses, sheep, and goats of the camping families. We also had 25 horses and a herd of about 150 cattle, an average size in Kham. We kept mostly *dri*, or female yaks, from which we obtained milk and the fine butter used both for cooking and as fuel for our lamps. Dri butter was so important to our culture that it was considered a proper offering in the temples and was used as an exchange in trade or even as payment in taxes.

Toward the end of October it was time to pack our tents and make our way down into the valley. My friends and I would sit one last time among the dry and fading wildflowers, looking around at the great open expanse. Some of us would not meet until the next summer, and so the parting was difficult, but we assured each other that when the snows melted, undoubtedly we would be together again.

◊ ◊ ◊

During winter all the family members congregated in the kitchen, enjoying the light and warmth of the hearth's fire and the security of each other's company while gales swept and whistled around the house. In moments of silence after evening had fallen, the howling of wolves could be heard. In those months, we ate all our meals together. Before eating we prayed to Dolma, the protectoress and female Buddha also known as Tara.

During meals, we sat on low, carpet-covered beds, with a low table between us. Our parents were at the head of the table, and we children sat in order of our respective ages. Our servants ate with us, as did any travelers who happened to be passing by. Travelers were always welcomed in our village. In a land without newspapers, those passing through from other places were a valued source of information and entertainment. The head of the household went outside to meet the travelers, supply hay for their horses, and invite them into the house, where they were immediately offered chang or tea and asked about the nature and length of their journey. After the evening meal our family, servants, and guests sat and talked or listened to stories while drinking endless cups of butter tea, a requisite beverage in Tibet.

During these times, our elders also spoke of their youth, transmitting to us their remembrances of the situation in Tibet in those days. In that way, though we did not attend schools, we learned something about the history of our land and our religious heritage. Sometimes my parents and my older brothers discussed the hardships that they had endured during the Manchu and Guomindang incursions into Tibet. Sometimes there were recollections of old feuds that had led to sorrow in the days the family lived in the province of Nyarong.

We also heard stories about the Holy City of Lhasa in the province of U-Tsang, or central Tibet, where the Dalai Lama reigned. He resided in the Potala, "the high heavenly realm," a palace of one thousand rooms and ten thousand altars situated on a hill rising above the city. They told us how the city, the most important center of pilgrimage in Tibet, held three of our greatest monasteries and the Jokhang shrine, where the sacred image of the ancient Buddha Shakyamuni was the site of many miracles. To visit Lhasa at least once was everyone's heartfelt dream, and to hear it described in the evening firelight made us wonder when we would be able to make our life's greatest pilgrimage.

My brothers loved to discuss their favorite subjects: trade, politics, and horses. Every Khampa, as we call the inhabitants of Kham, our region of eastern Tibet, learned to ride, and ride well, from a very young age. My father and brothers considered themselves experts in recognizing the necessary qualities of a fine animal. They sometimes mentioned a beautiful horse they had seen and how they wanted to buy it at any cost. Some women indignantly felt that men found their horses to be as dear as their wives.

The men sometimes recounted their rare travels to the trading centers of Amdo, the region of Tibet bordering Kham to the north, and their more frequent journeys to the important town of Dartsedo, close to the traditional Chinese frontier to the east. When they visited Dartsedo, my brothers saw lamas and traders from as far away as Lhasa walking through the streets. Great caravans of yaks carrying raw wool, precious musk, minerals, and medicinal items from Tibet ended their journeys in its caravanserais. In Dartsedo, the people of our region purchased tea, silk and brocades, needles, matches, and many other small articles. Sometimes even flashlights, pens, and other items were available from the United States, a modern country we knew little about, but about which we had great curiosity.

The activities of the Chinese in Dartsedo were a constant source of interest to my elders. Living as we did in the Tibetan borderlands close to China, the Khampa leaders were always watchful of our Chinese neighbors' actions. Our province of Kham bordered China's western province of Sichuan, and for two centuries there had been disputes regarding this easternmost territory of Tibet.

Dartsedo had once been the capital of the native Tibetan state of Chagla. In the late nineteenth century, the frontier state of Chagla had firmly allied itself to China. Chagla was converted to the seat of a Chinese magistrate, and in 1905 the king of Chagla became one of Tibet's first rulers to be deposed. A few years later the Chinese authorities burned his palace and decapitated his brother. The king's own relationship with the new rulers was never secure. Finally he died in sorrow.

After the disruption caused by the elimination of the former king, things had settled; the town returned to its foremost occupation, which was business. After the fall of the Manchu Dynasty, the region fell to the embattlements of ruthless warlords and eventually came under the increasing control of the warlord Liu Wenhui. The warlords, not receiving any salary from the provincial government, monopolized trade in items such as tea, gold, and opium in order to support their soldiers.

Sometimes our elders used the Chinese to frighten us when we children misbehaved. They said, "If you don't behave yourselves, soon the soldiers of Liu Wenhui will come and take you." Every child I knew was terrified of this image, and so when the evening conversation of the adults came round to the Chinese, I felt both a fascination and a desire for it to quickly shift to something more familiar.

One early spring day when I was around twelve years old, my abstract imaginings suddenly became a reality. My mother and I were sitting in front of our house cleaning vegetables. Standing up to stretch, I looked around and was surprised to see soldiers approaching in the distance. As my mother stood and watched them advance, she whispered, "They are *Gya mi* (Chinese people)." They were soldiers of the Sichuan Army, all dressed in khaki uniforms; and they came marching in a long line up the road that led past our house. As soon as I saw the odd sight, I hid behind my mother and felt safe only when peeping from behind her dress. It was the first time I had seen a group of people walking all the same way in a stiff military fashion. We never imagined that one day we would see so many Chinese soldiers walking through our town; but they came again six years later, as members of a different army and a new order.

2

FROM NYARONG

My family name is Tapontsang, meaning "Commander of Horses." For generations our family had been known as breeders of the fine animals that were a precious necessity to the inhabitants of our untamed land. My grandfather, who served in the Tibetan military, was assigned to breed and supply the horses used by the army of the governor of Nyarong district. Nyarong had experienced periods of freedom and alliance with Tibet in the centuries preceding my birth, and had also occasionally come under Chinese jurisdiction.

We lived in the northern area of Nyagto, which was ruled by the family of Gyaritsang, one of the oldest clans in the district. At that time, my father, Dorje Rapten, was the most trusted lieutenant of Gyari Dorje Namgyal, the leader of the Gyaritsang clan. First serving as a soldier and then a minister, my father's duties later included working for the clan in the capacity of *trimpon*, or "counsel of the law." If some manner of quarrel broke out between people, the trim-pon would be called in to carefully investigate both sides of the dispute and report the situation to the chieftain.

The residents of Nyarong are said to be the descendants of those who manned the garrisons of the great Tibetan king Trisong Detsen. In the eighth century, at the height of Tibet's military power, the king sent his armies throughout Tibet and Central Asia, conquering vast regions. Upon establishing his empire, he sought a means to establish Buddhism in our country, and so the king himself planted the seeds of Tibet's military decline.

Though the people of Nyarong grew to be religious in many ways, the spirit and honor of the warrior remained. Perhaps the greatest weakness of our people was a deeply ingrained sense of pride yet in some ways, that pride helped us survive. It united us in times of difficulty in the uncertain territories of Tibet's borderlands. However, it also added to our vulnerability, for when notions of honor were brought into question, long-standing feuds often erupted, dividing families and tribes. The lamas of Nyarong's monasteries always tried to remind the people of the Buddha's teachings, or the Dharma, the law that governs our existence. The lamas often aided in settling disputes, for even the most resistant parties felt that there was no choice but to respect their counsel—at least for a while.

In the early 1920s the Gyaritsang family found itself with no sons. In such cases an arrangement was often made by which a young man married a woman of the family and took on her family's name, living with them in order to carry on the hereditary line. The situation was solved by approaching the Shivatsang family of Karze, a region north of Nyarong. Jamyang Samphel Shivatsang was known as one of the most powerful and respected chieftains of eastern Kham; every chieftain from Nyarong hoped to create a link with his family. His son, Wangchuk Dorje, agreed to marry two of the Gyaritsang daughters and to take up residence in Nyagto. When the two families joined, many of their members shifted between Karze and Nyarong.

Unfortunately, a rivalry developed between certain members of the Gyaritsang clan, which was not unusual under such circumstances in those days. Some felt that the arrival of an outsider from such an influential family and his followers from Karze would undermine the interests of the Gyaritsang clan and bring instability to their position in Nyarong. They grew to resent his presence, and this led to a division in the clan. My father found himself torn and dismayed by the developing circumstances. Gyari Dorje Namgyal felt bound by honor to defend his son-in-law during the dispute , which resulted in a feud between the Gyaritsang and Shivatsang families. He gave my father, as his most faithful and trusted servant, the responsibility of assisting Wangchuk Dorje to the end. And so my father felt it his duty to fight alongside the Shivatsang family and their Gyaritsang supporters.

At one point, my brother Jughuma, not yet eighteen years old, joined the supporters of the Karze group. During the dispute, he killed a man who was known as one of the region's most exceptional marksmen. Although the incident gained Jughuma a certain amount of fame, according to the customs of our land, our family then had to compensate the family of the deceased in either money or goods. The price was a terrible financial setback. And some time later, the rest of our family fortune was lost during an accidental fire that destroyed our house.

The affair greatly saddened my father and completely changed his perspective regarding the use of violent means to achieve a goal. Jughuma, too, resolved to live a more peaceful life. By the time the dispute was settled, fifty-four people had lost their lives and many friends were separated for years due to various allegiances.

I was born in 1932, five years after the dispute ended. My mother, Sonam Dolma, who was forty-nine years old at that time, often recalled how embarrassed she felt when she was pregnant, for the matter attracted much interest in the community due to her advanced age. By then our family had again begun to prosper after facing many difficulties, and we were happy and stable. For this reason, my father decided to name me Adhe: the letter "a" is highly auspicious to Tibetans as it is considered the sound from which all others arise. Many Tibetan prayers and mantras, such as OM MANI PADME HUM, begin with that letter. (In Tibetan, the syllable *om* is made by adding the vowel *naro*, or "o," to the root letter "a.") In Nyarong, it is a common practice to give someone a pet name of two syllables, the first beginning with the letter "a." However, my father decided that Adhe would be my only name.

◊ ◊ ◊

When I was still a young child, our family moved to the vicinity of Karze. We settled in a village known as Lhobasha, which was about a four-hour horseride to the east of the town center. Karze was considered to be a major political and cultural center. Although no Tibetan towns were very large, Karze was thought to be more prestigious and peaceful than many other areas of Kham, perhaps because it was the home of thirty-one monasteries and nunneries. Also, Karze—meaning "white beauty"—is in sight of the sacred Kawalori Massif.

My family lived in a square, two-story house with thick walls constructed of stone and mud mortar. The houses in our village were only a short distance apart. When I wanted to meet my friends, I just shouted their names from the terrace in front of our house. We entered freely into each other's homes.

Not far toward the northwest of our village was Kharnang monastery, where 450 monks and lamas, or religious teachers, resided. The villagers looked to them in matters of spiritual guidance. On days of religious significance, they provided prayers and offerings on behalf of the families. Each family had a lama who regularly attended to the needs of the small chapel that most of the homes contained.

In the village itself was a small marketplace where we bartered or sold such commodities as salt, butter, and dried cheese. Some jewelry and copper cooking utensils were also available. However, the largest market of our region was in Karze, where we could obtain all sorts of items: fabrics ranging from cotton and wool to beautiful brocades and silks, fine saddles and gear for horses, imported foods such as dried apricots, farming implements, housewares, guns, and ammunition.

A wide river known as the Dza Chu passed through our village of Lhobasha and then flowed south to Nyarong, continuing on to unknown places. Our house was located very near the water's edge, and I often sat on its bank watching the reflection of the rising or setting sun on the water. Rising above the village in the distance was Kawalori. The mountain's three great peaks shone vibrant and alive with morning and evening light, changing in a few moments from vibrant pink to varying shades of transparent, delicate color. The mountain had four small lakes, one on each side, and was surrounded by thick forests abundant with snow leopards, bear, small animals, and birds.

The forests of Kham were considered to be our greatest resource. No one was allowed to use the land indiscriminately. Only the timber needed to build houses was cut. Other than that, the forests were never touched. We considered the trees the "jewelry of the mountains," and the varied and beautiful wildlife as belonging to these trees. Though most people refrained from hunting as much as possible, inevitably there were some exceptions, particularly nomads who would pursue certain animals that brought a high value in the marketplace such as the wild stag and the musk deer.

Though everyone over a certain age is acquainted with the unpredictable changes that life brings—age, fortune or misfortune, illness, and death—in Tibet there were two things that seemed constant: the Dharma, and the innate intelligence of nature to renew itself. We Tibetans revered the deities of the sky and perceived the earth as a manifestation of living essence. The deities of the mountains seemed as immovable as the mountains themselves. We never imagined anything would drastically alter our relationship to our natural surroundings any more than we could foresee that the ancient stones of Tibet's monasteries were not strong enough to weather many more centuries and would indeed crumble within our own generation.

3

FAMILY AND TRADITIONS

The chapel in our home was a special place. Only when our family lama came to do a special prayer ceremony did we gather in this room. Generally, we went inside only to quietly pray and then would leave. The room was very clean, with polished wooden floors. In the center was a stepped altar on which were placed statues of the Buddha and his manifestations in the forms of Tibetan deities: Chenrezig, the embodiment of compassion and the protective deity of Tibet also known as Avalokiteshvara; Jampelyang, the embodiment of wisdom, also known as Manjushri; Padmasambhava, "tamer of the wheel of the law"; and the green Dolma, the compassionate divine mother, also known as Tara. Below the statues we put flowers and seven prayer bowls filled with pure water. All families, rich and poor alike, were able to make this offering; thus it served as a reminder that true spiritual devotion had nothing to do with wealth.

As I grew older I loved to sit in the quiet, pristine atmosphere of the room amidst the small, flickering butterlamps and the smell of incense. Those were my quietest moments, and though I was rarely silent, the moment I stepped into the room silence seemed perfectly natural.

When I was eleven years old, my father told me that it was very important to learn the teachings of the Lord Buddha, which had been introduced in our land sometime in the seventh century. He told me that the central component of the Tibetan society is religion and then proceeded to explain the law of cause and effect. He said that I should always be good to others so that a positive reaction would be the result of my involvements. If I decided to treat others badly, sooner or later, a negative reaction would find its way into my life. He stressed the importance of always being truthful and having compassion for all living things. He discussed how one should not involve oneself in lying, dishonesty, or murder because they always bring unhappiness; whereas leading a life in which there is compassion and the practice of virtue brings clarity and peace.

My father told me the story of the historical Buddha, Prince Siddhartha, who had been raised in an atmosphere of luxury. Though he was carefully protected until after he had married and fathered a son, his compassion was such that when faced with the harsh reality of death and decay, which is humanity's only sure inheritance, he left all behind him and tirelessly devoted himself to finding the path of Dharma for all humankind. The Buddha stressed the importance of the "Eightfold Path," the fruit of his long years of introspection.

Upon entering our chapel, my father would do prostrations, or *chagtsel*, an act of devotion by which one repeatedly stretches full-length on the ground while praying. The sight of his devotion created an impression that has always remained with me. In my childhood it created my first glimmerings of interest in the spiritual nature of life.

My father taught me the prayer of the female deity Dolma. It was quite long, so I learned two or three lines a day. Dolma is depicted as green in color to remind us that her compassion is as far-reaching as the wind, which is also represented by the color green in Buddhist doctrine. My father said that praying to Dolma would help me to be successful in surmounting whatever problems and obstacles I might come across. Dolma is a *bodhisattva* (an enlightened being who returns to the worldly realm to aid others), who has vowed to remain in the form of a compassionate mother until all beings are free of the bonds of *samsara* (the beginningless cycle of suffering). I also learned the prayers to the Three Jewels, the prayers of Padmasambhava, and the OM MANI PADME HUM mantra of Chenrezig, the patron deity of Tibet.

My father told me of the great leader of Tibet, His Holiness the Dalai Lama, who is the human manifestation of Chenrezig—the perfect embodiment of unconditional compassion. During his first human incarnation in 1391, he vowed to protect and uplift the souls of all living beings, and he continues to reincarnate as the Dalai Lama to guide the Tibetan people. To see the Dalai Lama, and to be worthy of his guidance, is the heart of every Tibetan's aspiration. He is a symbol of perfect spiritual freedom, the perfect receptacle of the strength found in the teachings of Buddhism. To Tibetans, he is sanctity manifested on earth.

The Thirteenth Dalai Lama was Thupten Gyatso, who passed away in 1933, one year after I was born. As a political leader, he saw the need to reform many of Tibet's laws to initiate a balance of fairness between the nobility and the common people. He examined and amended the privileges of the monasteries and the nobility. He attempted to bring a renewed spirituality to the monasteries and stressed the value and uniqueness of each sect. After his death, the whole nation felt a terrible loss and entered a two-year period of mourning. Of course, I do not personally remember the sadness of those years, but from an early age we children heard our families speaking of our Dalai Lamas.

During the time of mourning, the administration of Lhasa was in the hands of the Regent, an incarnate lama known as Reting Rinpoche. Then, in 1936, search parties found the new incarnation who was destined to be the next spiritual and temporal ruler of Tibet. They were guided by images reflected in the visionary lake of Lhamo Lhatso and other signs that had occurred since the Thirteenth Dalai Lama's death.

In 1939 the child identified as the new incarnation was transported by caravan from his natal region of Amdo to Lhasa to take his place the following year on the Lion Throne as the Fourteenth Dalai Lama. All of Tibet celebrated the return of our leader and compassionate protector. I often thought of this child, who was younger than myself, living in the Holy City as my special friend and protector; and I prayed for his well-being. I hoped that one day I would have the good fortune of meeting him.

◊ ◊ ◊

My family often took me on pilgrimages. We visited Kharnang monastery countless times to receive blessings from the residing *rinpoche* (high lama). Any family member who was not feeling well would be taken to the monastery. We knew many of its monks and lamas personally. It would be a happy occasion to rise early and climb together up the mountain road. When we reached the monastery gate, we did three prostrations and then went inside. My father held my hand as we looked at the large statues of the Buddha and the deities. Very old *thankas* (religious paintings) hung on the walls. Everything was softly illumined by the glow of many butter lamps, the heavy smoky smell mingling with the delicate fragrance of incense. Sometimes we heard the monks chanting their prayers amid the reverberations of great horns and hand drums, the intermittent clashing of cymbals, and the low resonance of the ceremonial conch. As my father had taught me, I prayed for the happiness and uplifting of all beings. Afterward, we went outside to the large brass prayer wheels, which, he told me, contained thousands of prayers inscribed on paper that we spun to the heavens as we turned the wheels with our hands.

One of the lamas of Kharnang who my family knew well was Kharnang Kusho. I remember him as always being a part of our lives, and he always gave me special attention. When I was quite small, he was in his twenties. I thought of him as very beautiful and very holy. If I had a headache or the slightest physical discomfort, I asked my parents to give me some water we kept in our home that Kharnang Kusho had blessed. He often came to our house to do *pujas*, or offering ceremonies; and before his arrival, incense, water, and flowers were always made ready. He prayed in the chapel and then gave teachings to the whole gathered family. I remember taking part in an initiation during which he touched our heads with a very holy statue of Chenrezig. When he came to touch me, he pushed the statue a little hard into my head to tease me. Looking up into his eyes without moving my head, I did my best not to flinch or show any reaction.

Another important lama to my family was the incarnate lama Chomphel Gyamtso, whom my father and brother Jughuma had accepted as their root guru, or primary spiritual teacher. He was greatly revered throughout Nyarong. He was the son of Lama Sonam Gyal, a religious instructor to His Holiness the Thirteenth Dalai Lama. A lama of the Nyingma sect, Chomphel Gyamtso would be consulted for anything that seemed to require extra consideration. When someone in the family passed away, he performed necessary prayers for their departed spirit. And people turned to him in times of need for divination. I often heard my father and Jughuma refer to him, but I saw him only twice in my youth. One time when I was very small, my family decided to make a pilgrimage to Kalsang monastery, where Chomphel Gyamtso resided, so that I might have my first audience with him.

The journey on a rocky narrow path along the Dza Chu river took about three days. Close to the monastery is a sacred mountain known as Holo Drago, which people circumambulated three times. This devotion is known as *kora*; one always walks so the holy mountain or shrine is to one's right. When done with a prayerful attitude, it purifies and cleanses the devotee of defilements.

Due to my young age, I found the walk quite tiring and finally refused to go any further. My father patiently sat with me for some time and then said, "Adhe, I am going to place a mark here on the stone. It is your mark. Though it is a difficult thing to do, every time that you walk around this mountain you will earn a mark that is all your own." In that way he convinced me to continue the circumambulation. Because I was very small, I do not remember any of the words spoken between my family and our lama during that visit; I can only recall his smiling at me.

The next time I saw Chomphel Gyamtso was in my adolescence during one of his visits to Karze when he gave a public audience. There were so many people that there was no opportunity to speak with him personally. Years later, under very different circumstances, we would meet again.

◊ ◊ ◊

As was sometimes a custom in Tibet, my father had two wives, Bochungma and Sonam Dolma. My mother, Sonam Dolma, was his second wife. Even though they were not related, the two women were extremely compatible, and neighbors and relatives considered them to be closer than some sisters. They tended to each other's children without any feelings of separation. I often slept with Bochungma, and for several years I actually believed that she was my real mother.

I was the youngest in the family, and though I was a bit mischievous and demanding, I was adored by everyone, especially my father and my eldest brother, Jughuma. I was also very close to my other brothers and sisters, especially Dolma Lhakyi and Bhumo. Dolma Lhakyi was my oldest sister. When she was young, she was given the affectionate name of Sera Ma, or "yellow head," because her hair was light in color. I often went to visit her in her home, which was one day's horseride from my home in Lhobasha. Sera Ma had many children and was always rushing around to tend to their needs. I greatly enjoyed teasing her about this: when she was pouring tea and hurrying to serve everyone, I pretended to be crying and nagging for attention, or imitated her harried expressions and sighs. Because she was busy, she drank her tea very quickly, and I did the same just to tease her and then asked for more. Sera Ma laughingly scolded, "Don't tease, because one day you will also have children; and then you will remember your sister." Still, whenever I arrived, Sera Ma was delighted to see me and, with a smile of welcome, said, "Oh, Adhe, come." Both Sera Ma and her husband Phurba were much older than I; I thought of Phurba as a kindly uncle. Their whole family joined us in the mountains in the summer, staying until the autumn months.

My brother Jughuma, the object of my unparalleled adoration, was the only family member who could draw me away from my playmates. Twenty-four years my senior, Jughuma was married and had two children. He and his family lived with us; and, as our father aged, Jughuma increasingly took on more of the paternal responsibilities. He oversaw the care of our herds and crops, and in his free time he cut and stitched the boots and winter *chubas* (traditional Tibetan dress for both men and women) we all wore. Though Jughuma had a family of his own, he and I had a very special relationship. In many ways we were very similar, and Jughuma was infinitely patient with me. We greatly enjoyed each other's company, though I bore the brunt of his constant teasing.

When I was old enough, Jughuma taught me to ride horses. Although he didn't teach me very much of the trick riding so popular with men, under his rigorous instruction, I was fair competition in a race and was considered one of the best riders in the family.

Although our family now led a quieter life than we had in Nyarong, Jughuma and my other brothers still appreciated the precision of a fine weapon and the discipline of marksmanship. Jughuma allowed me to accompany him when he went for target practice. After a short while of watching him, I, of course, insisted that he should teach me how to shoot. Ever patient, Jughuma fulfilled my wish and enjoyed giving me lessons. It was quite exciting, because I did not know of any other girl who could shoot.

My brother, in teaching me to excel in interests reserved for men, attempted to transform my demanding nature to one of determined self-discipline. During those lessons I soon found he would coolly walk away from my childish outbursts of impatience and laziness, and I was the one who was left at a loss. He constantly stressed the importance of observation and concentration. Wanting to please him, and feeling a growing sense of satisfaction in my newfound capabilities, I came to accept the stern attitude he assumed as an instructor.

My mother would say, "Jughuma, you are a grown man. How can you spoil her so? You know it is considered improper for a woman to take up a gun." I always disagreed with her, for there were exceptions, including a woman of Nyarong, Chimi Dolma, who was a member of the Gyaritsang clan. Her intelligence and bravery had placed her in the position of a chieftain, and her leadership in battles with rival clans, the army of Liu Wenhui, and the soldiers of the Long March (a six-thousand-mile trek across China made by several Communist Army columns as they fled the Guomindang) who had at various times entered her region, made her name a legend throughout eastern Tibet.

Despite her fame, my mother decided not to allow me to continue accompanying Jughuma when he went to shoot. Of course I felt this decision was greatly unfair and a hardship. When the men went up into the mountains, I always tried to persuade my mother to allow me to accompany my brother. My mother scolded, "There are only men up there. Why should you want to go?" I simply did not want to be separated from Jughuma.

Jughuma compensated by taking me to camp across the river in a small, round yak-skin boat. The river was wide and deep, and the water was very cold. On the other side, we had our own ceremony during which we burned fragrant juniper branches and prayed to the deities. When our evening meal was finished, I nestled in my brother's arms as we sat near our campfire. He taught me to empty my mind and listen carefully to everything around me, and, in that emptiness, observe my surroundings. With the moon softly illuminating the three peaks of Kawalori, he told me stories or pointed out the constellations. Sometimes we saw myriad showers of meteors in the rarified clarity of the night sky. We joked together or just listened to the sounds of the forest until I fell asleep.

◊ ◊ ◊

My sister Bhumo was five years my senior. Whereas people loved me despite my impetuousness because I was the youngest in the family, Bhumo was truly admired both for her kind heart and her exceptional beauty. It seemed that somehow she was always capable of sensing what others were feeling. She always knew what to say and was very patient. Bhumo was the quiet one in the family. Though she and I were the closest sisters in age, I sometimes felt very childish beside her, particularly after my dramatic bids for attention. I wanted to be her equal in every way. Her hair was always fixed in perfect plaits. She wore beautiful necklaces and nice clothing that complemented her pretty face and gentle, smiling eyes.

At the time of Bhumo's marriage, I saw her fine headgear and started pressing my mother to provide me with a headdress "just like Bhumo's!" It was flat and long and held three amber stones at the crown; it looked very fine and regal. I had a great weakness when it came to attractive jewelry. I hadn't realized that this was something only for marriages. My mother scolded, "Shame on you! Your time will come. Don't worry."

It was quite upsetting when the day came for Bhumo to leave the house. My mother told me, "One day you will leave in a similar manner." Her words shocked me, and I immediately became completely opposed to such an idea. I had always pictured my entire family being together throughout our lives. I began to cry, and many times afterward I felt an overwhelming sadness and confusion at the thought of separation. From that day on, for many years, the idea of marriage was a dreaded subject.

Aside from my precious hours with Jughuma, most of my childhood was spent playing with my friends. I remember my mother telling me, "It is no longer your time to play; you are growing up." I always argued with my poor mother on these details. I told her that all my friends were my age and they were still playing, so it *was* my time to play also. "No, no, no," she would respond. "When you go around with those girls, you stand out." Most unfortunately for me, I happened to be quite tall.

My mother continued, "Tomorrow you will grow up. You will have to take responsibility; and because you are not a nun, you won't stay in this family. If you want to become a nun, then you will have to practice religion in a strict sense. You won't be able to wear jewelry and have your hair plaited. If you don't become a nun, you will marry someone; and when you go to his house, you will have to know how to handle everything. If you don't learn the responsibilities of a household, it will be very embarrassing for you and our family." I responded, "Why should I be sent away? Why can't I stay here with you and father?" She tried to explain that marriage was a natural occurrence in life.

On many occasions, Jughuma advised, "Better you become a nun, because if you get married, we won't be able to stay together." I quarreled with him because I didn't want to lose my jewelry, plaited hair, and nice clothing, and the opportunity to wear all this at dances and other gatherings. Why should I be forced to shave my head and give up all the pleasant things in life just because I loved my home? Often at such times, my exasperated mother scolded me for talking that way; but the issue of being thrown out into the world was always going around in my mind.

A suitable husband was found for my sister Bhumo in the person of Pema Gyaltsen. He came from a good family whose members resided in the same district. Unlike many Tibetans in our region, Pema Gyaltsen had received a formal education in a monastery and had attained a reputation for scholarship. From a young age he was noted for his courage. His face was quite handsome and he wore a slight mustache. As was traditional for the men of Kham, he had long braided hair that was wrapped around his head and fastened with red silk threads. As I watched him speak to the men in our family and their friends, he seemed to emanate friendliness and assurance. I realized that my father was very fond of him.

Although when I first met Pema I rather liked his appearance, especially his smile, I remained a bit aloof. He was an outsider who now had first bid on my sister's attention. Already I'd been ignored during the many preparations necessary for the wedding. For several months after my sister left, I felt rather dejected.

As time went by, my family told me about Pema Gyaltsen, what a good man he was and what a fine companion he would be for my sister; and so I began to accept the situation. Fortunately, they lived quite close to us, a distance of only about five kilometers. As I got to know him, I felt less shy about approaching them as a couple and found that I could visit them fairly frequently.

Pema always made a point of welcoming me in their home. Generally a happy person, he joked almost constantly. He easily embarrassed me with comments such as: "Oh, Adhe-la has arrived. Watch out she isn't hiding a gun. One day she'll raise an army and make herself queen of the territory." Then in a half-serious voice he would question: "Adhe, why don't you have a boyfriend? Maybe they're all afraid of you? Not only could you shoot one if he decided to stray, but you are taller than most of the boys your age." I strained to think of a brilliant answer with which to regain my dignity, but usually I was at a loss.

Although Pema was slow to anger in the presence of his family, he could suddenly become proud and impatient when he felt people were making foolish decisions regarding serious issues. It was not an easy task to win an argument with him, and his opponents soon learned the extent of his tenacity. At times he could be quite hotheaded in debates or matters of honor.

Pema was well versed in Tibetan literature and often read to us from the epic of King Gesar of Ling, the warrior patron of Tibet. Guided by Padmasambhava and many other deities, Gesar, in days long past, fought demons and evil kings to restore their kingdoms to the path of Dharma. The adventures of Gesar could fill one thousand pages, and many Tibetans memorized large portions of the king's life story and spent many hours delivering a rendition of it. They read or told the stories in a lyrical manner, reciting the metrical verses in richly intoned voices. Pema had an exceptionally fine voice for story-telling and rendered a very dramatic account of Gesar.

Pema Gyaltsen became another older brother to me. At that time, I could never have imagined the suffering that would one day befall him and Bhumo. Before too many years of marriage, they began to face hardships: neither of their two children lived to adulthood, and one day circumstances beyond their control forced the couple's separation. Eventually, Pema Gyaltsen and I served as examples of political opposition and rebellion and were branded as criminals of the worst sort. Yet, in those early years, we could not have foreseen the events to come, and we lived and grew as a family in happiness and peace.

◊◊◊

Pema Gyaltsen and my brothers were always interested in learning about China's relationship to Kham. Like many young men in our region, they were indignant about the Chinese presence in Karze, and when the men in my family and their friends got together, Pema often described the situation by using colorful and imaginative invectives.

The most outstanding difficulties that occurred in the region during our lifetime before the Communist invasion of 1950 came as a result of the far-reaching influence of the warlord Liu Wenhui, who had broken away from China's central government. Liu gained control of much of Sichuan (the Chinese region on our eastern border) and, later, the bordering Tibetan district of Dartsedo. By the late 1920s his power had spread to eastern Kham, where the cruelty and corruption of his troops created hatred and mistrust in Tibetans.

Only a disdainful coexistence based on bribery and compromise could be maintained.

Jamyang Samphel Shivatsang and his ministers observed with abiding interest the unfolding of events during a long and difficult twelve-year feud the Gyaritsangs fought against Liu Wenhui under Gyari Dorje Namgyal, and later under the irrepressible female chieftain, Chimi Dolma. In the early 1930s, Chimi Dolma was elected to the leadership of the clan during Gyari Dorje Namgyal's absence. Though Chimi Dolma had been one of the main opponents of the union of the Shivatsang and Gyaritsang families, my father still spoke with admiration of her abilities in strategic planning and her outspoken determination to regain Tibetan control of Nyarong. Armed and dressed in the clothing of a man, Chimi herself led the Gyaritsang army into many battles. She was finally captured in Nyagto by Liu Wenhui's army and was taken in chains to the Fort of the Female Dragon, where she was executed before a firing squad in 1939. After her capture, the Chinese set fire to and destroyed the Gyaritsang *dzong* (fort).

Before long, however, Liu Wenhui's own actions resulted in his defeat. Not only did he lose his position in Sichuan because of a war with his nephew, Liu Xiang, another warlord who was his greatest rival; but because he had so distanced himself from the central Chinese government, he eventually lost most of his control outside of Dartsedo. Liu Wenhui, who had once been so powerful as to be able to control and wage war throughout large areas of Sichuan and eastern Kham, began to have difficulty in providing for his soldiers and eventually controlled only a small detachment that would sometimes be hired by the central government in Nanjing to go here or there. During those years, the Gyaritsang fortress was rebuilt and the chieftains of Nyarong resumed their positions. The Chinese in Karze then rarely ventured outside their garrison to the outskirts of the region. They traveled only along well-established routes, mostly between Karze and Dartsedo.

Between 1940 and 1950 we carried on our lives without giving much thought to foreign authority: we who lived in Kham were undeniably Tibetan, and we lived as Tibetans live. I knew of the Chinese leaders only through some old stories, which, though frightening, did not seem quite real. But the Chinese continued to look upon Tibet as a land they wished to fully possess.

4

MEMORIES OF KARZE

When I turned sixteen, I began working in the fields with the adults. Surprisingly, I discovered that the work, though at times tedious, was actually enjoyable. The day chosen for plowing was an auspicious occasion. Several days before the ground was broken, the lamas conducted special prayer ceremonies, and no one commenced field work until the prayers were completed. Early in the morning on the day the plowing was to begin, we decorated the horns of our *dzos* (cross between a yak and a cow) with bows of red wool, red symbolizing good fortune. Then incense was lit in the fields; and our family lama, Kharnang Kusho, walked around their borders carrying religious scriptures and intoning a prayer of purification.

The men prepared the fields with iron-tipped plowshares. The older women carried baskets from which they sowed the seeds. I used to insist on joining them, but they told me, "You are too young. If you throw the seeds too much here or there, they will not grow properly." Still, I persisted.

During planting and the harvest, all the family members worked in the fields, except Jughuma. He divided his time between tending to the herds in the mountain camp and overseeing everything else that was happening on the farm. At harvest time pots of chang were taken to the fields, and in the evenings there were parties with songs, dancing, and wonderful things to eat and drink. The valley in which our farm was located was three to four miles wide and fifteen miles long; it was considered one of the most fertile areas of farmland in all of Kham.

◊ ◊ ◊

The time between my childhood and marriage was a beautiful one for me. My friends and I were very close, and we felt no pressing problems. My family often made trips from Lhobasha to Karze to visit the dzong in which the Shivatsang family resided.

The dzong was a huge square castle located on a large hill above the town. Meadows covered the lower part of the hill and above the dzong was Karze monastery, one of the largest in eastern Tibet. As we approached from the plain below, we could see the golden roofs of its main temple glittering in the sun. Its buildings were painted in several colors, with red and white predominating. The monastery's setting on the hill gave it the appearance of a *mandala*, the celestial palace of a Buddha.

The many temples and the living quarters of the monks and senior lamas were arranged on different levels, connected by narrow alleys and many staircases. On several levels were terraced gardens opening to glorious views of Kawalori. The buildings were supported inside by great columns of red lacquered wood. The temples were consecrated with images of the Buddha and Tibetan deities, their walls adorned with huge silken thankas and tapestries of great age. The monastery possessed a very large embroidered thanka of Dugkar, the deity who holds a white umbrella and symbolizes the pacification of evil. In order to destroy negativity, she assumes a semi-wrathful form with one thousand eyes and one thousand arms that reach out to all sentient beings. This renowned treasure, which was more than three stories high, was unrolled for public display once a year at the end of summer, when it was hung from the assembly hall of the dialectic school.

During my youth, two high incarnate lamas were in residence: Lamdark Rinpoche and Sigyab Tulku. Karze monastery was an important pilgrimage center; pilgrims could always be seen circumambulating its three-mile perimeter. During that act of piety, they stopped at certain shrines and joined together to turn the great prayer wheels, some of which were twelve feet long and six feet across. It is believed that turning the prayer wheel aids in concentrating one's attention on the recitation of the mantra.

Monastic dance rituals known as *cham*, and Tibetan folk opera, *lhamo*, were performed at the monastery during the summer. Tents were erected and many people came great distances to see the monks who dressed as kings and heroes in beautiful brocade robes, long swords, and turquoise jewelry. It was a wonderful sight.

The main themes of Tibetan operas involved a hero or heroine overcoming tremendous obstacles in the pursuit of the Dharma. Some lhamo were reenactments of the lives of religious kings and chieftains; and others, such as the Yak Dance, were comedies about everyday life. A lhamo performance lasted the entire day. People brought meals and settled down to enjoy the great communal event. Children learned the stories by heart and recounted their details for weeks after the performance.

Another important pilgrimage site was a temple on the outskirts of Karze that was dedicated in 1284 to the deity Mahakala. The performance of religious practices there was said to resolve medically incurable diseases from which a person had suffered for a long time. Perhaps the greatest reason for the temple's popularity was that prayers to Mahakala were known to enable barren women to give birth.

One of the most beautiful monasteries was Karze Day-tshal, which was not far from our village. It was located in the center of a settlement begun by people who had fled there from disturbances in Nyarong in the early nineteenth century. After becoming subjects of Karze, they were resettled in a nomadic region famous for its vast pasture land. This region adjoining the monastery was where our family camped when we moved to the higher ground during the summer months.

In the late 1860s, a remarkable *tulku,* or incarnate lama, was born into a family in Dra-Dha, about one-and-a-half day's journey by horse from Day-tshal. With the father's consent, the Day-tshal settlers took the young tulku to live in and guide their community. Gradually, the fame of the tulku spread, and the great monastery of Karze recognized him and assisted the settlers in building Karze Day-tshal. The settlers provided food for the monks, and a special feeling of harmony and tranquility existed between the monastery and the surrounding community.

The monastery was a favorite place for my father and Jamyang Samphel Shivatsang to visit. They enjoyed taking long walks together on the grounds and the surrounding area. Shivatsang always referred to the beauty of Karze Day-tshal as a perfect communion between the creations of nature and humanity, a place where one can walk in peace.

The Karze Gon, or monastery region, was one of the five regions in Karze District under the jurisdiction of various chieftains. It had been ruled by two chieftains from the same family who held the title of Mazur, rulers of the "separate corner." But long before, the family divided into two branches through marriage, and a son of the Mazur chieftain took over the rule of part of the territory; his family came to be known as the Khangsar, or "New House." The chieftain Jamyang Samphel Shivatsang belonged to the Mazur branch of the family. The Mazur chieftains were originally appointed by the Lhasa government as *pon*, or district commissioners of Karze.

◊ ◊ ◊

Our family and the Shivatsangs had a very close relationship. The chieftain's two daughters, Dechen Wangmo and Pema Wangmo, were my great friends. Dechen, the serious one, was a compassionate and patient person who took an interest in everything around her. All the work done by the Shivatsang family and the ten subchieftains of our region held her attention. She loved to listen to discussions between her father and brothers and would try to understand the problems in the community.

Pema Wangmo was a lively and pleasant companion. Like me, she was especially fond of new dresses and necklaces. We didn't have any of the modern makeup that women wear today, but we applied a certain white ointment with the fragrance of flowers on our faces, believing in its beautifying properties. The ointment was brought from Ziling by Chinese traders, who sold it to Khampa merchants in Amdo for trade in the local markets.

Pema Wangmo and I helped each other choose necklaces, blouses, and silk chubas that properly matched, and then romped about in our outfits, considering ourselves to be the great beauties of Karze. Most of the time we stayed within the confines of the dzong, but on certain occasions, such as when dances, lhamo, or cham were held, we were able to venture into the town. Because of our unusually fine dress, everyone looked at us as we walked together through the streets.

By that time, I was fully involved in all the household chores. Our family had four servants, three of whom were women who helped with the animals, taking them to graze, milking them, and making butter and cheese. Palmo, the senior servant, was around forty years old. Sometimes it seemed as if the whole household belonged to her. She took her job very seriously and looked after many of the requirements of the family. The other servants were Dolma, Tseloma, and Choenyi Dolma. Dolma and Choenyi Dolma worked in the fields, while Tseloma took care of the water supply and looked after the herds. Tseloma was especially patient when instructing me in preparing butter and other dairy products. Until my arms grew accustomed to the work, she took the churn from my hands as soon as she saw I was getting tired.

Another person who was often in the household was Paljor, Jughuma's assistant. They went everywhere together. When they camped in the mountains or traveled on business, Paljor saw that everything was properly packed on the animals, and when they stopped for the night, he pitched the tent. Jughuma had great faith in Paljor's honesty and ability. He always described him as "a man who is able to identify what is wrong and what is right." Though he had his own family, Paljor often stayed with us, for he greatly enjoyed drinking chang and having discussions with my brothers.

◊ ◊ ◊

By 1948 I had come of age to be married. Through inquiries made by my friends, my family heard of the availability of the son of a family that lived about a two-hour horseride from our home. The family, originally from Saten in Nyarong, had moved to the vicinity of our village. They still owned a small farm in Nyarong, and one near Lhobasha. The two farms were their main source of income. Though the family was not exceptionally wealthy, my father was satisfied that they were comfortably self-sufficient.

Though Sangdhu Pachen and I didn't know each other personally,

I'd often heard of him from one of my girlfriends with whom he had once exchanged bracelets. Though their union had not been possible, she continued to tell me of her high regard for him and his exceptional qualities. I had seen him several times when she and I walked together in Karze.

My father and Jughuma went to his home to speak with his mother and arrange a formal family meeting. Then one day Sangdhu Pachen, his mother, and his older sister rode to our home carrying *khatags* (ceremonial white scarves) and gifts. He was quite handsome and just three years older than myself. I felt very shy when we first met, and I am sure he felt the same; but we took an instant liking to each other. During the meeting with our families, he sometimes looked at me and gently smiled for just a second. I felt drawn to him, as if we already knew each other.

Slowly something within me began to accept that the time had come. I began to find the idea of marrying Sangdhu Pachen quite interesting. His unusually beautiful black eyes were bright with intelligence. He seemed quite kind, sensitive, and thoughtful. Though young, he had already adjusted to life's responsibilities; when his father died several years before, it had been necessary for him to take over the care of the family. I felt grateful for the understanding that my family had shown in choosing someone I could really love, and that Sangdhu Pachen found something in me that drew him to our union.

In the late spring of 1948, Sangdhu Pachen and I were married. On the morning of the wedding day, I dressed in a purple brocade chuba that had an embroidered design of a yellow dragon and flowers. I wore long golden earrings and three necklaces of gold, turquoise, coral, and Zi stones (rare patterned stones popular throughout Tibet). My arms were adorned with jade bracelets. Around my gown was fastened a belt of heavy silver. When the dressing was completed, my mother looked at me happily and said, "Adhe, finally your time has come." I remembered the time years before when I had quarreled with my mother about wanting to wear Bhumo's wedding jewelry, and I suddenly realized, "Yes, this definitely is the end of my childhood."

With my family and friends, all dressed in their best finery, I set off for my husband's home. Before we dismounted our horses, the praises of the bride and groom and the ancestral history of the two families were described in a traditional narration. When it was completed, I got down from my horse using a step fashioned of tea-bricks covered with a leopard skin.

At the door of the house, the family lama conducted a brief religious ceremony known as *tru-zo*. The groom and his family waited inside the house, while we remained outside until its completion. Then the whole bridal party entered the house, and everyone participated in a grander ceremony, the second tru-zo, held in the living room. The presiding lama sprinkled blessed water over our heads as he recited the prayers to consecrate our marriage and bless our future. All the relatives, guests, and servants crowded to get a glimpse of us. I was extremely shy and nervous, and hardly raised my head throughout the ceremony.

Then began three nights and days of celebration. Bonfires were lit in the evening. Many delicacies were eaten and vast quantities of chang were consumed. My brother Ochoe, who had never married, gave a speech on the coming together of our two families; he had inherited the gift of oration from our father, and everyone was very fond of him.

After the wedding ceremony, it was traditional for the bride to continue living with her family for six months to a year. After that period, both households were joined as one. The spring of the following year I was considered to be formally married. My mother came to me and said, "The time has come when you must go. It is time to begin your new life."

My things were collected, and the next day we all set out to deliver me to my new home. Although by that time I was mature enough to realize that I could not stay with my family forever, at the moment of my family's departure from me, I suddenly grew tearful and suspicious. But I was very fortunate to have been taken into an understanding family. Soon after my arrival, my mother-in-law, Sampten Dolma, told me that in her eyes, her son and I were equal. I soon began to call her Ma Sampten, *ma* being one of the Tibetan words for mother.

Ma Sampten was happy to have another daughter in the house along with Sangdhu's elder sister, Riga. A few months after I arrived, Riga came home from a trip with her husband, Pema Wangchuk, and she and I developed a close relationship. Ma Sampten, Riga, and I spent long hours talking with my close friend and servant, Choenyi Dolma, whom I had brought with me from my parents' home. I heard many charming stories of Sangdhu's childhood. Ma Sampten often discussed the happiness she had experienced bringing her children into this world. Sangdhu, her youngest child, seemed especially precious to her.

We lived in a three-story, sturdy wooden house situated in a field fairly close to a road. On the third floor were two shrine rooms. On the second floor were the family bedrooms, living room, storerooms, and servants' quarters. My favorite room was the living room with its fine wooden floors and small Tibetan rugs. The tables and ottomans were colorfully painted in flower designs, and Tibetan rugs and pillows added comfort to the ottomans. The supporting columns in the living room were painted red with delicate designs of blue, yellow, green, and white. The best feature of the room was its two windows, from which we could gaze on the ever-changing, high snow peaks of Kawalori.

Most of my household responsibilities were in being a hostess to visiting guests and taking care of my mother-in-law. I especially looked forward to the harvest season, when I enjoyed working in the fields with Choenyi Dolma, and celebrating at the parties we had afterwards—and so, there remained in my life a few more years in which there would be times for laughter.

As Sangdhu Pachen and I faced the early adjustments and closeness of married life, I felt myself becoming completely devoted to him. However, in the first year after I came to live with him, he sometimes found me crying. He assured me that I could go to Lhobasha to visit whenever I wanted; and sometimes he suggested, "Wouldn't you like to go and see them for a month or so?" Sangdhu was a wonderful husband, understanding me and always concerned with my happiness. If for any reason I felt sad or upset, he somehow managed to lift me out of my moods. He realized that in some ways I was still very young, and he was patient. Sometimes, looking at his sensitive face, I realized how many responsibilities he had to bear, and I resolved to behave more maturely.

Ultimately my family and Sangdhu's family became very close. My sister Bhumo's husband, Pema Gyaltsen, and Sangdhu had been friends before my marriage, and we frequently visited each other's homes, where we listened to Pema's many tales and recitations of the Gesar epic. As time went on, our house came to be full of visitors from both sides of the family. One of my brothers, Nyima, usually came when Sangdhu was away, since he felt that that was when I would be most lonely. My oldest sister, Sera Ma, and my parents joined us whenever they could, and the two families camped together in the mountains when the warm weather came. Thus, our lives seemed very fortunate.

◊ ◊ ◊

For most of my life I had never really sensed what the Chinese presence in our land could mean. When as a child I saw the soldiers walking on our village road one day, I had been overcome with fear. But since I was very young at that time, within a short while many pleasant and immediate things had distracted me from concerns of what the future might bring. Later, I could not have imagined the unfolding of events that ultimately threatened the stability of my marriage, the ties of my family, and everything we had known. Though we did not realize it at the time, the year of my marriage was a fateful one. The final victory of a war that had long raged in the east had been won, and this achievement soon resulted in tremendous upheaval and confusion in our own society. The first intimations of change occurred when we heard one day in late 1949 that the Communists had entered Dartsedo.

PART TWO

INVASION
AND
IMPRISONMENT

5

THE ADVENT OF COMMUNISM

In the spring of 1950, as always, the farmers of Karze region went to the fields to pick stones, spread manure, and plow. But in mid-April, we heard that a Communist force had just set forth from Dartsedo. By the last week of April, although the tender new shoots of wheat and barley brought a familiar vivid greenness to the fields and the buds were just beginning to open on the trees, uncertainty grew within our hearts. The moments passed in strained expectation.

The soldiers of the Eighteenth Army of the Southwest Military Region reached the plain below Karze in the midafternoon of April 28. That same day, Communist troops arrived in Lhobasha. My family gathered to discuss what the appearance of such a large force in the area could mean. At some point during our conversation, we heard some commotion outside. One of my brothers got up to look and, quickly turning his head, announced, "The Chinese are here." We all ran to the door and watched as the road filled with soldiers. We were very surprised by their discipline and politeness.

The army entered Karze under the command of Wu Shizang. For a full week, sections of their detachments continued marching into the region. We wondered at their numbers, which ultimately rose to nearly thirty thousand in Karze and the surrounding areas. We did not yet understand that the Eighteenth Army's Fifty-second Brigade was being prepared to enter Chamdo (the Lhasan administrative center nearest to us) and the regions of Kham under the jurisdiction of the Lhasa government. They would later march on the city of Lhasa itself.

The Communist army held a public meeting in a large field called Thogo, east of Karze monastery near the dzong. They announced, "We are very glad to meet you. We have come to liberate you from the corruption of the Guomindang regime, which is now forever finished. We have come to help you establish a true rule of the people, to better the living conditions of ordinary men, and to right past mistakes. We are guests in your region. We realize that these lands belong to you. After the completion of our duties, we will return to our native land. We are brothers and sisters, and we have come only to help you."

Brigadier Wu was accompanied by Sangye Yeshi, a Tibetan collaborator who as a youth had joined the Communists during the Long March and had adopted the Chinese name of Tien Bao. Now, word passed quickly among the people that he did not seem to remember how to speak his own language.

At the meeting, silver coins bearing an impression of Yuan Shi-kai, the second president of China's New Republic, were distributed as gifts to all the people present. The coins, which were called *dayan*, were the initial means that the Communist Chinese used to influence us. The soldiers walked through the streets of the villages and approached youngsters with their coins, but no one in Lhobasha had the courage or desire to accept one. When the children of our village saw the soldiers approaching, they ran away to find their parents or nearest elder, or quickly disappeared behind the closed doors of their homes. In the end, the soldiers gave the coins to the parents, telling them to buy sweets for their children.

The troops were quite ragged looking. Their clothing was not sufficiently warm, but they were well armed. They had faced great hardships traveling in high altitudes that they were not accustomed to. All the regular soldiers looked undernourished and many were experiencing nosebleeds; their faces were burned red by the bright sun. Only the officers were provided with oxygen masks to ease the adjustment to Kham's altitude, which made many people from the lowlands ill with nausea and headaches. The Chinese soldiers frequently took a mixture of sugar and water, which they believed would help their symptoms, and found some additional relief by visiting the hot springs near Karze.

Soon the streets of Karze were filled with processions of Communists waving banners and carrying large portraits of their heroes, Mao Zedong and Zhu De, as they shouted slogans we could not understand. In the beginning of their "peaceful liberation" of Tibet, the soldiers did not use force or threaten us in any way. Many were peasants who had been oppressed in their homeland. The Communist revolution put power into their hands. They sought to win our confidence through their many speeches and exemplary behavior. They were under orders not to harm anyone, touch any of the women, or damage any property; and to pay for whatever they took. They were inspired by the promise of a "new world order" that would be achieved through communism.

In the beginning, the Communists projected an attitude of reverence toward religion. We did not know at that time that a brief study of our religion and customs had been part of their military training for the purpose of winning our confidence. One day when I was visiting my family in Lhobasha, I went out for a walk. I saw some soldiers wandering up the road in our village, where they met an old Tibetan who was walking and praying aloud. One of the soldiers took his prayer wheel and tried to rotate it, and then another took it. Next they examined his rosary and took turns passing a few of the beads through their hands. As I drew near, I heard them repeating aloud the sacred prayer of Chenrezig, OM MANI PADME HUM, "Hail to the Jewel in the Lotus," which they had memorized. One of them commended the man on his devotion to spiritual practice and told him that they also loved the Buddha. At first, this often-exhibited attitude made some Tibetans think that the Communists were practicing Buddhists. This was a great surprise to my elders, who had for the most part experienced Chinese administrators as usually apathetic toward anything having to do with our culture. The Communists continued to say, "We are the same people. We have only come to help you and teach you to rule your own land; then we will return to our land. At that time, even if you ask us to stay, we will not stay." They said they had come to implement the policy of "Self-Determination and Self-Rule."

At the time of their arrival, the military leaders spoke only of unity; but we eventually learned that their ultimate goal was a classless society, which to them meant the establishment of class warfare.

Their actions soon divided the society, created mistrust between friends, and helped them to learn who was in possession of valuable properties and goods.

That summer, bundles containing rice and silver coins were dropped by parachute from planes that flew over our region. The Chinese soldiers did not like to eat barley, the most important item in our traditional diet. Since they received their supplies by air, we wondered if their ground army was meeting resistance somewhere below Karze.

◊ ◊ ◊

During the harvest, groups of smiling Chinese soldiers entered our fields to offer their assistance. If they saw someone carrying a heavy load, the soldiers would insist that it be put down; and then they would pick it up, saying, "Please let us help you. We are relatives." When visiting monasteries, they told the monks, "It is very good that you are involved in such spiritual practices," and would offer bags of their silver coins as donations.

My father, Dorje Rapten, was very angry about this and thought our people foolish for accepting these gifts. He felt that the Chinese were treating us like children whose trust they were trying to win, and that our neighbors were blinded by their promises.

Eventually, divisions of the Eighteenth Army moved on toward Chamdo. By that time, the large Sixty-second Division was firmly established in Dartsedo and had assumed the overall administration of our own and various other regions. Much of eastern Kham was overrun by the incredibly vast army. Many of the older people remembered the hard battles that had been fought during the Long March, when, due to the scarcity of resources, the Communists had been desperate and had done whatever they could to obtain food. Though many Khampas wanted to fight, they realized that they were greatly outnumbered.

Gyari Nyima and other Tibetan officials in contact with Chinese authorities had heard of a plan. If negotiations could not be reached with the Lhasa government, and if the Dalai Lama chose to flee, the Communists planned to install Sangye Yeshi as head of the government.

The possibility was a matter of great concern among the chieftains of Karze District and Nyarong, who were well aware of the Communists' superior military strength.

The Communists had become very powerful immediately upon forcing Chiang Kai-shek into exile, and world recognition of their government was a matter of great concern in Kham. Others felt that if we just humored the Chinese, they would leave before too long and that perhaps, in the meantime, we could outsmart them and benefit by what they were offering. A few, mostly those who had collaborated with the Communists during the Long March, believed their promises would create a better society for Tibet.

◊ ◊ ◊

Before the Communists arrived, there had been no source of electricity in Karze. They soon set up a small generator in the Khangsar dzong; it was operated by a man pedaling a stationary bicycle. By this means, they were able to send messages by a wireless transmitter. After about six months, other generators arrived and the Chinese began to show propaganda films in the dzong. The citizens of Karze, most of whom had never seen films of any sort, were at first amused; but we felt skeptical about the claims in the films: they constantly expounded on the greatness and integrity of the Communist Party, which had rescued the poor and was creating a new China in which all citizens would work together for the upliftment of the masses. They showed the hopeless inefficiency of the Japanese soldiers against the brave and able young soldiers of China. Before long, Pema Gyaltsen would grow quite indignant and bored, sighing and shifting in his seat. I remember walking behind Pema Gyaltsen one evening after such a showing; he sarcastically remarked to his friends, "After seeing this film, now I can feel confident putting my fate in their hands."

The Communists seemed earnest, but we found their constant humorless moralizing tiresome. They seemed to be completely lacking in spontaneity, and they constantly relied on quotes from Chairman Mao in their conversations, not only with Tibetans but with each other. During these meetings, we listened to Communist songs and slogans, but we found them stiff and dull. We just sat politely and waited until they were finished.

◊ ◊ ◊

Due to my father's position as trimpon, six Chinese officials regularly visited our home to discuss the Tibetan judiciary system. They inevitably commended my father for his reputation in the region for the fairness he employed in settling disputes and his concern for the poor. They told him they were interested in understanding the basis of our family's influence in the society. During those visits, I had the opportunity to further observe what I had heard and witnessed concerning their unusual interest in our religion. The officers who visited our home always asked permission to enter our family chapel; and my family was, at first, surprised to see them perform the prostrations and acts of ritual not known to be practiced by Chinese Buddhists. They spoke of Mao in almost a religious sense, declaring him "the great father who has come to liberate everyone of suffering, whose concern for the welfare and happiness of the Tibetans knew no bounds." They said that they had been sent by him to see if our people had any difficulties in which they might be of service.

My father and brothers were interested in the modern guns of the Chinese; and at some point during their visits, all the men climbed up to the roof for target practice, exchanging Jughuma's shotgun and Luger pistol for the officers' pistols. Jughuma was still known to be quite a sharp shooter, and they always praised him for his ability and gave him extra bullets for his gun. They told our family how good it was to have this opportunity to become friends and learn from each other. Of course, they always assured my father, "We are not thinking of staying. We are just here now and will be gone tomorrow." Several times after they left, father told us that all their actions were for the sake of appearance, to create a false sense of security in our minds in order to win our trust.

By that time, the Chinese had identified the most respected and influential Tibetans, the authorities of the society, the wealthy families, the beggars, the monks, and the abbots of the monasteries. Their main purpose in spending time with us had been to discern these things. They had effectively noted the wealth of the monasteries, how much livestock they possessed, and what types of statuary they contained. They had also collected information regarding the individual wealth of all the families in the Karze region.

◊ ◊ ◊

During the time of the Guomindang, work on an airfield had been started on the edge of Su-ngo sha, a village on the plain below Karze. With the help of requisitioned Tibetan labor, it was completed in the first week of December 1951. Though the Tibetans were paid for their labor, they complained heavily, for some had been made to travel many days' distance from their homes and thus were unable to work in their fields. The airfield was inaugurated with a great ceremony. I was not present, but I heard it was attended by many prominent people from Karze and other areas who were impressed by their first sight of a landing airplane. I don't know if anyone at that time imagined what the presence of such airfields would mean in the near future. Su-ngo sha, approximately five miles southeast of the Karze dzong, eventually became an enormous city of tents housing thousands of Chinese soldiers and officers.

As time passed, the number of soldiers stationed in the district greatly swelled. They were living in the Karze garrison and Karze Day-tshal monastery, and Lhobasha became the headquarters of the Chinese cavalry. Once a military compound was built, the area soon became one of their main camps.

The occupying force fulfilled their promises of building schools, hospitals, and veterinary clinics. A primary school for the children of poor families was built in Karze, and1952 brought the completion of a hospital that gave free treatment to Tibetan patients. When we rode by its entrance we often saw lines of people waiting for examinations. Later on, however, the hospitals in Kham were used mostly as a back-up for the Eighteenth Army.

It soon became apparent that the Communist instructors in the schools were teaching the children to consider our people one of the

minorities of the great motherland. They said our land was an insepa-
rable entity of the vastly superior Chinese culture, and that the
Chinese language, history, and customs must be learned and put into
practice in order for Tibetans to understand their true identity. The
elders could not accept this even from the beginning. They quietly
discussed among themselves the idea of schools where children were
taught to believe that the traditions of their families were something
to be ashamed of.

◊ ◊ ◊

During the *Losar* (Tibetan New Year) of 1953, a large celebration was
held at a place called Chendha, in the monastery district of Karze. It
was attended by all the prominent families of the region and most of
the townspeople, as well as many Chinese officers and soldiers. At the
banquet they told us, "This is your land, so enjoy your freedom. We
are not here to interfere with your lives; and today, during this celebration, we can take the time to enjoy each other's company." But during
the party, photographs were being taken of certain people. Those who
were particularly curious watched carefully and noticed that the people
being photographed happened to be wearing a lot of jewelry.

A few months later, the Chinese selected leading individuals from
the monasteries and the families of the region and told them, "Since
you are the most capable people of your society, we want you to go to
China to see our country." There were twenty to thirty members of the
delegation, including my father and Kunga Gyaltsen Shivatsang, the
son of the Karze chieftain. They traveled to China by plane. There they
were shown only the best factories and farms to instill trust in them
that everything was functioning perfectly under Communist rule.

They were taken to several different towns during their factory
tour. In one town, my father noticed that Buddhist statues and
thankas were being sold in the market. At one point during the tour,
his part of the delegation became separated from the main group.
Their translator was a former member of the Guomindang who had
recently, for the sake of self-preservation, converted to communism.
My father became interested in an elderly Chinese man and, with the

help of the translator, struck up a conversation with him. While they were talking, a truck full of Chinese Guomindang prisoners drove by. "You see there," the old man told Father, "all of those prisoners will be executed. The Communists are slowly plundering every family for their riches." My father was horrified.

A few moments later, a truck full of women prisoners arrived. All the women were pulled down from the truck and lined up to be shot. They were so terrified that many of them were falling down; their shaking legs simply couldn't support them. Suddenly, my father felt he knew the Communists' true intention, what their real policy was behind all the seemingly noble speeches and promises. In his mind, all trust disappeared.

Before the delegates returned home, each was given two large portraits of Mao Zedong and Stalin. Later, my father told us, "These people do not plan to leave our land. Of course, when the portraits were given I couldn't refuse them; but I won't have them in our home." He then threw them in the fireplace, and in silence we watched the paper burn.

One day, soon afterward, an announcement was made demanding the return of all the silver presidential coins that had been distributed. As the collection began, we were warned that if any coins were found later, there would be severe consequences for those who had kept them. Most people returned the coins; but some had made them into rings, and there were a few who took chances and hid them. The coins were then declared to be non-negotiable in the marketplace. The Chinese told us that these coins were too heavy to be carried for daily use. This was the first time the Chinese paper currency known as *yuan* would be used in Kham. Previously, we'd had our own currency in coins of various denominations and paper notes, although most trade within Tibet was by means of barter.

◊ ◊ ◊

In early 1954, we were informed at a public meeting that the Chinese planned to set up a political consultative committee comprised of educated people in the area. All the most respected, influential, and wealthy people of Karze district were made officials. They were to be paid by the Chinese to influence the rest of the society to appreciate the benefit of following Communist Chinese policies. The committees were to be assigned Chinese advisors who would aid the members in the dissemination of new policies. An announcement was made regarding a program of "Economic Change for the Welfare of the People." The Chinese spoke of voluntary land distribution and attempted to convince landowners to give a certain portion of their land to the Communist government so it could be distributed among the people. The landowners in Karze were not enthusiastic and ignored the proposal. Those on the political committee were told that it was their work to help initiate these practices. In the first years after the Communists' arrival, various types of farming implements were handed out to the citizens; and many Tibetans accepted interest-free loans.

The Chinese announced that free grain and clothing were to be distributed to the people in Karze and the surrounding regions. The only prerequisite for receiving these gifts was that the recipients had to declare how much wealth and property were already in their possession. It was said that this would ensure "a fair distribution of the gifts." Chinese officials would visit homes to make certain that everyone was satisfied with the distribution. Many people were quite happy to receive these presents. They accepted them without hesitation because they viewed these actions as having no future consequences. The Chinese always stressed that this was their way of showing service to the people. During that time, people willingly answered questions on the situations and attitudes of their neighbors.

My father was made a member of the political committee. However, ever since witnessing the executions of the Chinese women, he'd had a black spot in his heart and was never happy with anything the Communists did. He had begun to quietly call on trustworthy friends and advise them, "These people have no good intentions. They are going to spoil our society and take everything away." One day, new orders came, stating that the members of the political consultative committee were to be "reeducated."

At that time, my father fell ill and was bedridden. His health had not been good since his return from China; he suffered from diarrhea and was always weak. His heart was filled with sadness. Soon, some soldiers came to our door and announced that they were going to take him to the hospital. My brothers went to visit him every day. One day as Jughuma sat by his side, Father waited for a moment when no one was around and told him, "Now there is no use in staying here. It is better if you take all the capable men and leave. Everything is in the hands of the Chinese. There is not much hope. Being that I am old, my time has come." He asked Jughuma to tell my husband that he must find some way to take me away from Karze. He felt that perhaps we would be safe in Lhasa.

The Tibetans in the locality, including my family, suspected the Chinese were purposely delaying the proper medical treatment for my father. At first, he had been quite stubborn about accepting any medication from them, but my brothers finally convinced him to try. He then began to grow steadily weaker, and people who saw him began saying, "He never recovers; maybe they are putting something in the medicine." In the late spring of 1954, my father died in the hospital. The last words he uttered to my brothers Jughuma and Ochoe were, "Whatever assurances they make, don't trust them. They will soon attempt to spoil our society and eliminate us. You must try to find a way to save our land from this course of action that is bound to end in destruction."

The authorities expressed their regret to the public, saying that my father had been a genuinely honest and moral man. After his death, they decided to force Jughuma to take Father's place on the political committee.

My father's body was disposed of by sky burial. Traditionally, when a person dies, we thought it highly beneficial for the sake of the departed spirit to collect a small amount of the bones and hair of the deceased and bury them in the cemetery beside Sera monastery in Lhasa. Partly to avoid joining the political committee, Jughuma decided to do this. The Chinese agreed to his plan only after my brother Ochoe agreed to join the committee until Jughuma's return.

◊ ◊ ◊

Immediately after the invasion, the People's Liberation Army (PLA) began to speak of the need for new highways and how this would be of great benefit to the Tibetan people in furthering the political, cultural, and economic development of our country. Shortly afterward, work was begun on widening the traditional caravan trails and building bridges to link the major regions of Tibet. Some Tibetans believed the roads would benefit us, but most realized they would more greatly benefit the rapid deployment of Chinese troops and military supplies throughout Tibet. The Xikang–Lhasa highway began in Sichuan, passed through Dartsedo, and would eventually pass through Karze and further east.

During the highway construction, thousands of Chinese who had been taken forcibly from Chengdu and other cities in Sichuan were seen working on the road between Dartsedo and Karze and further east. Quite a few were Guomindang prisoners. They were totally unfamiliar with the Tibetan language and customs, and they suffered intensely due to the difference in altitude and the conditions under which they were expected to work. Many of them died. Those who survived the building project would be the first Chinese settlers to live in a Tibet under Communist rule.

Tibetans from Minyak and other regions between Dartsedo and Nyarong who were taken for labor were at first kept separated from the Chinese labor units and were paid well with silver coins. But as more PLA troops entered Tibet, the amount of wages paid to Tibetans suddenly declined sharply. The Tibetans quit and could not be convinced to return to the projects. Finally, they were threatened with reprisals unless they agreed to work. Many Tibetans taken for work simply disappeared and never returned. As reports of the road's progress trickled into Karze, Pema Gyaltsen cursed certain wealthy Tibetan traders who at first had provided tools and supplies for the Chinese. "What could they have possible thought would happen?" he bitterly asked. "Did they really believe the main concern was that we could buy our tea from China at a cheaper price? Have so many

Chinese lives been sacrificed only for the sake of our comfort and prosperity?" At one point, soon after the road opened, Gyari Nyima came to visit Karze and told us about some Tibetans from southern Nyarong who discovered that family members who had been taken for road-building and never heard from had, in fact, been transported far north to Golmud, an important location in northern Amdo that became the last point of a railway link to Ziling and Lanzhou, in Gansu Province.

In August 1954, the road from Dartsedo opened, and for the first time, we saw motorized vehicles enter Karze. On the old caravan routes, the time required to journey from Beijing to Lhasa was three months; with the road's completion, the journey to Lhasa from Beijing could be made in twenty days. With the opening of the Lhasa road on December 25, 1954, the journey from Karze to Lhasa would take twelve days.

◊ ◊ ◊

During that same year, His Holiness the Dalai Lama was invited to visit China. The Communist Chinese National Assembly was about to draft a constitution, and he and nine other Tibetan representatives were invited to participate. His Holiness saw this invitation as a possibility for helping his people, and he looked forward to an opportunity to meet with Mao Zedong.

The Tibetan populace was greatly agitated about this proposed visit, for we suspected the possibility of treachery. We asked "How can they take the gem of our eyes and the heart of our bodies?" No one wanted His Holiness to make the journey.

The Dalai Lama's party began the long journey from Lhasa by automobile. After ninety miles of travel, the new road was found to be washed out. They continued the journey by horseback along the as-yet-unfinished road, which after a period of heavy rainfall had become prone to landslides and falling boulders. Members of the Dalai Lama's party insisted that the group travel by the old route; but this was taken as an insult, and the Chinese escort insisted that they press on according to plan. Three people were killed, along with many mules and horses. Finally, the party reached a section of road over which, though very rough, they were able to travel by jeep. In this way, they reached Karze, where more than fifty thousand people had gathered from all over the province and from several regions in U-Tsang province to receive the audience of the Dalai Lama.

Many elderly people between seventy and eighty years of age came to Karze monastery that day for what they felt would be their last earthly opportunity to see the Dalai Lama. Bedridden people suffering from serious ailments were carried by their able-bodied kin to receive his blessing.

Under the prevailing circumstances, we felt our only choice was to engage in extensive religious services to ward off any trouble toward our spiritual leader. Everyone did their best to propitiate the national deities, and we held constant prayer vigils that included the chanting of one million mantras for the success of his trip. I was greatly worried about his trip and, for the sake of his long life, fervently sought the benevolent protection of the invisible powers that be.

We Tibetans consider having the opportunity to offer the Dalai Lama all of our personal or family effects a great benefit to our present and future lives. Many who sought his audience that day begged him to accept their offers. They feared that their valuable things might at some point be confiscated by the Chinese. However, His Holiness, on his way to China, was in no position to accept the offers of property.

Everywhere I looked, people were crying. We knew that we stood no chance in challenging the military might of China. Most realized that if we attempted to take on the Chinese physically, we would further endanger His Holiness and the populace would be bound to suffer terribly.

As the delegation proceeded through eastern Kham toward Sichuan, some Khampas, fearing both for the safety of the Dalai Lama and the possibility that the Chinese would try to use him for propaganda purposes, tried to intercept his party before it entered China so that they could somehow take him back into Kham. But the Communists had anticipated such an attempt and had stationed large numbers of troops along the Xikang–Lhasa highway. One of the

THE ADVENT OF COMMUNISM

Dalai Lama's last stops in Tibet was an airfield called Ra-nga namthang in Minyak Ra-nga gang. Approximately thirty thousand people, including some of my family members, went to receive him. They were delighted to see him and tried to race each other in the hope of being the first to receive his blessing, but their hearts were heavy with thoughts of possible treachery and their feelings of help-lessness. They appreciated that he was facing immeasurable problems and this was the means he had chosen to establish a working relation-ship with Mao Zedong, and they knew that his decision must be respected. But, they asked themselves in agony, when would he return, if he ever did?

◊ ◊ ◊

The Dalai Lama remained in China for nearly one year. He has stated in his memoirs that he was constantly told that China was the great-est power in the world. He was taken on tours to various areas. He observed that although China had materially benefited in its drive for industrial progress, it seemed as if the Chinese people themselves had lost all sense of individuality. They all wore the same clothing. Their actions were highly regulated. It was illegal for them to possess foreign newspapers or a radio. All information given to them was delivered through government-sponsored radio programs and newspapers.

Mao assured the Dalai Lama that the PLA generals who were sta-tioned in Lhasa were only there to help him and the people of Tibet and that they had not gone there to exercise any kind of authority. He said that it was the mission of China to bring progress to Tibet by developing its natural resources. Mao appointed the Dalai Lama chairman of a "Preparatory Committee" for the Tibet Autonomous Region. The stated purpose of the committee was to prepare Tibet for regional self-government. But His Holiness realized that the ulti-mate aim of Communist policies was to reshape all who came under Chinese rule into an image of Communist China itself, and this was the ultimate concern that he and his ministers had to face.

Finally, news came that the Dalai Lama would be leaving China. It had been arranged that he would enter Dartsedo and then travel a northern route through Amdo. Because people in many regions of Kham were deeply disappointed in not having the opportunity of his blessing, His Holiness sent representatives to meet the people: Trijang Rinpoche, his junior tutor, visited Gelugpa monasteries; Chung Rinpoche, the Mindoling Lama, was sent to the Nyingma followers; and the Karmapa was sent to those of the Kagyu sect. The visits brought more hope and unity among the Khampas. To the intense relief of the Tibetan people, His Holiness arrived in Lhasa in April of 1955.

◊◊◊

Upon his return to Nyarong in early 1940, Gyari Dorje Namgyal had discovered that a lama named Aten had been appointed by Liu Wenhui to serve as district commissioner of Nyagto, the position the Gyaritsang chieftain had formally held. The Gyaritsang family asked Aten Lama to step down, and he complied; but for years he insisted on the right to retain certain privileges and finally filed suit in Dartsedo a year or so after the Communists had entered the region. To resolve the situation, the Communist authorities summoned Gyari Dorje Namgyal and Aten Lama to appear in court in Dartsedo in 1953.

In China, Gyari Dorje Namgyal had learned enough of Communist ideology to realize that now that the PLA had entered Tibet, the private fortunes of individuals would eventually be confiscated. Traditionally, when a very influential member of Tibetan society passes away, the family makes a large contribution to the monasteries. And so Gyari Dorje Namgyal left instructions that in the event of his death his family was to donate a major portion of the family treasure to various monasteries in the hope that all would not be lost.

The key members of the Gyaritsang clan, including Gyari Nyima, who had been appointed chief administrator of Nyarong, accompanied Gyari Dorje Namgyal to the meeting in Dartsedo. When they arrived, all were placed under house arrest. The Communists had seized that opportunity to weaken our traditional leaders. In detaining Gyari Dorje Namgyal, they removed from action one of the last of the powerful chieftains. His detainment meant that he was not allowed to see the Dalai Lama on his journey to China or to receive the blessing of Chung Rinpoche when he was sent in spring 1955 as the Dalai Lama's emissary to Nyarong. The old man was greatly saddened to miss these rare opportunities. In autumn 1955, Gyari Dorje Namgyal passed away while still under detention.

For some time after the death of Gyari Dorje Namgyal, my brother Ochoe stayed quietly to himself, considering the unenviable position into which this highly respected man had been thrust. Remembering also the circumstances of our father's death, Ochoe recalled the long years of friendship the two older men had shared and the reason for their ultimate separation. The lives of the two friends had taken very different directions. It seemed their troubled last years marked a transition from all we had known of Tibet's past. Now, with our father gone, we realized that our lives would never again be the same; and we could not help but wonder if, ultimately, our destinies would be at all different from his.

6

FORGOTTEN PROMISES

Day-tshal Tulku, the incarnate lama of Karze Day-tshal monastery, died shortly before the "liberation" of our land, leaving behind a four-page document of prophecies of future difficulties to be faced by the people of Tibet after an upcoming invasion. Aware that his own end was coming, he had instructed the monastery to construct four small *chortens*, or religious reliquaries, in each of its corners to hold his ashes. Due to Chinese interference, the people were able only to pile four small mounds of earth over his remains.

Soon after the Communists arrived in Karze, they occupied the Day-tshal monastery and established the *Xiang*, or Village Administrative Office, there. We were told that the function of the office was to peacefully deal with Tibetans in all necessary interactions. Soon afterward, the monastery was overrun with PLA troops.

In 1955, the first persecutions of the monasteries began. Suddenly, the Chinese declared religious life useless to the society. They dressed a few young beggars as monks and nuns and presented them to the monastic community of Kharnang monastery, where the "monks" and "nuns" declared that they were going to marry. The Chinese said that the other monks and nuns should follow suit in order to play a more useful role in the society. This strategy was implemented in many monasteries. Suicides within the monastic community began to occur on a large scale in order to prevent the breaking of vows. Many others pretended to accept a new life as lay individuals but quietly continued their religious practice.

Sonam Dorje, an elderly monk of Kharnang monastery, had been born in our village and was a close friend of my brother Jughuma. One day while visiting my father's home, Sonam Dorje set down his cup of tea and closed his eyes, softly declaring, "All my life I have committed myself to renunciation and the practice of my faith. I cannot now be forced to live as a lay person; it would be better to die than to live under the Chinese and forget religion." Jughuma was concerned about his friend's despondency, but he could not think of anything to say as we rose to say good-bye. Not long after, Sonam Dorje hung himself from a large tree next to Kharnang monastery.

◊ ◊ ◊

In summer 1954, I discovered that I was pregnant. The following spring, I gave birth to a son, Chimi Wangyal. His birth brought great happiness, yet his life began in the spring of a most uncertain year. By that time, my husband Sangdhu Pachen, my brothers, and my brother-in-law Pema Gyaltsen no longer spoke of trade, horses, and the other interests that had occupied them all of their lives. Instead, they gathered to discuss in somber voices the procession of events in the region. No longer was there laughter and lightheartedness during our meals. Remembering our father's warning that the Communists would ruin everything in our lives, we discussed how to evaluate their activities and resist their cunning objectives. Frequently, while reflecting on the seeming futility of the situation, we were overwhelmed with silence. In those moments, as our private thoughts were punctuated by the crackling hearth and the rising wind outside, I looked around at the faces of my family and friends illumined in the firelight and wondered what would happen to them in the next month, in the next year.

Pema Gyaltsen became increasingly serious about the possibility that the men might have to gather together to fight the Communists. It was decided that Sangdhu Pachen would try to take Chimi and me to Lhasa, where he had some close relatives who were prosperous traders. Making arrangements for our departure was very difficult, for any movement had to be carried out secretly. Permission to leave, if applied for from the Chinese, was certain to be refused; and applicants were in danger of being placed under surveillance. The situation was highly unpredictable and volatile, and fighting had already broken out in areas of Karze region and many other places by early spring 1956. Finally, later in that season, we completed the necessary preparations.

Just before our departure, my family hosted a banquet for the community. My sadness at leaving my friends and family turned to shock and disbelief when, immediately after consuming some meat at the banquet, Sangdhu became very ill. Clutching his stomach, he cried out and fell to the ground. I ran to his side, feeling helpless and terror-stricken as I told him to hold on, that help was coming. Though some people immediately set off to find the lama who was our village doctor, Sangdhu died before the lama arrived. No one witnessed the poisoning of his food, but everyone suspected that the Chinese had planted someone to commit this act. Many of our friends and family stood around his body crying. Everything happened so quickly; I first felt numb, then came the realization, "We have waited too long." After that, a terrible weakness swept over me. As tears began to fall from my eyes, I collapsed.

At that time, my son was one year old and I was two months pregnant. Without Sangdhu Pachen, I could not go to Lhasa. Life became more uncertain by the day as changes began coming quickly. The day after my husband's death, I awoke in fear. I tried to calm myself by recollecting things my father and Jughuma had told me that had influenced me throughout my life. Having been a protected and privileged child, I had grown to be a typical wife, fully dependent on husband and family. Now the men of my family were disappearing, and I remembered the brief period of my life when my brother had sought to teach me the value of properly directed determination. I didn't know what to do. But it was obvious that each individual could not rely on others to take initiative and provide protection. My sorrow turned to anger and then to a conviction of determined responsibility as I realized that the only course for the moment was to watch carefully and wait.

From that time on, after realizing the uncertainties and subtleties of the Chinese policies, the Tibetans began comparing the Chinese presence to a Tibetan proverb about leprosy—that it kills one slowly as the fingers fall away from the hand.

After Sangdhu Pachen's death, my mother-in-law, Ma Sampten, grew ill. She was in a state of constant despair. I returned to her home to take care of her, and we spent months scarcely speaking as she grew progressively weaker. Finally, she could not even stand or walk without my help.

My poor little son never experienced the moments of joyous spontaneity that are natural between parents and young children. I tried to make his life pleasant and interesting, but the effort was exhausting. I could only wonder what would happen next. Ma Sampten never recovered from the shock and died about six months after Sangdhu. I then returned to my family's home.

◊ ◊ ◊

In spring 1956, the first of the "Democratic Reforms" were introduced in the Karze region. The properties and herds of the monasteries were seized, and it was announced that in the future they would be transformed into "farm cooperatives." The lamas were told that they must participate in agricultural cultivation and other types of manual labor that involved digging. The monks always had chores they tended to in the monasteries; but because farming involved taking the lives of many small creatures, these practices were traditionally not acceptable for monks and lamas in Buddhist custom.

While doing their forced work in the fields, the monks were made to carry and spread human excrement, which was used as fertilizer, with their bare hands. The Chinese also insisted that the monks and lamas take part in killing birds, insects, rats, and other small animals considered to be pests, as well as sheep and goats. In the evening, they had to satisfy the Chinese soldiers by showing them their quota of dead houseflies and birds and counting the bodies one by one. I witnessed this several times when visiting the monasteries.

The main thrust of the Democratic Reforms was to nationalize all private property and set up "mutual aid teams," or working units of six or seven families. These units were to be the first step toward a more broadly based commune system. It was said that under these reforms Tibetans would finally enjoy liberation.

The populace was informed that all personal land, herds, seeds, and agricultural implements would be collected and used for the betterment and modernization of the collective Tibetan society. Landowners were given receipts for the value of their property with promises of eventual payment, but they were never actually reimbursed. People were told they could keep other personal property but would have to invest a certain fixed sum from their personal holdings into the system.

We soon realized that the long-term plans of the Communists were to take everything we possessed. The initial benefits we had experienced from the completion of the Xikang–Lhasa highway, such as lower prices for important goods like tea and salt, did not last. Ever-increasing restrictions were placed on our actions, including new controls on the caravan routes, which made our traditional methods of trade more difficult.

The PLA supplied us with new fertilizers and introduced insecticides, and told us to grow two additional crops each year. But the soil of mountainous regions like ours is very fragile, and planting must be rotated so that areas can lie fallow and regenerate themselves. Though crop production increased in the first years, eventually the land was not able to take the burden imposed by overcultivation. It became clear to us that although the PLA had claimed they would introduce improved agricultural methods, they lacked even a basic understanding of farming practices necessary in our terrain and climate.

Tibetans consider the earth a living being. The deities of the soil, mountains, water, and sky protect it and give nourishment. Our culture had always existed in perfect balance with our surroundings. We grew only what we needed and it was always enough. In the Communists, we saw only greed. Now it seemed they were planning to cultivate all the available land in order to feed their armies.

For some time, the Communists had been trying to convince everyone to hand over all their arms and ammunition. The rationale was that if these arms were kept in our homes, there would be internal conflicts that would be harmful to the society. They told us, "You don't have to worry about external conflicts or invaders now because we will guard you against them." Of course, our people were not children—we had spent generations in our own land protecting ourselves.

In Kham, it is a tradition for the men to have long swords. The

65

Communists said that the Khampas could not keep these swords because they might fight among themselves and kill somebody. This decree was not very successful because the men did not feel themselves to be in need of outside protection from each other, so the Communists tried to use the political committee of local Tibetans to influence the people. Those on the committee told the Communists, "We don't have any right to insist these people hand over their weapons. That is up to individual Tibetans."

A huge meeting was then called, and the Chinese tried to make my brother Ochoe tell everyone to hand over their arms. My poor brother stood with his head bowed like a prisoner surrounded by Chinese soldiers. The meeting went on for two days. Although Ochoe was frightened, he stood his ground and refused to personally advise people to hand over their arms. Finally he raised his head and, looking into the eyes of his friends gathered before him, only said, "The Chinese are telling us to do this." After the meeting, the soldiers scolded him, saying, "You should have said you yourself felt it was important for the people to turn in their weapons. Of course they wouldn't comply when you just say this is what we want."

Ochoe's position was very precarious. The Chinese had targeted him as a person they wanted to use as an influential mouthpiece. He was totally at their mercy with no hope of escape, yet he knew the necessity of not saying anything to influence the people to do something that could be harmful to them just to save himself. No matter what the consequences, he would never act as a puppet. The others on the committee always wanted Ochoe to speak for them because of his strength of character.

By that time, my brother Jughuma, who was in Lhasa, had come to comprehend the PLA's intentions. He wrote a letter to our family, which fortunately reached us without the knowledge of the Communist authorities. It said, "All arms and ammunition belonging to our family should be handed over to them because our brother is in their hands. As far as the public is concerned, we don't have any right to decide for them."

In a subsequent public meeting, Ochoe said, "We have decided to hand over our weapons because there is no other alternative for our family. As for you in the public, it is your own decision. You have your own right to decide." Our family had seven rifles, three pistols—one of which, a German Luger, held several rounds of ammunition—and swords. All the families had rifles and ammunition, but no one had such weapons as machine guns.

After the PLA attempt to use the political committee to influence the people to hand over their weapons, those on the committee were taken to Karze, where they were quartered in a large house with guards outside in the western section of town. From that point on, though no charges had been brought against them, they lived under conditions that amounted to house arrest; and the public had no access to them. We were not even allowed to bring them food or speak alone with them for a short while.

◊ ◊ ◊

In 1956 the struggle sessions known as *thamzing* first occurred in the Karze region. The purpose of thamzing was to divide the members of the populace. Children were called on to denounce their parents; servants their employers; and the peasants and monks of the monasteries their lamas and abbots. In thamzing, the prisoner could be manhandled and humiliated by twenty, fifty, or even one hundred people. Children and family members sometimes were forced to commit acts of violence against their own families, through fear of being tortured themselves. Many Tibetans died as a result of these sessions.

One day, all the townspeople were called to attend a thamzing session. Several villagers and a lama had been arrested. To our horror, the first lama in our town to be humiliated was our family's special lama, Kharnang Kusho. One of the female soldiers walked over to where the prisoners were standing. The beggars were told to observe how she dealt with the lama and then they were to do the same. Kharnang Kusho was forced to kneel, and the soldier knelt on his legs behind him. She then took a rope and put it in his mouth, as one would do to a horse, and jerked his head backward. She poured urine on his face, trying to force him to drink it. When he refused, she just spilled it on his face.

As the struggle session was going on, the kneeling prisoners were forced to face the crowd. Watching Kharnang Kusho being treated so badly, some townspeople stood up and shouted, "What has our lama done that you are prosecuting him in such a way?" Immediately, soldiers removed those who had spoken out and put them in a truck to be taken to prison. The Chinese explained their religious persecution by telling Kharnang Kusho, "In the name of God, you have been evil and have been fooling the public by using your doctrine for your own benefit."

After witnessing the humiliation of our lamas and friends that day, the whole crowd was crying, saying, "Now our time has come to suffer under the Chinese Communists."

◊ ◊ ◊

One day, our family was informed that there was to be a trial in Karze the following morning and we were expected to be present. The soldiers in Karze brought out all the detained members of the political committee, including my brother Ochoe and other capable Tibetans, as well as several lamas from Karze monastery. They were taken to the center of the town and told to kneel before the people. They were then beaten and verbally abused.

Before the implementation of this violence, public meetings had been held regularly in the villages. The Chinese told us the populace was officially divided into five classes: the religious community, capitalist landowners, the middle class—including merchants, artisans, and peasants (farmers who owned their own land)—agricultural laborers, and servants. The Chinese said that there should be no such thing as rich families and poor families, that all must be the same. They said that the affluent of the society had accumulated their wealth by depriving the beggars of their rights.

Neither the ideology nor the thamzings made sense to us. It was as if suddenly the Communists had gone completely mad. Though we did not trust them, we never imagined this kind of cruelty. The people of Kham had seen many battles but believed if battle was necessary, it must be clean and bravely fought.

There was no longer any room for doubt that the PLA was our enemy. We began rebelling at the plan for the forced communalization of our region. Most of the able-bodied men decided it was time to take their arms and ammunition and retreat to the forest to prepare to fight. Only the elderly, women, children, and the beggars and the very poor who had nothing to lose remained.

The Chinese had influenced some of the beggars and the poor by telling them, "All your wealth was taken by these people and now is the time to retrieve it. We are behind you." They Chinese gave them "titles." They were dressed in uniforms and were armed. Now they were to be recognized as officials. To some, especially women beggars, the Communists said, "We will supply you with plenty of money, but first you have to beat that incarnate lama." Some beggars took money but wouldn't touch the lamas, while others were very greedy and would do almost anything for the Chinese.

The new cadres came to be known as *hurtson chenpo*, the diligent workers. At first they could not use the guns properly, and we laughed at their attempts. But our humor was short-lived. It was a matter of great sorrow to see former beggars, who had always been allowed to live their chosen way of life and had been generously cared for, turn against their own people in this time of need. But one major drawback for the Chinese was that none of the new officials really knew how to be leaders. They didn't know how to properly express themselves when working, and this created much confusion.

The new officials used religious thankas as the carpets underneath the saddles of their horses, and they laughed and joked about other Tibetans as they rode by. One of their songs compared Tibetans to vultures and the Chinese leaders to eagles that the vultures tried to imitate—that we imagined ourselves to able to soar equally as high. They compared us to an ox trying to be as flexible and graceful as a *drong* (wild yak), or a jackal sitting in a tiger's cave pretending to be the tiger. For us, it was quite upsetting to see that many of their horses were so ill-treated that they died.

Before the beggars were given any responsibility, they had to be fully indoctrinated to believe that the wealthy Tibetans and local leaders were their enemies. They were told that their main work was to monitor the society and tell who among the populace was fostering nationalistic feelings. Among those awarded such positions, more than half still thought of themselves as loyal Tibetans; but because they were receiving food and extra amenities, they kept quiet. One beggar prominent in my region in 1956, Yulo Gonpo, was elevated to the highest administrative position afforded such people. He was placed at the secretarial level, allowing him to sit in on planning committees.

Servants and genuinely poor people were also given these positions; but more often than not, they tried to help the Tibetan community. Of course, even if a Tibetan was given a high-sounding title, it had no meaning. An ordinary low-level Chinese staff member always had more actual decision-making power.

Our close friends, the Shivatsangs, were in a difficult position. Like all prominent families, they were closely watched; and anyone seen in their presence was in danger of constant observation. Reluctantly, they decided to leave Karze after Shivatsang's mother died. The Communists had openly declared that anyone could travel freely; but, of course, that was not actually the case. However, it would be difficult to restrain the movements of such an important family without creating an incident. When an important Chinese official who was stationed in Dartsedo came to Karze, Shivatsang took the opportunity to inform him that he and his family were going to Lhasa on pilgrimage. The family left and never returned. We hoped that somehow they had managed to escape to a region where they would be safe.

Soon after the Communists had first arrived in Karze, the Khangsar chieftain, Yeshi Dorje, decided to go to Dartsedo and attempt to reason with the new administration. He was given the political appointment of general secretary of Karze Autonomous Prefecture. However, his attempts to reason proved to be ineffective. From then on, he and several other Tibetan leaders from different regions in Kham were saddled with obligations to attend meetings and engage in never-ending assignments; this made it impossible for them to return to their respective regions and influence the populace in any way. In the following years, Yeshi Dorje's family suffered heavily under Chinese rule during the Cultural Revolution.

◊ ◊ ◊

The situation in Karze soon reached a point where Chinese soldiers took family members from their homes and marched them up into the forest, where they were forced to shout to the men in hiding, "If you don't give up the arms, our family will be prosecuted." The forest was so thick and our men so familiar with its depths that it was impossible for the Chinese to see where the men were hidden, but it was hoped that they would hear their names being called out.

It was not long before everyone was asked to hand over all their riches, including the silver ornaments that most people possessed and the gold that only a few had. All of our rings, bracelets, and traditional ornaments worn over our dresses—even our better clothing— were confiscated. We were left with only old, worn clothing to wear. The soldiers also took statues from the altars of people's homes. They said, "Now we will see if your statue goes up to heaven when I shoot it," and then they shot and damaged the statue.

Some families were able to hide some of their things underground. Certain people were caught doing this and were punished. One resident of our village was tortured, beaten, and suspended from a pole with his hands tied behind him. A fire was built below to create a lot of smoke. The soles of his feet became red and blistered from the heat, and his face turned completely black. Soon he was incapable of saying anything and then fell completely unconscious. Some people were tied by rings around their two thumbs and then suspended. By this method, the flesh would be torn off by the pressure. People who couldn't stand the pain anymore would call out, "Oh, yes, I have hidden it. I will show you where it is. Please take me down." But even after the Chinese had been taken to the hiding place and the valuables had been dug up, the person would not be released. The Chinese still did not believe that the person being interrogated had no more hidden wealth and no further information. The next day, they might torture him or her again, using the same fingers, repeating the process on the same sores, though there was no answer to satisfy them.

These were typical prosecutions employed by the PLA in the Karze region. But the Chinese decided that since so many people were dying, they would shift to such strategies as the bamboo method—the insertion of fine bamboo underneath a fingernail, forcibly pressed downward until the bamboo broke through the skin. In this way people could be kept alive for the purpose of obtaining information and would still be effectively intimidated.

Even before returning to my family's village, I realized the necessity of aiding our men in the forests and keeping them informed of what was happening in Lhobasha and Karze. Now it seemed this was my best opportunity for taking a course of action. Approaching only trustworthy friends, I formed a small underground group of Tibetan women. They in turn brought others to work with us. We decided to fight with whatever means available. We laid out most of our plans in 1956 and brought them into action the following year. We met at night, always covering the windows of our meeting places, and posting guards. We spoke in hushed voices as we listened for the *Gong An Ju,* the police who might be passing in the street.

Ultimately, between fifty to sixty women became involved. In the daytime, we made sure to appear as unconcerned, foolish women, just hanging around the town. If we came across each other during the day, we pretended not to know one another. We had a network of people who passed on messages.

Our group monitored the military installations and the prison. The Communists never suspected that we were observing their whole military situation. We discovered which leader was working in which house in the compound, where the doors were, how many new soldiers were coming in, and what kinds of ammunition they carried. Sometimes people who were arrested for minor offenses such as theft or fighting among themselves told us after being released what they had overheard or seen in the prison.

My work was mainly in arranging contacts and communications and going to inform the men of new developments on the Chinese side. I made appointments for certain women to meet at a designated place after nightfall, when we took supplies and information to the men in the forest. I didn't go out in public very often because we thought they might suspect me due to the prominence of my family. When I did go out, I gave the impression of having gone mad from grief due to the suffering that had been imposed on me. I was pregnant and had let my hair loose. No longer bothering to wear clean clothing, I presented a pitiful appearance. People would say, "Oh look, see what has become of Adhe."

One of the leaders of the resisting Tibetans was Pema Gyaltsen, my brother-in-law. During the afternoons he would come down a little way toward the town to talk with me and arrange a meeting place for later. Toward evening, some men tried to come down to communicate with their families. But the people who had remained behind in town always sent this message to the men in the forest: "Don't come down. Never surrender. This is what they have done to us; they will do worse tomorrow. We will always try to reach you with supplies." And we brought them *tsampa* (a staple food made of roasted barley flour), butter, and whatever was available.

Since the Chinese had had no success in coercing the men to come out from their hiding places in the mountains, they turned to the use of airplanes. The planes were able to locate the men through an aerial survey. Three divisions of calvary were brought into Karze, and other troops followed. It was then that the real battle started between the Tibetans and the People's Liberation Army.

7

DESPERATE BATTLES

Compared to the Chinese, our men were poorly equipped for battle. The ammunition of the resistance came from private stock, and it was usually limited to one or two hundred rounds. When that was finished, the men would have only their swords and daggers to rely on. Because of that, whenever a Chinese soldier fell during battle, the Tibetans immediately tried to grab his gun and bullets. When our men finally ran out of ammunition, they broke their guns so that they could not be used by the PLA.

In spite of our efforts, every day our numbers were decreasing. No matter how many Chinese were killed, more always kept coming. The replacements were fresh troops, completely equipped with modern ammunition.

In 1956, destruction was rampant in all the districts within Karze Autonomous Prefecture—Nyarong, Lithang, Karze, Derge, Bathang, Markham, and Setha. By introducing aerial bombardment, the Chinese had found a method to deal with the Khampas, who were physically better suited to fighting in the high mountains. Russian-made planes set out on bombing raids from airfields in Karze and Chengdu and created widespread panic and devastation throughout Kham.

It was a desperate year for the people of my land. No such devastation had ever been seen. The monasteries of Lithang, Bathang, Derge, Gyalthang, and Changtreng were bombed. Almost all their wealth, including many sacred scriptures, was confiscated and taken to China. The lamas of some monasteries managed to save only a few religious objects by hiding them.

Numbers of Tibetans who belonged to the upper three levels of the five strata into which the Chinese had divided the society were arrested, and many were shot before public audiences. Many lamas and monks were imprisoned without sound reasons, or subjected to public humiliations, or condemned to death after public trials in which the Tibetan populace had no voice. Between 1956 and 1957, several thousand people in the Karze region were executed for taking part in the revolt or aiding the men in the forests.

The event that touched off the simultaneous uprisings throughout Kham was the announcement, in all the districts, of "Democratic Reforms." It united all of eastern Tibet in the struggle for freedom. Even though it was impossible for the leaders in such distant areas as Bathang and Lithang to be in contact in the first month of 1956, the similar circumstances in their regions drew identical responses from their people. To Tibetans, it seemed clear that the creation of communes strictly controlled by Communist Party members would completely destroy our religion and culture.

By spring 1956, citizens of Nyarong region had experienced the same conditions as the rest of Kham. In every village, lamas and leaders were subjected to humiliation, violence, and sometimes death in thamzing sessions. The members of one family of an administrator in eastern Nyarong that refused to give up their weapons were shot. This incident led to a decision throughout the region to fight the PLA.

The Chinese had made one mistake in planning: the Eighteenth Army left a reduced number of troops in Nyarong after they passed through on their way to Chamdo. Although their divisions passed through at intervals, many areas were left with insufficient guard. In early March 1956, two major battles occurred. The Tibetan populace arose and attacked Chinese encampments; under the direction of Dorje Yudon, one of Gyari Nyima's wives, they also attacked the Communist garrison in the Fort of the Female Dragon, laying siege to the castle for about one month. The Chinese suffered great losses throughout Nyarong. Replacements sent from Karze were defeated, until later in the month, when a column of at least fifteen thousand soldiers of the Eighteenth Army was sent in to deal with the rebels. After heavy fighting, the Communists brought the situation under control, and the rebels were forced to flee to the mountains.

The reduced numbers of Tibetan men engaged in the fighting began to concentrate their efforts on attacking the convoys of Chinese trucks that traveled along the new roads. Due to Tibetan resistance, the Chinese were bringing in increasing numbers of supplies guarded by heavily armed soldiers. Large convoys of trucks traveled together, but the Tibetans could stop them by creating landslides.

Afraid that the rebellion would spread to the interior of Tibet, the PLA deployed an additional eighteen divisions, numbering forty thousand troops. The number of refugees from Kham and Amdo entering Lhasa rose to nearly ten thousand. Many of these refugees were men between twenty-five and thirty years of age.

◊ ◊ ◊

In Nyarong, there is a large plain known as Bu na thang. It was there in the latter part of 1956 that many scattered resistance fighters from different localities decided to regroup into a large body. Many women, children, and elderly Tibetans were with the men, for the situation by that time had become unbearable in their homes. Most of the Tibetans from eastern Kham had run out of ammunition and had only their swords with which to fight. Unfortunately, they were spotted by air surveillance and, shortly after they arrived, surrounded by three rounds of Chinese infantry.

The men fighting there were desperate. They had not only themselves but their families to protect. They were undernourished and exhausted. The battlefield was a scene of panic and desperation. Women, children, infants, and the elderly were trapped in the fighting.

Many Tibetans of our region who were able to fight were killed in this battle. It was found that when they died, the grip of their hands on their swords had been so tight, so intense, that their hands turned brown from the blood.

There is one man named Aghey who is alive today in Nyarong. My family was closely associated with him and his parents; his mother was an older sister of Pema and Dechen Wangmo Shivatsang, my friends from Karze. Their family lived in the nomadic region of Phitsha, between Nyarong and Lithang. On the plain of Bu na thang, Aghey lost his parents and all the rest of his family members. He was only fifteen years of age at the time. His legs and one of his arms were injured.

After the battle, the Chinese scrutinized each body to make certain it was really dead. Any people pretending to be dead and found alive were summarily shot. Fortunately, they somehow decided not to shoot Aghey. Standing beside the bodies of his parents, he raised his hands in surrender. Looking around the field, he saw so many bodies that they seemed like countless pebbles scattered about. He saw the body of one Tibetan mother who had been shot. Her child was beside her, and not knowing that she was dead, the crying baby was attempting to breastfeed, trying first one breast, then the other. The Chinese came and took the child.

Hundreds of vultures began to circle in the sky above. There were many small streams running through the field, the water running red from spilled blood. For several days these streams remained stained.

Immediately after his arrest, Aghey was taken to a hospital. The Chinese tried to learn more information from him regarding how many were still hiding in the forests, who was aiding and bringing information to them, and the plans of the remaining Tibetan fighters. Aghey was sentenced to twenty years of imprisonment. Meanwhile, from the Karze side, Tibetans were still fighting in the forest.

In Setha—a region lying north of Karze on the Golok border of Amdo and Kham—is a very high mountain whose summit is always shrouded in fog. Known as Sergyi Drongri Mukpo, Abode of the Golden Yak, it is considered to be a sacred mountain, the site of the deity Mahakala. At one point in 1957, several thousand Tibetan fighters were hiding around the base of the mountain. One of the leaders was a nomadic chieftain named Washul Tolho. Pema Gyaltsen had wanted to join that group, but since Ochoe was under such close surveillance, he had decided to stay near Karze.

A major battle took place there in the winter. The horses the Chinese had brought with them from the plains—unused to those surroundings—had great difficulty, for they wore horseshoes that caused them to slide in the snow. However, the Tibetans, who were down to their last guns and swords and the remnants of ammunition from their homes, were caught again by air surveillance. Before long, their ammunition was spent and they had to resort to fighting with their swords. In battles such as this, Khampas seldom surrendered. It was a matter of do or die. In the end, although some Tibetans were arrested and taken as prisoners, most were killed. Washul Tolho and his wife Sonam Dolma were among the Tibetan fighters who were captured. Washul Tolho was beaten and dragged around before the other captives. Rope was tied around his neck, twisted around his arms, and fastened with his hands behind his back. Then they brought him before his wife. Looking at his face, she could see that he was almost dead. He was unable to utter a word, and within a few moments, he died. Years later, I would meet Sonam Dolma and learn the details that led to her imprisonment.

Afterward, when people went to the scene of the battle of Sergyi Drongri Mukpo, it seemed that wherever one looked, there were the carcasses of horses, decaying bodies of human beings, and bones. A strong odor of death hung over the place for some time.

◊ ◊ ◊

At this time, there was a Chinese military leader who was regarded as the deadliest prosecutor among the Chinese in our area. He was the *Xian Zhang*, a subdistrict official in charge of both military and civil administration. (Throughout Kham, civil administrators were military officials who just exchanged their uniforms for civilian dress.) His house was located outside of the military compound in Lhobasha in the northern section of the village, known to us as Drushi. He spent a good deal of time at his house; but being the main official in our district, he often traveled to the garrison and Karze dzong. Whenever he walked through our village, he gave the appearance of great confidence. He was always armed and followed by a group of soldiers.

It was this official, who arrived in Lhobasha in the wake of the initial Communist military force, who began to instigate the terrible tortures inflicted on the populace in Karze region. Tibetans of my generation had never been exposed to the actions of such a cruel and calculating person. His heart seemed to be made of stone. Through him we learned that the Chinese considered us worthless barbarians—which is what they generally considered everyone who is not Chinese. Although they had been given orders not to use their traditional word meaning wild barbarians, *mantze*, it began to be heard.

The unusually cruel behavior of this Chinese administrator, his overpowering nature, his disregard for our identity, and the atrocities that he initiated caused the populace to hate him. He turned our district into a region of mistrust and fear. He was especially interested in accumulating precious gold and Zi stones, and he even tortured elderly people to find out where their jewelry was hidden. One day we learned of orders issued by him that resulted in the hanging of a married couple in Karze who had openly opposed Chinese policies. This incident triggered our decisive action toward him.

We informed the men in the forest of the location of his house in Drushi and how many soldiers were guarding it. One winter night, near the end of 1956, Pema Gyaltsen and four of his men raided the official's residence. Surprising the armed guards outside, they killed them by stabbing them. The Chinese officers were relaxing inside, confident that the soldiers were guarding them. Pema Gyaltsen and the others quietly entered the house and found the administrator and two other officers. The officers had their guns hanging on the walls, but they were so intimidated by the long, sharp, traditional swords that they just cowered, covering their heads with their hands. All three were killed. News of the attack spread like wildfire throughout the Tibetan community. Its success gave our people a surge of hope; yet at the same time, we did not know what it would lead to.

The Chinese described the slain military superior as a "martyr" and a "freedom fighter," a loyal Communist who had given his life for the great vision of Mao Zedong. They held a big funeral procession with many flowers and speeches. His body was later taken to China for a hero's burial. After his death, the torturous forms of persecution stopped for a while in our locality.

One day, I decided to try to visit my brother Ochoe in Karze. I bundled Chimi in warm clothing and the two of us rode on my horse. Though I was happy to be allowed to meet with Ochoe and to see that the sight of his nephew cheered him, we weren't provided the privacy necessary to have a serious conversation. While Chimi and I were in the building, one of the Chinese officers took notice of us. Perhaps it was the sight of my poor clothing that caused him to offer a large quantity of silver coins in exchange for my son. I thanked him but, looking downward, shook my head, hoping he wouldn't notice that my knees had begun to shake as he explained that Chimi could have a very good life if I were only willing to make a personal sacrifice for his sake.

Holding my one-year-old baby harder, in that moment, I felt what he meant to me. He and the unborn child I carried were all that remained of my life with my husband. Looking at his face, I could see vestiges of his father, along with similarities to me. The love Chimi felt for me was the most precious remaining aspect of my own life, and I could not imagine him being taken to a place where he would never know the memory of his father and his heritage, where he would be separated from his mother and taught to accept a different life which, though perhaps more comfortable, would be a lie. Hurrying outside, I decided not to bring my son to Karze again until perhaps some change in the situation occurred.

One day, during the winter of 1957, my brother Ochoe and other members of the political committee were charged with the official's death. It was announced that Ochoe was to be executed.

When Pema Gyaltsen heard of this, he and four other men decided to surrender. He didn't want Ochoe to be executed because, besides being a member of his family, Ochoe was a very capable, hardworking, and practical man in the society. Pema and his men descended from the mountain and surrendered. He told the Chinese, "My brother-in-law has been under house arrest most of this time, so it is not possible for him to have had any hand in the assassination. Actually, it is I who did it. There is no reason to execute my brother-in-law for things he has not done." Immediately, Pema Gyaltsen was manacled. The PLA officers present commended him for doing a very good thing by admitting his crime and said that he would soon be released. He looked in the direction of his family just before he was led away. For a second, our eyes met, and then he and the others were helped into the back of a truck. For almost one year, Pema was kept in chains in solitary confinement.

When the Tibetans remaining in the forests heard what had happened to Pema, there was another fight, a very intense battle during which most of the remaining men perished. Only a handful remained in our region.

It seemed that all hope was gone for us. The Chinese had taken everything. We didn't know what they would do next, for they had already surpassed our worst expectations. The remaining villagers were hungry. We were being forced to attend political meetings during which we were told of the glories of China. I was glad that my father was not alive to see these things, and I found comfort only in the possibility that somewhere my brother Jughuma might be free.

◊ ◊ ◊

In the autumn of 1957, six months after my husband's death and one month after my mother-in-law's demise, my second child was born. I had returned with the remaining villagers and the herds to the nomadic region for the season. However, none of us felt like taking part in our usual celebrations. So many of our close relatives and friends were either gone or living in danger and discomfort. We could not imagine what we would face next in a few weeks when we had to descend to the village.

I was staying with my son, Chimi, in a tent near my family. My sisters helped with the delivery of my little girl, who was given the name Tashi Khando. Her birth immediately reminded me of the birth of my son and of the care my husband had given me. He had been there to share my joy and my pain, but now there was no one to look after me or the child. Now that she was born, the truth of his loss became painfully, crushingly vivid. I kept feeling how unfortunate it was, how sad it was that my husband would never see her. Falling into a state of deep despair, I found it difficult to concentrate on caring for the children. My sister Sera Ma watched them while I stayed alone crying in my tent.

My baby was a pretty child with lovely skin and red cheeks. She was usually very calm and seemed to be quite happy. People who looked at her said, "Oh, what a beautiful baby." It seemed so odd to have given birth to a child in those dangerous, uncertain times. Remembering my own childhood, I wondered, what could I ever possibly offer her? What kind of life would be her inheritance?

8

ARREST

After some time, one of Pema's men, Lhoyang, broke down under torture and gave my name as one of the people who had helped the resistance fighters. Jughuma's assistant, Paljor, had been enlisted to work as one of the Tibetan translators for the Chinese. He came up to our camp in the nomadic regions to warn me that I might be arrested and that if that happened, I would be subjected to public manhandling by people I might not have liked before or who didn't like me. He admonished me, "You will suffer if you don't accept the Chinese and keep your mouth shut." He promised that he would try to cover for me by saying that I had never opposed the Chinese system.

As I gazed at the beautiful meadows around me, I wondered if this was the last time that I would see them and feel the freedom of the high mountains. As a child, I had never conceived of leaving this place. It was a most important part of me. I'd always felt that I belonged to the meadows, as did the flowers, the clouds, and the brilliant stars that filled the night sky above our evening fires as we laughed together and told stories of our land. I thought of my happy childhood friends with garlands of flowers in their hair and remembered how free we were in our innocence. I recalled the loving care of my brother Jughuma and the security of his company and how we had laughed as we rode together, sharing our special understanding.

I refused to bring more fear to those who were close to me, and so it seemed there was no one to whom I could speak of my fears and uncertainties. I remembered how my husband had died an early death at the Communists' hands; and I knew that, like him, there was nothing I could do to change my destiny. I could only wait.

Every night, I held my children close to me and wondered when my time would come. I looked hard at their faces and tried to memorize everything about them. At any moment, I might be taken away from them and I did not know when—or if—they would be returned to me. My little daughter was only one year old. My son, Chimi Wangyal, now three years old, could not stand to be separated from me. He could not remember his father. Even though he was just a young child, he had somehow developed a very protective instinct toward me.

I wondered what kind of life my husband and I might have been able to give him if we had managed to escape to Lhasa. What would become of this sweet child when I was taken away?

Very early in the morning of October 16, 1958, I arose. Little Chimi was just waking up. I hugged him and dressed him in his tiny yellow chuba, securing its red sash and adjusting the cloth above it, as he stood sleepily looking into my eyes, gently holding onto my braids. Then I glanced at my still-sleeping daughter and smiled. Suddenly, the sound of barking dogs attracted my attention. Lifting the tent flap, I saw six armed Chinese policemen and three Tibetans. "They're here to arrest me!" I thought, and my legs began to feel weak. As they came closer, I realized that Paljor, Jughuma's servant, was among them.

One of the Tibetans ordered, "You must come with us now." I told them that it wasn't possible because I could not leave my children. At that point, first one man, then several more came forward and started beating me. They kicked and hit me, and I was struck very hard on my right ear. I fell on the floor and was tied with rope. As they tied me, my little daughter, now awake, laughed happily as she sat on the bed. She must have thought that we were playing a game.

My son kept crying, screaming, and calling, "Ama, Ama." He kept trying to reach me to grasp my dress, but the soldiers kept pushing him back, kicking him hard with their boots. Looking up, I saw that Paljor was in tears. He tried in vain to comfort Chimi, whose eyes were wild with fright. I still refused to walk, insisting that I couldn't leave my children, and so they dragged me outside. Everyone had gathered outside their tents, and they begged them not to take me. But it was useless. Pulling the ropes, they dragged me along the ground a distance of about one kilometer to Karze Day-tshal monastery.

As I was being taken away, I could hear my women friends crying and my children's voices calling from a long distance. For a while, it was possible to see the small terrified figure of my son running, trying to catch up, and calling to me. I do not know how I didn't die then and there.

When we reached the monastery, they were angry with me for having refused to cooperate. They complained that I hadn't listened to them and had been unwilling to walk. One of the Chinese policemen said, "We can see that you are just a woman. Do you know what you have done? Now you will realize whether you or we have won. Now we will see how brave and strong you really are."

They tied my hands behind me, pulled them upward with a rope, and then suspended me from the ceiling. My arms felt as though they would break, and my chest felt very tight. Initially, all that registered in my mind was the sound of them laughing at me. Then the thought came that I mustn't say anything. I decided not to plead for mercy. Suddenly, everything below me started spinning, and I lost consciousness. Afterward, Paljor told me that mucus had been coming out of my mouth.

When I woke up, I was lying on the floor. Shortly after I regained consciousness, they came and pulled me to my feet. I was taken to the courtyard. While they complained that I would "never listen," they pushed me up onto a horse and again tied my hands from the back and then tied my legs as well. In that manner, they took me to Karze prison. As we went along, I had no balance and kept falling over to one side or another. Just before I fell off the horse, they would push me up again.

The first thing that they did at the prison was take away my chuba belt, bootstraps, the silk cords that tied my hair, my rosary, and my amulets. This, of course, was to prevent suicide. Then I was taken downstairs and put into a cell for women prisoners. Inside were four women who were staring at each other, afraid to speak. Conversation was not allowed. The female guard showed me one spot where I was supposed to stay. There was no type of bedding and no mattresses.

A wooden bucket in the center of the room served as the only toilet. There was no water available inside the cell, which was about nine by fifteen feet. It had no electricity or any form of lighting except for a small hole through which the guards looked. Every morning at ten and in the evening at five, someone would be allowed to go out and empty the toilet pot. The food given to the prisoners was quite poor and meager. There was no form of cleaning whatsoever.

Sometimes we heard people walking outside, and occasionally a child among them was heard crying. That sound always gave me a burning sensation in my heart. I hardly slept at night, and when I did, I dreamt of being with my children, embracing them, breastfeeding them, preparing their meals. In the morning, I woke up feeling completely lost, and wondered, "What is happening to them?"

Immediately after my arrest and imprisonment, they executed two Tibetans. In the early morning of the fourth day, I was called upstairs to an office where five Chinese policemen and a translator were waiting. I learned then that Pema Gyaltsen and I were being charged as two of the key rebels in the Karze region of Kham.

The head officer said, "You'd better distinguish between the black sheep and the white sheep. Now you must confess. If you don't confess everything, you will have a very hard time. Your children are outside with no one to look after them. If you tell us the truth, you can go."

They accused me of being the leader of the women's resistance. I told them that I knew of no one involved in any such thing, and I gave them several personal reasons that gave me cause to hate the Chinese. I told them, "My father died in your hospital shortly after he began speaking out regarding your policies. My husband died before my eyes. Look at what has happened to my brother and brother-in-law. Under these circumstances, what do you expect me to feel? Still, there was no need to involve other people in my actions." The head officer said, "We have already heard from your mother and your friends all that you have done. We are now just asking for the sake of formality."

During our resistance meetings, my friends and I had all promised each other never to divulge anything under questioning about what we were doing or even about knowing each other. Until the Chinese brought someone face to face with me who had been involved or who had known about our activities, I decided to say nothing.

While being interrogated, I was handcuffed, kicked, and struck with rifle butts all over my body. They forced me to kneel on two sharpened triangular pieces of wood with my hands raised above my head. Every time I lowered my arms, they struck my elbows with rifle butts. Somehow, though, I managed not to tell them anything.

The first interrogation ended. The senior Chinese policeman told me, "You should now consider whether you want to go back and take care of your two children or whether you would prefer to be executed. If you tell us what your mother has already told us—how you people met, who the leaders were, who else was in the group—then you can return to your family."

I was given three days in my cell to decide whether I wanted to go back to my children and my mother by informing on all the members in the group, or whether I was prepared to die for the sake of not cooperating.

When I was brought back upstairs, the senior officer said, "Now tell us what you have concluded." I responded, "You have given me three days to think over these two choices, but now I can only tell you that I have nothing to confess. If I concoct things, it won't do you any good, so what can I do? I have no names to give you. I have nothing to say."

The interrogator replied, "You have chosen death for yourself." After translating this for me, Yeshi Dorje, the Tibetan translator, warned me in our own language, "If you don't tell them anything, they will kill you." Then the interrogator said, "So you still think that you are very brave and bold." He ordered the soldiers to handcuff me, and I was returned to my cell.

Conditions there were very uncomfortable. The floors were cold and damp, and the room smelled terrible. All these days I hadn't been able to breastfeed my daughter, and my breasts had swollen and were causing me pain. There was a pain in my right ear, and I found that I could no longer hear from that side. I constantly imagined that I could hear a child crying.

Because I was handcuffed, I realized the great extent to which a human being is disabled by not having the use of one's hands. Even to stand up made me feel uneasy. I could not even go to the toilet without someone offering to help me by lifting my chuba and holding me steady.

Some of the women in my cell had decided to risk whispering a few words to each other in the night. Their names were Lhaga, Lhamo Dolma, and Dolma Yagtso. These were my most compatible companions.

Lhaga, the daughter of Gyapontsang of Dhargye, was related to the leading families of the five Hor States, including the Sandhutsangs and the Chagzotsangs. The Gyapontsang family also had very close ties with Reting Rinpoche, the regent of the Fourteenth Dalai Lama. Lhaga had been given in marriage to the house of Beri Pon, and from that time she had been known as Beri Lhaga.

Lhamo Dolma was a nun who was known in the society as someone who could give good divinations. She was always consulted by the Khampas in her region when they were planning attacks and strategies. They asked her when and where they should fight in the mountains or whether they should surrender. For this, she was arrested and detained.

Dolma Yagtso, my third cellmate, was arrested after an incident that occurred in 1958, after the Tibetans had finally run out of arms and ammunition and were forced to participate in the communes being organized in Karze. The remaining lands, property, and animals of the Tibetans in our region were seized. People were made to work twelve to fourteen hours a day, and a system of political workpoints was introduced. Each day, the amount of work each member of the commune had completed was tabulated, and the worker was awarded a certain number of points and a commensurate amount of grain. Party policy demanded that the people "tighten their belts," and this policy was enforced with the slogan, "Eat Less, Produce More." Every commune was required to meet a production quota fixed by the Party. If these quotas were not met, the members of the commune were punished. If the commune produced more than the production quota, they were rewarded with higher work-points. The workers were told that based on the work-points, in time they would receive currency and coupons that would entitle them to a certain amount of grain and small quantities of butter or oil.

The communes were required to hand over a portion of the food production as tax and sell another portion to the state for a very low price. Ultimately, the bulk of the communes' produce was sent to China. After the commune system was in place, the Chinese began the propagation of winter wheat, which they preferred, and the fields under barley cultivation decreased. It soon became very difficult even for Tibetans who were not imprisoned to obtain our traditional tsampa.

Communal kitchens were established. The food most commonly served was a watery soup with a sprinkling of vegetable parts that would ordinarily be thrown away, such as the parts of radishes that join the leaves. The commune workers lived in a constant state of hunger. Those who had more strength bore the responsibility of sharing what they earned with the aged and infirm. During those times, families could not have a fireplace; everyone was supposed to cook and eat their meals from a communal kitchen.

One day, the house that Dolma Yagtso was living in caught fire. She was blamed and charged with the possession of an illegal stove and cooking her own meals, and was brought to Karze prison.

When the prisoners were interrogated, for the sake of saying something, they spoke about very insignificant things. After four days, I was called again and did the same kind of generalizing. The interrogators got very angry and started manhandling me. I'd been continuously handcuffed for four days, and my hands were still cuffed behind my back. They kicked me so heavily on the thighs that a lump developed; it can still be felt thirty-nine years later.

As I fell to the ground, I was manhandled by seven or eight Chinese policemen. Except for Yeshi Dorje, everyone was hitting me where they liked. Sometimes they pulled my hair; other times they stood me up, then forced my knees down on pieces of sharpened wood. Once they inserted fine bamboo all the way under my second fingernail until the skin below the nail was broken at the base of the first joint. Pushing bit by bit, they tried to force me to give them information. However, the faces of my family and friends kept coming before me, and by now it was apparent that if I began to talk, there would be no end. Finally, I passed out from the pain.

These types of beatings began to happen frequently. I was called up for interrogation and then was beaten and thrown back down into the cell. All the prison staff considered me to be the worst of the condemned.

Every night I thought about my friends. All of us were one in heart. If I said anything about even one of them to the Chinese, ultimately they would want the names of all my other colleagues and the other Tibetans who had revolted. I realized that then they would undergo the same kind of ill treatment and detention, and that they also had parents, children, and husbands. Considering these things, it was simple to see that it was definitely better not to say anything about them. After suffering tremendously and undergoing so many atrocities, I couldn't bear the thought of inflicting this on my friends. Every night, I reaffirmed my resolve to be silent, no matter what.

About two months after my arrest, Lhoyang, under severe torture, broke down again and told the Chinese everything. One day, I was called up to the interrogator's office. As I walked into the room, I saw Lhoyang standing there. Immediately a feeling of blackness came into my heart. My legs felt weak. I was told, "Now you'd better listen carefully. Since you won't say anything, Lhoyang will tell the truth for you."

By that time, Lhoyang had been tortured so severely that he no longer had the inner strength to withstand anything. They had told him, "If you tell us everything about Adhe and make her confess, we will release you immediately." Lhoyang began to speak. "Oh Adhe, now it is better that you confess and accept. When we were in the mountains, it was you who brought us information regarding the Chinese. When we killed the Communist official, it was you who always kept a gun under your pillow and volunteered to come and fight with us, but Pema Gyaltsen wouldn't allow it." He continued, "Your mother taught you to hate the Chinese, and it was you who influenced your friends to work against us."

Every time Lhoyang said something, I would make a sighing noise to imply that he was lying. At one point while I was doing this, they picked up a stoker from the fireplace and hit me on the head shouting, "Still you are not accepting the truth of your crime!"

I replied, "You and Lhoyang are insisting on the truth of these things. I cannot open my heart and show you. All these names that Lhoyang mentioned mean nothing to me. I cannot force other Tibetans to take responsibility for your accusations. Whomever I might conjure up for the sake of giving you an answer would not have any reason to accept them. You wanted to kill me. I don't have anything to add, so it is better that you kill me now."

Then once again they uttered the words that frightened me the most, "Today, Lhoyang has told us everything. Tomorrow, we are going to bring your mother, who is also detained." I have no way out, I thought to myself. Lhoyang has told these things. My mother is going to tell. There is no hope.

I raised my eyes and, looking into the eyes of the main official, asked, "Please...kill me." They began shouting, "You don't have to tell us to kill you. You will die." I was hit a few times, and then a senior official ordered them to stop.

Approaching me, the senior official asked, "Why do you keep insisting that you are not the main one responsible? Pema Gyaltsen is saying that you are the main one responsible. Your mother is saying that you are the main one responsible. It is better for you to confess so that you can return to your children. Why don't you think of their well-being? Otherwise, your time to die is nearly at hand."

After many days, I was again called to the office. When they knocked on the cell door and yelled, "Adhe, come out," the first thought that occurred to me was, "What if they brought my mother?" My heart was beating very rapidly. I knew that Pema Gyaltsen would not divulge information; I had absolute trust in him. But I worried about my mother, who was old and would not survive the kind of beatings and torture the prisoners were made to endure. Out of fear and confusion, she would probably tell them everything that they wanted to know.

As I walked into the room, I was very happy to see that she was not there. An official looked into my eyes and said, "Now your mother has told us everything, and Lhoyang has stood before you and revealed the details of your crimes. There are two paths that you can choose. One path leads to your mother and the other is to face execution, which you do not have to tell us to do—if you follow this path, it will happen."

By this time, after being constantly handcuffed for months, my hands were very swollen, even the palms. My inmates had to take care of me like a baby, feeding me, lifting my chuba when I needed to relieve myself, helping me to stand and to sit. These things came into my mind and, finally, I said, "I am seriously telling you that I have nothing more to add. Of course, the earlier that I could be with my children, the better it would be for me; but at the same time, I cannot lie about other people. Instead of ill-treating me with these handcuffs and making me suffer with all this pain in my breasts, it is better for me if you kill me immediately because I cannot concoct things and I don't have anything more to speak of regarding what you are saying."

Later, I learned that my mother had never been detained. They had just been using her name to convince me that it was hopeless not to talk.

All the time we were in Karze prison, Pema Gyaltsen and I were not allowed to meet. At first, he had been imprisoned in a very small structure built by the Chinese. Later he was moved to a cell not too far from my own.

A new prisoner, Bhumo Yalu, came to our cell. Her husband was in the resistance, and she was imprisoned for having helped him in a manner similar to what my group had been doing. By the time of her detention, she was very depressed and quite terrified by her experience. Seeing this poor woman who was quite a bit older than me made me feel that she was more in need of help than myself.

Sanitation in our prison cell was growing worse and worse. We were never allowed to wash. At that time, I did not realize that it would be eleven years before I had an opportunity to bathe my body.

Most of us had no extra clothing. When we women experienced our menstrual cycles, we had nothing of any sort to check the flow of blood. It went all over our chubas, and later, after it had dried, we tried to scrape it off. Of course, we never had the opportunity to wash our clothing. Ultimately, I was to wear the same filthy dress every day for five years.

These conditions were embarrassing and demeaning. We were people who were accustomed to exercise, light, and open air. The only compensation was that we were all in the same situation. Outwardly, we might as well have been animals, but somehow this increased our determination not to be reduced to behavior that would undermine our humanity. We tried to assist each other in whatever small ways we could as we waited in the darkness for a day when something out of the ordinary would happen.

◊ ◊ ◊

Very early one morning, my name was called. Many policemen were standing outside the door. It was still quite dark outside and seemed to be the middle of the night. The handcuffs were unfastened from in front of me and refastened behind my back. I thought they were taking me to the execution ground. I began thinking about how I would never again see my mother and my children, but at least I had a feeling that my friends would look after them. As we climbed the stairs and went outside, I walked with my head down.

Suddenly, I looked up and saw a crowd of people. Ten other Tibetans, all men, were also handcuffed. A truck carrying armed guards came into the courtyard. We were thrown into the truck like inanimate loads. Armed guards positioned themselves at the head of the truck, and we were tied together with rope. The truck took us to Lhobasha.

I was amazed to see a huge gathering of thousands of people, much greater than the population of our village. The people of Lhobasha were standing in the front of the crowd. I could see my brother Nyima and many of my colleagues, all of whom were crying.

We were made to kneel down with our heads lowered and were told not to look up. Every time I tried to look around the crowd to see familiar faces, the police hit me. Years later, my friends told me that after seeing me in that situation, they found it impossible to eat without thinking of me and had difficulty sleeping at night.

Choenyi Dolma, Bhombi, and Sonam Gyurme, the servants from my husband's family, were brought forward to beat me. I later found out that the three had been indoctrinated for one week to prepare them for this day. They had been told, "Adhe is a counterrevolutionary who is responsible for killing a Chinese officer," and such things that were useful to justify the thamzing. But none of the three wanted to ill-treat me. One of them spoke out, saying, "If her husband was alive, we would have done it to him, but she has not hurt us in any way." None of them could be persuaded to beat me. A female Chinese soldier was sent forward in their place. The woman glared at me as she walked past and then behind me. Then, she yanked sharply on my plaited hair and repeatedly jammed her knee into the back of my neck. She also repeatedly hit my right eye with her fist, attempting to damage it. I felt tremendous pain and noise in my ears. The woman's anger was probably compounded by the refusal of my former servants to beat me.

All eleven of us were kneeling in a line. Each was accused and beaten in turn. Among us were blind Palden, a subchieftain who came from Karze—known by this nickname because he was blind in the left eye—and Tsewang Tashi, a neighbor from Lhobasha whose home was very close to our own. These two had been aiding the men who were fighting in the forests. Three rinpoches also suffered humiliation. The meeting lasted from early morning until almost noon.

During the morning, our ropes had been untied; and after the struggle session, I tried to dust off my chuba. This angered my guards, and so they again wrapped the rope around my arms and tightened it, pulling from both sides. The circulation in my arms stopped. In this way, I rode back to the prison.

Before we were taken back to our cells, we were all put into one room. I tried to pull myself out of the ropes and in the process fell unconscious. Upon awakening, I saw the guards staring at me. I looked around the room and saw that Tsewang Tashi was looking directly at me from the other side. Tears were falling down his cheeks.

Back in the cell, I was again handcuffed. My right eye was swollen and blackened from the beating, and I could see only from the left one. Lhaga was quite concerned for my eye and was very helpful in tending to my needs. She sat near me and was very kind in kneading my portion of tsampa and helping me eat. Of course, we were not allowed to help each other, but it was impossible for us not to.

After a few days, I was called back to the office, threatened with my mother's confession, and sent back down to my cell to think. Before long, I was summoned again and told, "Now you realize your situation and the situation of the society outside the prison. Now you are the enemy of the society." Of course, I did not believe that the people considered me their enemy, especially since my friends had not been willing to harm me. It was just another trick.

The round of interrogations lasted for many days. I continued my plea of "not guilty." Each time I said, "I've already told you whatever I can. My two children are without anyone to take care of them. Why would I purposely leave them alone?"

One morning, Bhumo Yalu and I were called out of the cell and taken upstairs. They took off my handcuffs, which were difficult to remove because they had begun to be wedged deeply into the skin. My hands were then tied in back with ropes. We were driven down to the plain below to a place where an army headquarters had been built. When we arrived at the grounds, a huge crowd was gathered. The furthest person in the crowd could be seen only as a tiny object. A sign about eight by four inches was hung around my neck. We were taken to a large open area in front of the buildings where they had collected thirty other prisoners who were tied and kneeling in a line.

Before long, I heard a commotion, and then I saw Pema Gyaltsen being brought out. He also had a sign on his chest. His was written in red letters with a red cross, whereas mine was written in black letters with no cross. As they walked along, Pema Gyaltsen was smiling. He was jumping here and there and shrugging off the guards on each side who were holding him with one hand and waving a pistol with the other. He was giving them a difficult time.

When they reached us, we were made to stand. Pema was made to walk at the head of the line, with me behind him, and then the other prisoners. When we reached the final site, Pema Gyaltsen and I were separated out and made to kneel down facing each other for some time. I saw that the rope tying him came around his throat, wound around his arms, and was pulled back tightly, tying his hands at the back. Because of the rope at his throat, he couldn't speak or breathe properly, and his face was becoming swollen. As we faced each other, he just kept smiling at me.

Since my arrest, I had seen Pema only from a distance on two occasions when we were allowed to go and empty the urinal pots. We had never been able to get close enough to each other to speak.

A voice came over the loudspeaker, saying, "Today we are going to execute Pema Gyaltsen. It has been decided that Adhe Tapontsang will suffer throughout the rest of her life. Today she is sentenced to sixteen years of 'Reform through Labor.'"

Then the others were all charged as reactionaries and rebels who had revolted against the Chinese. They received sentences of five, seven, eight, or ten years.

Pema Gyaltsen and I were made to stand up. As we stood, Chinese music began blaring over the loudspeakers and a voice said, "Today we are going to take revenge for our leader's death." I said to Pema, "Quickly now, just pray to the Three Jewels." He nodded and became still.

After a moment, I heard two gunshots, and Pema fell before me. Pieces of his brain and his blood splashed onto my dress. He had been shot from behind. His execution occurred when he was thirty-three years old, around eleven in the morning, on a day in the late winter of 1959.

I immediately felt as if there was no sensation in my body. I asked the Chinese to kill me also; but they said, "No, if we kill you, it's like Pema Gyaltsen in front of your eyes. It will be over too quickly. We want you to suffer for the rest of your life. Now you see who has won." Then over the loudspeakers they announced, "You can see today what will happen if you follow the Communists, and what will happen if you follow people like Pema Gyaltsen and Adhe Tapontsang. Who can help you then? Tell us. Now you can see whether America comes to your aid, whether the Dalai Lama comes to your aid. If you listen to us, you will have a happy life; otherwise, you will meet the same end as Pema Gyaltsen."

Bhumo Yalu was so frightened by the execution that her legs crumpled and she was unable to walk. Two guards grabbed her on each side and dragged her in the same way I had been dragged when arrested. When we returned to the prison, she was roughly thrown into the cell. I thought perhaps she had been badly kicked with their boots and that was the reason for her condition. I quietly asked, "Where did they hit you?" She answered, "They didn't hit me, but now I am feeling no sensation in my feet and can't seem to move them." After a little while, though, she did recover fully.

After I was sentenced, there were no more interrogations. I simply sat with my inmates in the darkened cell day after day. For a while I had been quite fearful of losing sight in my eye, but fortunately it healed. Sometimes late in the night we risked whispering to each other, but it was impossible to speak much.

We sat and listened to the sounds going by outside and wondered what was happening. When one is imprisoned, the smallest sound takes on a magnitude of importance. The sound of approaching feet can mean that someone is about to be tormented, or it can mean that the terrible monotony of the day will be broken by some type of meal. The sound of a bird means that it is light outside. The sound of a voice can give a scrap of news. The sound of trucks can mean that a major change is about to happen.

I was haunted with worry for my children and family and by the memory of Pema Gyaltsen. Before his execution, I always knew that he was alive because I could hear the sound of his chains whenever he moved about in his cell. From that day, there was no such sound.

9

"WE WILL SEE THAT YOU SUFFER FOR THE REST OF YOUR LIFE"

One morning in late June or early July of 1959, a prison guard brought some steamed dough for us to eat and two large pots of black tea. Due to the small rations of food, we normally tried to drink a lot of tea in order to fill our stomachs as much as possible. While drinking our tea, we heard the sound of an approaching truck outside, and suddenly the guards began calling out the names of prisoners. From our cell, they collected Bhumo Yalu and myself, took us to a group of prisoners gathered in the courtyard, and told us to get into the truck. The other prisoners were all men. Among them was blind Palden, the local subchieftain from Karze who had been in my thamzing session in Lhobasha. The majority of the prisoners were high lamas. We were tied together two-by-two; I was tied to a tall, elderly lama I did not know. In the front of the truck was a soldier armed with a machine gun; two others had climbed up and taken positions in back.

The truck's engine started with a roar, and the soldiers shouted some final words to a few others who were standing nearby on the ground below. Then, with a jolt, we pulled out, heading toward the southeast. We all turned to look between the soldiers standing behind us and watched until Karze monastery, our valley, and finally the peaks of Kawalori disappeared. Throughout the entire day, we were driven continuously. They never stopped to allow us to relieve ourselves. For a woman to urinate in the truck in front of monks and lamas would have been disrespectful. Religious people would never do this, so with great discomfort and difficulty, I somehow controlled it as the truck lurched and bounced over the steep road. If we had known about the journey, of course, we would not have drunk so much tea. Finally, after ten hours, the truck slowed down and pulled off the Sichuan–Lhasa highway. I felt quite sorry for some of the elderly monks who had urinated on themselves in the truck, knowing that they felt ashamed.

We'd stopped in front of the entrance to a guesthouse. One guard helped us down, while the other two kept their rifles trained on us as we slowly shuffled, still bound together, toward the building. After a head-count, we were allowed to urinate. A young Chinese guard untied Bhumo Yalu and me from the lamas we had ridden beside on the truck, and bound our hands together. Then he took us outside behind the inn and allowed us to relieve ourselves. Once inside, we were provided a meal and hot tea by the Chinese hosts. Bhumo Yalu and I had to organize how we would slowly lift our food and drinks to our mouths, for a clumsy movement would mean we would lose whatever we were holding in our tied hands. We spent the night sleeping on raised platforms that were heated from underneath. Early the next day, we awoke to Chinese voices and soon felt the prods of rifle butts. Bhumo Yalu and I were separated and again tied to men. Then we all climbed into the truck and set off again. Later in the day, we slowly descended the narrow, twisting road through the high mountains until we saw a town nestled in a valley. "You see," the lama closest to me spoke, slightly inclining his chin toward our destination and moving his hand an inch or so forward as he tried to point, "We are entering Dartsedo."

The truck pulled into the courtyard of Ngachoe monastery. The ransacked monastery, which had been one of the largest in the area, was now a prison and had been completely sealed off from the public. We could see that many of its rooms were being used as prison cells. Approximately sixty monastic prisoners, including learned *geshes* (monks who have received the highest degree possible within the monastic educational system), incarnate lamas, and ordinary monks were detained in what used to be the assembly hall. Male lay prisoners were held in rooms surrounding the courtyard where the sacred cham dances once had been performed.

Upon our arrival, we were each given one piece of steamed dough and a cup of tea. Then we were brought into the prison office to be registered. As evening fell, I was taken to a cell occupied by a group of women. Once again, no bedding was supplied, although some of the inmates had managed to carry a few things with them. Unfortunately, when I was arrested, my only possession was the clothing that I was wearing. My chuba itself was my bed. I used the sleeve for a pillow. As I lay down, I looked around me.

The room, about nine by fifteen feet, served as a cell for sixteen women. Eight women lay on each side, having about one and a half feet of space to themselves in which to sleep. In the center of the room was a wooden toilet pot. Whether one wanted to urinate or defecate, there was no privacy. Many prisoners, being unaccustomed to the poor food, had diarrhea; and the smell was very intense. As I tried to sleep, I was overwhelmed with the all-too-familiar stench of close confinement. As I settled into my small, cold space that first night, images of the last twenty-four hours came before me, but weariness soon overcame my scattered thoughts and I fell into a deep sleep.

The following morning and every morning thereafter, the prisoners were awakened at seven. At eight, we were given a small cup of watery gruel; and at nine, we were gathered together in the courtyard and then escorted by guards to work in lines of two. We generally worked for four hours and then were given something to eat. After lunch, most of the prison guards rested for an hour, and the prisoners worked for another four hours. My first assignment was to carry stones for the construction of new cells. The monastery was not large enough to accommodate the hundreds of prisoners being sent there. There were about eight hundred men detained at Ngachoe, and women lay prisoners numbered about three hundred. Altogether, about 1,200 Tibetans were being detained there in midsummer of 1959.

We carried the stones from the stone quarry to the construction sites at the prison, perhaps one kilometer. The stones were transported by means of a wooden plank that had several holes for straps and a wooden base on which up to four stones would be laid. A strap held them in place, and there were other straps for one's arms. My first day at the quarry I had no idea how such an implement was to be used. The first time I tried to use it, I put it on upside down. Immediately, the guards began to shout at me. They ran to where I was standing and began to beat me. Several struck me in the face, demanding, "Why did you put it on upside down? There must be a reason for doing this. What are you trying to do?" I replied, "I've never seen this before. I've never done such work, so how could I know?"

I was relatively young and healthy, so the work was not too much of a hardship for me; but I was devastated by something else: each day we watched elderly lamas being forced to carry heavy stones as they were kicked and beaten with rifle butts.

Since the advent of Buddhism, Tibetans have understood that there is much more to life than obtaining one's daily bread. We have striven to comprehend the unity of life, to pray for the upliftment of all, and to fill our lives with acts of good merit. Our lamas took strict vows and devoted themselves to serious study and contemplation of the truths espoused by the Lord Buddha. They spent years memorizing the basic principles of Buddhism and then learned to put the precepts into practice—mentally, through dialectical debate, and spiritually, through years of meditation. Now these lamas, so revered in our society, were being treated in such a lowly way. It greatly upset me and the other prisoners, for we could do nothing to stop it.

The Tibetan population outside the prison witnessed this also, and they cried at seeing their lamas being treated in this manner. While carrying stones in the prison, I could look outside and see people who were free. I then remembered my childhood and all the happy times I'd had with my family and wondered, Why? Why were we undergoing this now? I cried and constantly wondered how such sufferings and atrocities could be happening in this world. What was the purpose of such cruelty? They had invaded our land and taken away our possessions, our family members, our way of life, our religion, all our hopes and dreams, and then were forcing us to work as slaves for them. Yet, they were saying that we were evil for opposing them. What could we do?

In order to survive these sufferings, my cellmates and I felt that there was no other means than to pray to His Holiness and to the deities. In the nights, I could only pray.

As time went on we learned that most of the monastery's statues and other valuable articles had already been taken to China. Images made of clay had been crushed. The stone chortens of the monastery had been demolished. Wooden religious articles and all the religious texts had been burned. Monks and lamas who had been associated with the monastery and prisoners who had arrived earlier quietly told the other prisoners what had happened. Everyone was hungry for news and anxiously searched for opportunities to exchange our observations.

There were moments when the guards were not looking as we carried the stones, and Bhumo Yalu and I quietly talked. We shared such information as what had happened at Karze prison, who had been executed recently—just a few words and then we would have to beware. Most of the women were very concerned about the welfare of their children, and we always asked each other if we had children somewhere. There were women from many different regions of Tibet—all the regions of Kham, areas of Amdo, and from as far away as Lhasa. They were piled into trucks and transported to Golmud and Ziling, from which they were taken in freight trains to Chengdu, then again by truck to Dartsedo. We had great difficulty in understanding each other's dialects. A woman from Amdo quietly asked for Amdowas. Lhasans and people from other towns in U-Tsang Province searched for those who might have news of their region, and the nomads did the same.

The work we were doing was terribly tiring, and everyone was weak from hunger. Food in the prison was poor and meager. We quickly tired of being served the same food for breakfast, lunch, and dinner: one small cup of porridge made from poor-quality barley or oat mixed with maize flour. As time went on, dying prisoners also ate grass and roots.

A few months after my arrival, we were herded into the monastery's courtyard for an evening meeting. A Tibetan named Thupten Dhargye was brought forward to kneel on the ground. The Chinese doctor had caught this starving prisoner attempting to eat the calf of a dead prisoner. The body had recently been thrown into a hut that served as a morgue. Thupten Dhargye was beaten and loudly scolded in front of us. When asked to account for his actions, he replied, "I haven't eaten anything, because nothing but skin remained on the corpse; and anyway, I am too weak for my teeth to be able to bite through the skin." Then it was announced that, thereafter, unless they were assigned, Tibetans were not allowed to go to the place where the bodies were thrown.

We emerged from the meeting hardly believing what we had come to. "It seems as if the events around us are happening slowly, slowly as if we move and have no weight, no substance, no voice." Bhumo whispered. "How can this be real?"

One afternoon shortly afterward, I began to feel weak. Then apparently I passed out while carrying stones. It was morning when I awoke to the rushing sound of a river. I couldn't remember where I was. Looking up, I saw a corrugated ceiling and wooden walls. My head felt so heavy that it was difficult to move. As I looked around, I realized that I had been put in the hut that held the bodies of the dead prisoners.

I immediately remembered the faces of my mother and my children and felt a swift rising of panic and loneliness. When one has suffered that much, tears don't come easily, so I didn't cry; but the sight in the hut was terrifying. The bodies looked like skeletons. The eyes had blackened; the cheekbones were protruding. The sickening smell of rotting flesh was overwhelming. Normally people could only walk in that area by covering their noses. For a few moments I was too terrified to move or to shout. Finally, I slowly made my way off the pile of bodies and knelt in a corner. After a while, I heard the voices of those whose work it was to dispose of the bodies. As they opened the creaking, makeshift door and the light fell on my living face, they were quite startled. "What's this? How long have you been here?" they asked. I couldn't bring myself to answer. But one Tibetan said to his friends, "She must have been thrown with the last pile we brought last night." Two of the men helped me to my feet. Another pointed to the corpses and quietly said, "You see, when the clothing is removed, except for the head, which looks very big, there is only skin covering the bodies' bones." Though the men were accustomed to the sight, they remained shocked and saddened by the work before them. One of the men looked at me and said, "Come. Until the wagon returns, you might as well just sit over there in the sun."

On the outskirts of Dartsedo, there is a junction of three roads: Minyak Tago, the western road, which leads to areas in Minyak Ra-nga gang; Gyayi Tago, the eastern road, which leads to China; and Yhagra Tago, the northern road, which leads up through the mountains to Karze. There were military posts on all three roads that made it impossible for anyone to enter or leave Dartsedo without being noticed.

On the northern road, a short distance from the prison, prisoners had been made to dig an open pit. The bodies of prisoners who had been executed or had starved to death were dumped into it. At least ten to fifteen prisoners died of starvation every day, and a truck carried a load of bodies to the open grave every twenty-four hours. When the hole was full, it was covered and another pit was started.

After a few days, when I was again able to move about normally, I was transferred to working in the pig sty. I was happy to discover that within days my physical condition began to improve because I was able to steal some of the food reserved for the pigs. The Chinese loved pork and kept pig sties in every prison and labor camp. The pigs were fed well and then slaughtered for their meat.

At that time, I saw many lamas in the prison who were hungry. Many of the elderly ones simply could not endure the physical labor being asked of us. Finally, the oldest lamas were locked up in their cells and only the younger ones were called to do the work. The rations of the elderly lamas were severely reduced. I began to take some of the pigs' food and leave it where the lamas would see it when they came outside twice a day to empty their urinal pot. I signaled to them when the guards had gone, and then they picked up the food and ate it.

It was under these circumstances that one day I again met our family guru, Chomphel Gyamsto Rinpoche. His relationship with my father and Jughuma had been a very close one. After my father's death, he wrote to our family warning us to remember what father had said about the future of our land and advised us that it was perhaps time to make arrangements to leave the region. The letter was delivered and read to us by one of the lamas of Karze Day-tshal monastery. Unfortunately, by the time the letter reached us, it seemed as if it was already too late for us to attempt escape. Not wanting to bring any trouble on our spiritual teacher, the letter was destroyed and never mentioned outside of the family.

In 1957, all the lamas of Nyarong were instructed by the Chinese to attend a meeting at the Fort of the Female Dragon. From the assembled group, the soldiers chose the most revered of lamas, forced them to dress in women's clothing, and subjected them to a long public thamzing session. Chomphel Gyamtso was among them. At that time, there were more than sixty monasteries in Nyarong. The monasteries were almost simultaneously surrounded, and all the monks and lamas were arrested. Most of them were sent to prisons, where they perished. Chomphel Gyamsto was imprisoned for one year in Nyarong and was then transferred to Dartsedo.

Chomphel Gyamsto had an unusual problem: whenever he was handcuffed, the handcuffs would come unlocked by themselves. Worried about more beatings and of being accused by the prison guards that he was somehow purposely trying to do it, he tried to relock them, but he couldn't. He asked the guards to lock them, and again, they immediately came off. After that, he was not made to wear handcuffs.

◊ ◊ ◊

Before a prisoner was subjected to thamzing, he or she would undergo an interrogation. The period of questioning always began with the Chinese trying to fool a person as one would a child. They said, "If you confess that you did this, tomorrow you can go home and be with your children." Then, "If you give us the names of Tibetans who want to flee their native land and who are opposing the Communist Party and Mao Zedong, we will release you." By promising amenities, they were able to encourage a few of the detained to work for them as spies within the prison.

At some point, a Tibetan who was working for the Chinese as a spy noticed that I was giving the lamas extra food and reported me. This was the first time that I was sentenced to thamzing in Ngachoe monastery. I was brought before a large group of prisoners, and the officials made me kneel on a sharpened piece of wood. They told me of the charge and asked if it was true. I did not feel I'd done anything wrong, but I realized they would never understand my perspective. It seemed the best action at that moment was to make no outward response. I remained silent. They began to scold and hit me, as the translator said something about my aiding criminals and being an enemy of Mao Zedong.

The second thamzing occurred after I was assigned with nine other prisoners to clean a garage for military trucks. We noticed that the trucks were loaded with religious statues and other sacred objects that were about to be transported to China. Most of the prisoners were fearful of raising their heads, but a few of us looked around as carefully as we could. We told some other prisoners what we had seen. Somehow the Chinese came to know about this and subjected us to thamzing.

The third incident involved two newly arrived Tibetans who were native to Derge region. They had been wounded in the legs in battle and had been left behind. One day, when I was working in the pig sty, I heard someone shouting "Arro? Arro?" In Khampa dialect, this word means "hello there." At first when I looked around, I could not tell where the sound was coming from. Then again I heard, "Arro? Arro?" I followed the sound to a small window in the building next to the pig sty. I looked inside and saw the two men, their legs heavily bandaged. Immediately one of them asked me, "Are you Jughuma Tapontsang's sister?" My brother and I were remarkably similar facially, and most people who met us assumed that we were related. Fear swept through me, and I began to cry because I was afraid that my brother, for whom I constantly prayed, had been killed.

The injured man told me, "Do not cry. His Holiness has been able to escape without harm and your brother escaped, also. They are in free territory in India. Unfortunately, we were not able to follow them because we were hit in the legs while the Chinese were bombarding the border. The Chinese arrested us, and now they are keeping us alive by giving us some kind of injections. They are not doing anything else to help us but are using this opportunity to interrogate us. It is the only reason they are allowing us to live."

I felt quite sorry for these two men and the helpless position in which they found themselves, and so I began throwing some food into the room whenever I had a chance. I had to aim the food at their chests or someplace within reach.

None of the Tibetans in prison had known anything of the whereabouts of His Holiness. To know that he had escaped, and also that my brother was free, made me ecstatically happy. All of us had spent much time wondering and worrying about the fate of the Dalai Lama. We knew only from the prisoners from U-Tsang that the situation in Lhasa had grown increasingly worse and uncertain. We all prayed to the deities for his safety.

I had not seen my brother Jughuma since late 1954. Our last communication had been a letter that came just before the announcement of the "Democratic Reforms." For several years I'd been afraid to imagine him dead. The thought of meeting him again was one of the fantasies that gave me the strength to endure the long days and bitter nights. Now I knew for certain that my dream was possible.

I began to repeatedly sing a well-known proverb that had been made into a song my father had taught me: "Don't worry if today the snow falls heavily, because after heavy snowfall, the sun is bright."

I had no means of directly informing the prisoners of the wonderful news of the Dalai Lama's safety, so when feeding the pigs, I stopped to sing those two lines from time to time and then resumed my work. As soon as the prisoners heard the singing, they tried to come close to hear what the words were.

Unfortunately, one of the prisoners had been influenced by the Chinese promise, "If you bring news, we will release you." He told the staff in the prison office, "This woman's song has deep meaning. When the prisoners heard it, they became very happy; and they seem to be sharing a secret." A small group of officials and a guard came to where I was working. They took one of the small troughs that were used for feeding the pigs and ordered me to kneel on it. Then a guard hit my elbows to force me to raise my arms in the air. I was interrogated in this position and, ultimately, forced to kneel there for four hours. One of the officials said, "First, instead of feeding the pigs, you were giving their food to the lamas. Second, instead of working when you were sent to clean the garage, you were looking at what was in those trucks, and then you informed the other prisoners. Third, by singing those words, you were trying to encourage the other prisoners and make them more determined. What is the meaning of the song? What happier times are you referring to?"

I insisted there was no meaning, that it was only an old song about nature that my father had taught me when I was young. I asked them, "What happier times can there be for us now that everything is lost?" The official answered, "You are the worst of the prisoners. You above all the others have most stubbornly opposed our reforms. Of all the women in the prison, you are the most seriously condemned prisoner; and if you don't change your ways, you will have to be executed." He told me to "think carefully," and then I was lifted to my feet and—because my bruised, bleeding knees could not support me—half dragged to a small cubicle. I was warned to carefully consider the result of my actions and then was subjected to solitary confinement for several days.

When I returned to my cellmates, Bhumo Yalu and I talked during free moments. I tried to encourage her. We had received word from another prisoner that Bhumo's husband had escaped and was living in Nepal. I told her that since His Holiness the Dalai Lama had escaped, we could hope for better times. With external support, he and the Tibetans who had followed him might be able to drive the Communists out, and one day we might be able to live in peace and happiness as we had before. We discussed how we must somehow get our land back from the Chinese.

Chomphel Gyamtso Rinpoche tried to assure and comfort me. He once said, "Whatever we are passing through regarding this experience is a result of our karma, so we must bear it gracefully with faith that truth is its own witness."

◊ ◊ ◊

We all dreaded the nightly two-hour reeducation meetings during which prisoners were prosecuted for various reasons: perhaps a prisoner was caught saying some mantras, or someone was not working diligently. Often there were "statistics meetings" during which the officials mentioned the names of different kinds of bombs they had acquired. They said, "America does not have these things. Only we have them." We found such statements difficult to believe, as we had heard something of the amazing devastation of the atomic bombs dropped on Japan. The Chinese also told us that their military divisions had "achieved this" or "installed that." They would say, "We have found a new source of petrol, and it is running in abundance like water. All is in abundance. The reserve is in abundance."

They also said, "We have discovered so many different kinds of medicine in Tibet. We want medicinal herbs, and your people want money. Our medicines are so well known that all over the world people are pleading to us for them." We did not believe that they were giving money to our people. They recounted how much China was earning in exports and how many orders they were receiving from different countries in the world.

Basically, the purpose of those meetings was to make the prisoners believe that in every respect—politically, economically, militarily—China under the Communist Party had no equal in the world. The impression was given that no other country could compete with the Chinese. These were the basic points of indoctrination.

The warden of the prison, Zhang Su-dui, was one of the rare Communist officials who spoke fluent Tibetan. He was the son of a Guomindang porter from Sichuan, but somehow, after the Communist occupation, he had risen to a position of senior officer. He was in his late twenties and had a round face and staring eyes. He took an interest in young and attractive women prisoners. They were often called by him to clean his rooms and do his laundry. During this work, he also repeatedly raped them.

I was one of these women. Three others were also selected for this duty: Nangtso Wangmo, from Lingkarshe, a region bordering Lithang district, and Dolkar and Yangchen from Chatring. We were called in rotation and raped. As a precaution against us getting pregnant, he forced us to drink musk water immediately after intercourse. If we resisted, we were threatened with harsh punishments, even death. We could only obey and keep silent.

For us, this was an ultimate degradation. We had lost everything; we didn't know the fate of our families and our children; our people had been turned into a work force of slaves—but this was one of the most difficult things we had to bear. We were powerless. We came to hate Zhang, who was always rough and crude and would purposely say things to try to make us feel ashamed and hopeless. Although such activity was officially illegal according to the Communists' military rules, there was no one to come to our defense. There was no question of reporting the matter to higher authorities, for the only result would have been that we would be locked in our cells without food. Moreover, Zhang Su-dui was himself the authority.

There was no way to console ourselves. We regarded the times when each of us was called as a sort of execution. After one was called, the rest cried over the deplorable situation, and we tried to console each other as best as we could. After some time, Zhang grew concerned that we might somehow speak out. We noticed that if he saw us stealing vegetables, he ignored the situation, looking the other way. These were the things we thought of as we sat in the nightly classes in which they explained to us that we had been liberated by the world's most advanced and powerful government.

Chomphel Gyamtso Rinpoche, in trying to comfort me, often said, "You must always remember that His Holiness the Dalai Lama has been able to escape. Even though we are suffering very dark times, it will not be possible for them to destroy our religion and culture. Ultimately, the doctrine of Tibetan Buddhism will prevail."

An odd occurrence happened at the prison: seven rinpoches died on the same day. This was not due to any external causes. It seemed as if it was a conscious decision on their part. The Chinese were very surprised by this event. Some of those who passed away that day were Chomphel Gyamtso Rinpoche and Tongkhor Shabdrung of Nyagye and Rongbatsa townships, near Karze district.

◊ ◊ ◊

One morning in autumn 1960, our work was interrupted when trucks pulled into the courtyard and many doctors and their staffs alighted. We were rounded up to stand in lines as they noted down basic information, such as which regions we were from and how many years we had been sentenced. Of course, they knew everything already—it was all in the reports they had before them—but they were interrogating us to see if we would tell the truth. Every Tibetan who is arrested, sentenced, and imprisoned is followed to any prison or labor camp by full documentation.

The morning after the doctors and officials talked with the prisoners and checked our physical strength, we were all called to the courtyard. They shouted, "*Ji kho lo!*" which meant that all prisoners must come quickly and assemble. They told us, "Whoever hears her name called out must stand to this side." Out of three hundred women, I was among the one hundred who had been called aside.

We were told, "Everyone from this new group whose names were called out will be going to a very happy place. It is a place where only by eating fruits your stomach will be full, and there is no need for other food." Some prisoners believed this story and were quite happy about it, but I told myself, "It has to be a lie. All they do is commit atrocities." I didn't believe any of it and simply kept silent.

Separated from the other prisoners, we were no longer allowed contact with them. I managed only a fleeting glimpse of my friend, Bhumo Yalu. I knew that we would not meet again. Carrying whatever belongings we had—none had very much, maybe just some clothes, a bowl, a cup—we prepared to go. I had only a mug and the clothing I wore.

When we left Dartsedo, we were arranged in lines of two with soldiers on both sides and soldiers in the front and back. We were tied together in groups of five, six, or seven. No prisoners could break out of the line. We walked throughout the day until we reached a bridge called Chak Sum. We halted there for the night, and after some time, the soldiers brought us each a cup of thick gruel and a piece of steamed dough. Cold and unable to sleep, I spent most of the night in prayer.

My only desire was to commit suicide by jumping off the bridge. The guards were ordered to shoot anyone who might make this attempt. The ropes were tied very tightly, and I could not manage to loosen them. Of course, I realized that it was actually impossible to carry out my plan because it would have endangered the others with whom I was tied up. After crossing the bridge, it took four more days of trekking, sometimes traveling through difficult passes, to reach our destination—Gothang Gyalgo. It was not very far, but because we did not receive adequate food, we did not have much strength.

10

GOTHANG GYALGO

On the fourth day, we climbed slowly upward along a high, narrow, rocky path. At one point, the guards started pointing and shouting to each other: "Gothang Gyalgo." Approaching the region, we were impressed with the sight of immense mountains which soon surrounded us. In the late afternoon, we began the steep descent. Far below us, we at last saw the labor camp, surrounded and shut off by three mountains, which gave the whole area a feeling of wild and overwhelming isolation. As we began our descent, the prisoners in the camp situated in the valley far below us became visible, moving around like an army of ants inside. Finally, we arrived and walked through the gate.

Looking around at the prisoners, it seemed everyone was Tibetan. Later, I realized that approximately four hundred Chinese prisoners were also detained there.

The prisoner's faces were like skeletons, with deeply sunken eyes and sharply protruding cheekbones. Everyone was moving in an odd, slow manner. My next thought was, "Oh, they have transferred me to die here. These people look as if they come from the realm of hungry ghosts."

The prison was surrounded by a high concrete wall, with guards stationed in towers at intervals along its length. I didn't see what happened to the two hundred men who had come in our group from Dartsedo, but initially all the women were taken to a grouping of huts made of wooden planks, straw, and twigs. We each found a little space and laid down in exhaustion. We were filled with dread and uncertainty and wondered how long it would be before we came to resemble the unfortunate inhabitants of Gothang Gyalgo. The wretched memory of Dartsedo diminished before the reality of our present condition. I had not expected anything beneficial to come of our transfer, but the severity of our fate numbed me.

Later that evening, we were moved to a rectangular concrete building, inside of which were cubicles where groups of ten or twenty prisoners were kept. We spent the long night cold and hungry. At some point, my awareness of my aching legs and the hollow feeling in my stomach ceased, and I drifted off to sleep.

The morning after our arrival, we were awakened and taken to a large room where we were given a half cup of very diluted gruel of corn and oat. This was to be the main source of nutrition served at the camp for the length of my stay. My friends and I felt strangely disoriented and weak at the sight that surrounded us. Wherever we turned our heads to look at the long lines of seated prisoners, we couldn't see a single person who looked like a normal human being.

"What is this place?" the woman next to me asked. We hesitated to try to speak to the closest group of listless prisoners who were some distance away. It was difficult to imagine myself becoming one of them.

At the time of our arrival, there was already a large number of prisoners detained in the camp—I estimate between ten and thirteen thousand—even though the camp had only opened in the beginning of 1959.

After our hurried meal we were made to stand as a Chinese official spoke. His words, translated by a Tibetan guard with a megaphone, explained our duties at the camp. "You prisoners have been brought to this mine to be given an opportunity to redeem yourselves for crimes you have committed against Chairman Mao Zedong and the People's Republic of China. You have not understood the importance of your liberation from old and evil ways and the fact that the old must be destroyed to make way for the new. Under the leadership of Chairman Mao, a new world order will soon be established, of which it will be your privilege to take part. Now you are being given the opportunity to contribute to the needs of the People's Republic by working in this mine." The official took a moment to look at the faces of the new prisoners and then clapped his hands, shouting, "Assemble!"

We were then escorted by armed guards close to the proximity of the mine. Gothang Gyalgo was a border region, not far from Chengdu. At the base of the mountain near which the camp was situated, a big tunnel had been dug and raw lead was being extracted. There were many prisoners inside the tunnel. My group was not allowed to go beyond the entrance. Prisoners from inside were carrying the raw leaded stone in two baskets attached to a pole held by a strap fastened around their shoulders and delivering it to those who waited beyond the tunnel entrance. We were given similar baskets and told to carry them to prisoners who were working to separate the lead from stone in various locations below the mine. While working in the mine's proximity, I saw some of the prisoners taking hammers and iron rods inside: these implements were used to pry the leaded stone from the walls of the mine. I never heard any machine noises coming from the mine, but since two fast-moving rivers flowed nearby, one bordering the camp's edge, it was hard to tell. Due to the noise of the rivers, everyone at Gothang Gyalgo had to speak loudly; otherwise, you couldn't hear. All that week I didn't speak to anyone, and no one talked to me except to give me instructions.

The following week, I was transferred to work at a place about half a kilometer below the mountain. The raw materials containing the blue-colored lead were very hard and difficult to break off, so when the leaded stone was brought down from the mountain, sets of ten prisoners would be assigned the work of separating the lead from the stone by hammering until the stone became powder. The extracted lead was taken to Chaksam Kha (Lu Ching Qang in Chinese) and then transported to China's interior by trucks.

Prisoners did not converse during work for they saved their strength to try to complete the quota set for the production of cleared lead. Prisoners who could not fulfill their quota received only half a portion of the daily meal, or sometimes none at all. The officials would say, "You haven't finished your work. How can you expect to have the right to receive food?"

I soon learned there were two main units of prisoners: the healthier prisoners, and those whose health had totally deteriorated and were soon to die.

During the work hours, prisoners wanting to relieve themselves had to shout *"Pao gao jie shou!"* and then had to wait for the prison guard's glance. The guard's name could not be used, for the structure of protocol was designed to impress upon us prisoners that we were inferior outcasts. If the guard acknowledged the prisoner, he or she could go. Otherwise, one would just have to wait there until attended to by the guard. Sometimes when I called for attention for this purpose and was ignored, I just relieved myself next to the guard post. The prevailing attitude of randomly ignoring such a basic physical need infuriated me, and so I had a tendency to break the rules.

The schedule of the labor camp was four hours of work in the morning, four hours of work after lunch, and then a two-hour reeducation meeting each evening during which we were usually told, "Mao Zedong is the father of everyone." They said he was a "father" because he had helped the beggars and the poor. They said, "There is no other leader in the world who does that. The citizens of the world are shouting, 'We also want leaders like Mao Zedong. The People's Republic of China is the most progressive country on earth.'

"That is why America and Russia don't like China. Maybe some of you think that the Dalai Lama will be able to get help from the outside world, but this won't come even in your dreams. The Dalai Lama, without any other means, is pleading with the Americans; and the United States is only a name. America is actually like a drawing of a tiger on paper. If you look at the drawing, it seems to be very frightening; but if you throw it in the water, it dissolves. The paint is gone.

"You prisoners, in order to be happy, must follow what the Communist Party of China says. If you have hatred and resentment against the Communist Party of China, it will be just as if you are throwing a stone on your own feet." These were the main points with which they always tried to indoctrinate the people.

In addition to our nightly lessons on Communist ideology, we were often humiliated. Many were forced to undergo thamzing sessions. The Chinese dealt very harshly with the political prisoners, but they didn't really care what the actual criminals were doing. At one meeting I attended in the first month of my imprisonment, they singled out such a Tibetan prisoner and said, "This man has committed a crime just for his own benefit, but now he has acknowledged his guilt, has been thoroughly reformed, and is no longer opposing the progress of communism. Moreover, he has pledged to struggle against 'bad elements and harmful acts' and has given us information concerning what the counterrevolutionary prisoners are talking about in the cells, so we are going to release him." Then, in front of all the prisoners, that criminal was released.

◊ ◊ ◊

Throughout my imprisonment, I always tried to pray to my tutelary deity—Dolma, the protectoress—but as time went on I found it increasingly difficult to concentrate on the long twenty-one-verse prayer that my father had taught me. Perhaps due to starvation clouding the mental faculties, I found that my mind would go blank at certain points in the prayer. I simply couldn't remember, which was very discouraging. It was also impossible to pray in my free time without being interrupted either by guards or by other prisoners.

One time the opportunity arose to consult one of the imprisoned lamas regarding this problem. Kathong Situ Rinpoche was a Nyingma lama, originally from Kathong Gonpa, a monastery between Chamdo and Derge. He had continued his studies in Lhasa and had been arrested there. I had often watched him from a distance while he worked, and something about his quiet acceptance of the situation was calming. He still wore his lama's robe, but by that time it was filthy and stained. Still, just the sight of him was somewhat comforting. Sometimes I saw him watching the interactions of other prisoners; and from his expressions, I got the impression he was praying for them. His eyes, in contrast to the usual listless look of the other prisoners, seemed calm and deep as a deer's, embracing with interest and compassion the sights surrounding him. I felt quite shy to approach him but realized that he probably wouldn't mind. He seemed quite moved to hear of my predicament, and taking my hand, he looked into my eyes and gently said, "Under this situation we have no time of our own to devote to traditional practices, so I will teach you this shorter prayer, and you can recite it with the same devotion. I am glad to know that your spiritual practice is still of such concern to you." He then taught me an abbreviated prayer of nine verses to Dolma, which was to become my refuge in all future times of trial and loneliness.

◇ ◇ ◇

One time, after having worked and grown progressively weaker for some months, I just slept for a week. I had decided the system was such that you had to work and then had so little to eat that you'd most probably die of starvation. I felt I had nothing to lose. Finally, one of the prison guards came into my cell with a gun and said, "What are you doing? Everybody is going to work. Why are you not going?"

I replied, "I can't. I don't have any strength. My stomach is empty, and so it is impossible for me to work."

He then tried to drag me by my hair to the cell door. He began to threaten me by reaching for his gun. The second he pulled it out, I thought, "My time is up." By this time, I had undergone immense suffering, the execution of my brother-in-law in front of my eyes, and the arrests and tortures at Karze and Dartsedo, so at that moment I realized, "It is better that they kill me rather than continue to subject me to all these atrocities." Pulling open the top of my chuba and pointing to my chest, I shouted, "Yes, please! Shoot me!" The official was quite taken aback, so he didn't pull the trigger. Instead, he knocked me to the floor and began kicking me with his boots on my hips and thighs. I just rolled up in a ball and, without saying another word, waited until it was over. With a final kick, there was silence. For a few seconds he stood looking down at me before he walked out of the cell, slamming the door.

I still decided not to work; since everybody was dying of starvation, it seemed useless. The only thought I had was, "I am going to die here," so I tore a strip of cloth from the bottom of my blouse and, making one hundred and eight knots, fashioned it into a rosary. I felt that to do some religious practice was the only thing left for me.

During that period of solitary confinement, I recited the Dolma prayer as long as my strength held out.

I would recite, then fall unconscious. I would wake up again and try to walk while reciting the mantra, then I would fall down. From that time until I decided to try working again, they didn't give me any food. They said, "Only if you work will we give you anything to eat." Finally, one day, a feeling came over me that I should not try to force the end of my own misery. I remembered the others in the camp who were in the same position, and I thought of my family and of how fearful I had been of never seeing them again that time I'd been thrown in with the dead in Dartsedo. And so I decided to go back to work. There was no other way.

◊ ◊ ◊

There was another Tibetan prisoner from somewhere near my Nyarong region. This prisoner knew that I had taunted the prison official to kill me. And one day, before I had come out of confinement, he also decided to stop working. He asked for permission to relieve himself. The guard did not turn around to look and, assuming it was an ordinary prisoner instead of one known to be troublesome, absentmindedly gave permission. This Tibetan prisoner quietly went behind the point where the guard was positioned. Instead of relieving himself, he hit the guard with a pointed stone, then immediately took off his chuba. He snatched the soldier's gun, put on his uniform, and somehow managed to escape.

Many search parties were sent out, but they were unable to find him. They called a meeting and an official accused me of instigating the man. "She refused to go to work, and then she wanted us to shoot her. She is a very bad woman, but we are not going to kill her because she has been brought here to suffer," he said. Then, one of the officials announced, "We have already caught that prisoner and killed him." But we knew they were lying, because normally, when they captured and killed an escaped prisoner, they brought the body to show everyone.

Slowly I began to know a few inmates who had not given up completely and were willing to speak to me, perhaps partly because word had spread regarding my having been punished for my refusal to work. As the Chinese always considered me to be a most heavily condemned prisoner, I had to be careful in my contacts every time, everywhere. When new prisoners arrived, it took at least two weeks to a month to first study where they came from and what their backgrounds were in order to determine whether they were trustworthy for me to talk with them.

A most fortunate acquaintance was a Chinese prisoner who befriended me. Her name was Xi. She was from Chengdu and had been born into a very wealthy family aligned with the Guomindang. She was an odd woman with a certain gruffness about her, but perhaps she had not always been that way. She was filled with bitterness. I could only imagine what it must be like to be imprisoned this way by her own people. Before Xi was arrested, her brother—who had openly criticized the Communists and was subsequently labeled as an "ideological reactionary"—had managed to flee to Taiwan. The Communists assumed all the family members were reactionaries of the worst sort, and soon afterward, they were arrested, their properties confiscated, and they were sentenced as "capitalist class counterrevolutionaries." When Xi and I first met, she was quite fat; later, of course, we were all the same. She used to tell me, "Before, when I was heavy, people always called me 'Fatty, Fatty'; but now, only bones are left."

Xi came to take an interest in me because I never listened to orders. One day, with the help of a Chinese-speaking Tibetan, she took my arm and said, "When you asked the guard to kill you, he was greatly confused because they have been told that you must suffer properly and thoroughly. It was rather enjoyable to witness such a disturbance. The guard's face was red when he came out of your cell, and he kicked the side of a building. I was glad I wasn't in his way at the time."

We became quite friendly. In her own way, Xi was very kind. She was helpful in teaching me to speak the Chinese language. She often pointed things out when we were working, saying their Chinese names—for example, pointing to a bucket and telling me to bring it to her. These lessons continued after we left Gothang Gyalgo through our detention in two more labor camps. They proved to be extremely valuable.

Xi always wanted to oppose the Communists. At one point, the prisoners heard that China and the Soviet Union had become antagonistic toward each other. Although the countries once had had close ties, differences in the methods of spreading the Communist doctrine had developed. Perhaps also at that time, these two countries had individual designs on how they hoped to control the world through communism. Eventually, diplomatic relations between them dissolved. The Chinese Communists labeled the Russians "revisionists" because the Russians had begun to feel that revolution can be achieved by means other than violence. This news greatly encouraged the Guomindang prisoners, for they hoped that the strength of the Communists might somehow be weakened.

◊ ◊ ◊

One day before dawn, about thirty of us prisoners were assembled and told we were going to work some distance away. Escorted by around fifty soldiers, we left at dawn and walked out of the camp into the mountains. On the high and narrow path, the soldiers threatened us with death if we broke the line. Fortunately, we were not tied together. During our walk, Xi and I trudged silently alongside each other. I couldn't help wondering if we would meet any other Tibetans on the path and what they would feel upon seeing us, but though in the distance we saw several homes along the way, no one came outside. Our destination was a large monastery known to us as Gothang Gonpa. I had an eerie feeling when we entered the grounds that, though in good condition, were completely devoid of a monastery's most common feature: there was not a single monk to be seen. The buildings were completely deserted. The monastery was being used by a local commune as a storehouse for the corn harvest.

Our group was the first to be sent to obtain corn for the labor camp, and the last, the reason being that we could not control our hunger and began quietly eating the raw corn while working. The guards discovered us eating it and declared, "Instead of working, you are stealing!" With shouts and random strikes, they forced us to our feet and assembled us to leave with whatever we had managed to collect. Xi was furious. Spitting on the ground, she began to curse and declare: "If one is to live under communism, it is better to be born as a pig. We will all die, but at least they will throw some corn to the animals."

We managed to return to the camp by evening. But because we were unaccustomed to walking so far, we had consumed excessive water, and having eaten the raw corn, our stomachs had begun to swell, which made walking and carrying the heavy bags of corn difficult. Many of us suffered from diarrhea in the following days. That first night, after trying to sleep for some time, I clutched my cramping stomach and tried to relax. I closed my eyes and drifted into a dream of walking alone through the gates of a monastery, calling for anyone to come. Receiving no response, I walked through the darkened temples, the chanting hall, the kitchen, and the courtyard, feeling only a mounting silence in response to my queries and wondering where the inhabitants had gone, what had become of them.

During our venture to the monastery I had become interested in a young nun named Yigha from the Tawo region of Kham who hadn't said a word during the expedition. She normally remained very quiet and just sadly watched what was going on around her. I always felt that I wanted to talk to her, wanted somehow to help her, but what could I say? At that point, it seemed any encouragement would appear callous and sound ridiculous. Each of us had to face our inner strengths and weaknesses. Though we shared the same suffering, each was alone in finding some reason to carry on. Yigha had been assigned to picking stones out of the vegetable garden. It was a time when I was no longer in any state to work, but sometimes I would be sent to the vegetable garden to help there. Too weak to move about, I just sat. Sometimes I watched her from a distance.

The nun always tried to evade the guards and move toward the corner of the garden that was very close to the river. When they looked at her, she lowered her head and pretended to be concentrating on picking stones. This activity went on for about a week. One time, she managed to move sufficiently near the river when the guards were far enough away not to be able to reach her. With a final glance in my direction, then toward the guards, she ran and jumped into the fast current. I sat and watched as her body was swept away.

Like every other prisoner, she had been deeply depressed because the Chinese were condemning the Tibetan religion and were always singling out the monks and nuns. Starvation, of course, was another factor. Given those circumstances, even though our religion teaches that to be born into a human body is a great gift and that suicide is one of the greatest of sins, she thought it was best to take her own life.

At that time, the other prisoners had to agree with her. The years between 1960 and 1962 were the hardest. None of us had ever imagined that human beings could subsist in this manner. We had heard there was a famine but were told nothing of its source, and we could not understand what had happened to the additional crops grown in Tibet as a result of Chinese agricultural policies.

◊ ◊ ◊

In the kitchen of Gothang Gyalgo, the food was served from a large wooden container. We prisoners were so weak that we had to support ourselves on sticks as we walked, so as soon as we received our serving, we drank it on the spot. If we tried to walk away with our cups, inevitably the food would be spilled as we fell down trying to balance it, and that would be it. On seeing the prisoners swaying and staggering from side to side as they tried to support themselves, you could not help but think that you were observing a dance of the dead.

After the food was served, the cook pushed the pot into the center of the area where the prisoners were seated. The healthiest prisoners immediately moved forward to grab the food. Some put their whole hand into the container to get as much as possible and then licked it off their hand. Some just used their fingers.

The pot was pulled by some prisoners to one side, then by others to another side. They fought with each other trying to get the last little bits of food as the staff stood by laughing and taunting. At that time, I was too weak to try to get some of the extra food and just witnessed these scenes. It made me angry, but there was nothing that I could do.

By then, most of us had already eaten the leather from the soles of our shoes. The soles were made of only one thickness of leather. With a rock we pounded a shoe until the seam separated and then we pounded the leather to soften it. Whenever an opportunity arose, we chewed the leather to give us a feeling of satisfaction of having something solid to eat. The various pieces of it were shared, passed from one prisoner to another. Ultimately, it was soft enough to be swallowed.

Perhaps the most difficult test to be faced in Gothang Gyalgo was when the staff found a means of amusing themselves at the prisoners' expense. Sometimes the guards and officials poured tea leaves on the ground to form a mound. Then they dropped more tea around on the floor. Because every prisoner was dying of hunger, almost everyone tried to grab some of the tea leaves. Because they had no strength, they fell over as they tried to reach the tea, and then there were fights among them. Ultimately, someone reached the mound and got the tea, and then you would see his face and mouth turning black from the leaves. The officials and guards stood by clapping and encouraging one prisoner or another. They laughed and cheered while pushing each other and pointing at the scene.

There was one Tibetan prison guard who was known as Tenzin Tuta, "Tuta" being a title that means something like lieutenant. Before joining the PLA, he had been a beggar in the Bathang region of Kham. Tenzin was very helpful to the inmates. When we were stealing vegetables or the pigs' food, he always pretended that he didn't see what we were doing. During times when the Chinese were amusing themselves at the prisoners' expense, Tenzin stood off alone, looking very annoyed. The anger showed in his face as he stood with his hands clenched into fists. I could not help but wonder what he was thinking since he was obviously not a heartless man. He had obtained a position of comfort and security yet was constantly reminded of the suffering of his countrymen from whom he had been singled out. Tenzin Tuta stood alone, a helpless witness to the result of the promises of "liberation" made by the Communist Chinese. I did not envy him.

◊ ◊ ◊

The few Chinese prisoners in the camp dug up and ate two varieties of worms that could be found in the soil. There were always a great number of cockroaches, which were quite difficult to capture; but many prisoners tried to grab the quick creatures and then crush and swallow them. I was never able to bring myself to do this, but I picked any small green plant and put it in my mouth, not caring whether or not it might be poisonous. The garden was well guarded, so only occasionally could one manage to grab something from there. The gnawing hunger was maddening. One could only forget it during a few hours of restless sleep. Even then, we dreamt of food. In the night, one often heard dying prisoners calling out in delirium, "Couldn't I have some good tsampa to eat? Please give me a piece of bread, just a cup of tea." They also cried out to His Holiness the Dalai Lama, asking for his blessing in their last moments.

At first we greatly feared the lethargy and inability to concentrate that was brought on by the lack of nutrition. Conversation in the camp was difficult; and, after a while, even when the opportunity arose, we were too weak and found it necessary to remain quiet for the sake of reserving our strength. Finally, every thought was dulled by the incessant pangs of hunger in our stomachs and the resulting weakness, and we could only think of such things as how to manage to stand without falling, how to negotiate taking a step, how to escape beyond the freezing discomfort of the night into sleep. Often I awoke in the morning to find that the next prisoner, whose body had afforded some measure of warmth, had died in her sleep. One means I found of forcing myself to carry on was in setting small goals: I created a mattress by tearing the inner lining of my chuba. During the days, I looked for small clumps of grass or anything that might be a little soft that I could put beneath it to give some slight insulation from the cold.

◊ ◊ ◊

My friends and family had not seen me in five years. They found out that I had been sent to Gothang Gyalgo and encouraged my brother Nyima to attempt to make a visit. He made the journey alone.

Approaching the guards at the entrance to the labor camp, he was told that he would not be allowed inside, for prisoners were not allowed visitors.

But there was a Guomindang Chinese doctor at the labor camp who was a very kind man. For some reason, he had taken an interest in my welfare. When he heard that my brother had come, he somehow arranged for me to go to the gate and see Nyima for a few moments. When Nyima saw my condition, he began to cry. I was so sorry that he had to see me in such a state because I knew when he returned home and described my condition to the people in my village, they would no longer be able to hope for my survival.

It saddened me that perhaps his last memory of his sister would be of a hardly recognizable creature, starving and already half dead. For a moment, I held his hand and just stared at him. I'd been warned against saying anything about our conditions in the labor camp, but of course he could see. Then it was time for him to go.

Though Tibetans were not usually allowed to see the prisoners, they sometimes came and left donations of food for them. Sometimes the prisoners that the food was meant for received a small portion of it; but just as often, they didn't. The officials were not going to allow me to keep the food that Nyima had brought. The doctor intervened, saying, "I'll keep the food and give it to Adhe slowly." He called me to his office and said, "You'd better calm down and stop arguing with the officials and prison guards. You must stay a very simple prisoner, and then maybe I can help you. If you insist on quarreling with them, I won't be able to do anything."

At first, he gave me only a little tsampa with butter. He told me, "If you overeat at this point, you will die. I will give you the food your brother has brought little by little." When I came in contact with the other prisoners, they began to say, "Oh, Adhe is smelling of tsampa." More prisoners came around and asked me, "What did you get? What did your brother bring you?" This made me feel very selfish. After that, I was really disturbed because I knew that every prisoner was burning with hunger inside and wherever I went, everyone was looking at me.

I decided that the only thing I could do was to go to the doctor and tell him that I wanted to use my food to prepare something for all the prisoners. "How would this be possible?" he asked. "The amount of food that was brought for you is not much in quantity." There were small bags of tsampa, butter, small pieces of meat, some cheese, and tea leaves. I told him, "I want to put all these things together to make a thick soup for everybody."

Again he asked, "Are you really sure that you want to give everything away?" I replied that I was indeed sure, and so he began to make the arrangements for the food to be prepared. I don't know what means he found by which to help me, but he was the chief physician and was very respected by the Chinese for his knowledge. He arranged for the cook to provide a big pot, and he himself helped me with the cooking. The meal was served in the prisoners' kitchen. The doctor, dressed in his medical gown, stood by and watched silently as I gave every prisoner a cup of soup. All the prisoners were so happy in getting their share that although it was still very hot, they drank it immediately. You could see their faces glowing red. Some licked the cups, then put in some water, shook the cup, and drank again. All of them came forth to thank me. Some kissed my hand. They said, "At least before we die, we are having our native food. You have given this to us."

There were many lamas from the region of Lhasa in Gothang Gyalgo. Kathong Situ Rinpoche, the one who had taught me the Dolma prayer, was one of them, and he was present when the soup was offered. He said, "In independent Tibet, we used to have so many rich families making offerings and sponsoring meals and teas in the great monasteries. We can understand that situation because of the families' wealth. But today, your sharing of this food with everyone has far more meaning. You have done a greatly meritorious work, and you will live. But for us, there will only be death. There will be no way to escape from this atrocity."

There was one Tibetan who had been arrested in Lhasa and taken first to a labor camp in Amdo and then to Gothang Gyalgo. He was always seen wearing a particular hat. When I knew him, he was so weak that he could not stand or walk properly. For some reason, he always used to look at me. At that time, my clothing was in rags. I was always stumbling and catching the front of my chuba on my shoes, so the hem of my dress was torn apart in the front. The soles of my shoes had been eaten long before.

This man was among the prisoners who received some soup. He hardly had the strength to lift his hand to his hat but tried slowly to get hold of it. Then he took it off, and with his hands folded in prayer he presented the hat to me. I thought that maybe the hat had belonged to some lama, so I was very happy. I felt that somehow the hat had been blessed, and I put it on my head. Later that evening, I felt something hard like a button in the center of the hat. Taking it off, I looked at it carefully and saw there was a rolled piece of paper tied with thread. Unrolling it, I discovered that it covered a portrait of His Holiness the Dalai Lama. After that, I always wore the hat. I purposefully made it a bit dirty so that the guards wouldn't want it. Otherwise, if they saw that I had a nice warm hat, they were likely to take it away. This most precious gift gave me hope.

◊ ◊ ◊

The head jailer of Gothang Gyalgo was Ma Kuchang, who headed both the military police and the staff of the labor camp. Whenever Ma Kuchang appeared, he made an entrance as if he were the only leader left in the world. It was as if he considered himself the emperor who held sway over this dying and starving populace. He had a full, rather fat, glowing face that dramatically contrasted with the Tibetans, who looked like skeletons. Due to starvation, our faces appeared to be sub-human. Also, our complexions were jaundiced. There was no facility for washing or any way to obtain new clothes at the labor camp, so everyone smelled bad. When Ma Kuchang came around, he always covered his nose and mouth with a perfumed cloth.

In 1962, Ma Kuchang was to be transferred. The man who was to take his place was named Pei. As they were going over various documents together, they came to the list of prisoners. Ma informed Pei that in three years, 12,019 prisoners had died. Tenzin Tuta happened to overhear them talking and went to the doctor and told him this

information. Both found it quite shocking. Other prisoners overheard their conversation because Tenzin had approached the doctor
while he was doing his rounds.

One day shortly afterward, we learned that Kathong Situ Rinpoche
had passed away. Inmates who shared his cell reported that he had died
in a state of prayer. Early in the morning, his body was found sitting
erect in a meditative posture with his hands in the position of a *mudra*,
or ritual hand gesture. The body had the appearance of a statue.

Upon hearing the news, I immediately recalled his beautiful eyes
and the kindness he had shown me. I remembered the sound of his
voice and the encouragement he had given me. I couldn't imagine
how what he'd said could be true: that somehow I would survive.
There seemed no order, no justice, no sense to the events we were
experiencing. But I was certain that as long as I lived I would not forget him and the calm assurance behind the words he had spoken.

◊ ◊ ◊

Throughout my imprisonment in Gothang Gyalgo, my thoughts basically revolved around three subjects: I thought about His Holiness
and the Tibetan exiles, and wondered if they would be able to gain
support and regain Tibetan independence. I considered my detention
itself and all the prisoners who were dying. I wondered about my relatives who were left behind and about my children. Would there ever
be a time when I would meet them again? How could they be faring
with their mother starving in one of the prisons? At the same time, I
hoped that a brighter time would come and that one day I would be
able to leave the prison as a free human being and be with my children. But after imagining freedom, I felt there was not much chance
for experiencing it because everyone around me was dying and perhaps I would die here also. By the time I was transferred again, there
were only about sixty prisoners still alive at Gothang Gyalgo.

One day in 1963, the remaining prisoners were called and told,
"Now you will have to go back to Dartsedo. Gather your belongings
and prepare to leave." By that time, out of one hundred women who
were transferred with me in 1960, only four, including myself, had

survived. The local authorities had realized that the prisoners were too weak and died too quickly for the mine's activities to be profitable.

As we assembled and waited for the guards to signal our steep ascent from the valley, we leaned heavily on our sticks as the roar of the rivers filled our ears. As the order was shouted to commence, we began to walk in a double line. Each of us had just a small bag to carry. We walked slowly through the places where all the prisoners had been buried, and I realized that my own remains could easily have been left there. As we passed the graves, I silently spoke to my fellow prisoners, saying, "If only you had survived a little longer, you would be walking with us today." I prayed to all the deities of Tibet for their departed spirits.

Normally when a Tibetan dies, particular rites are performed for the sake of the departed, which extend for a period of forty-nine days. In our culture, a proper funeral is considered to be essential to free the spirit from the confusion and bonds of the earth. As we walked, I prayed for those who had passed away to have a good rebirth and promised that all through my life I would pray for them. It was as if one's own relatives were buried there because we had all endured the same suffering. Every Tibetan passing there was deeply moved as a witness to these unfortunate deaths. Walking through those starkly desolate burial places, I could not help but cry.

After climbing the path for some time, I turned and looked behind me. At last, the camp was completely deserted. I and the other survivors were left to walk forward along the uncertain paths our destinies would lead us. The hollowness that rose in my heart upon witnessing the rapid disintegration of human lives, the sudden silencing of voices to which not long before I had listened, brought to mind prayers from the great lama Tsongkhapa's *Essence of Nectar* prayers regarding the path to Buddhahood:

> If I carefully examine all the beings, distinguished and lowly, who lived in the past, I find that now only their names remain. And of all the beings who are living now, every one of them will someday pass away.

Since my present status, house, relatives, friends, possessions, and even this body must all pass away without remaining for long, to what am I attached in this dream-like present?

A good life that is truly meaningful is always difficult to find, and even when found is impermanent and will quickly be destroyed like a dewdrop that clings to a blade of grass.

Our teachers had deeply considered the nature of this earth's impermanence and the fragility of a single life, and our people had always placed importance on learning something of these teachings according to their individual capacities. Though I never could have imagined the test of such pain and numbing loss, I continued to meditate on our prayers, to ask the deities of Tibet for strength and guidance for myself and others. However, even though I practiced these things, my heart was heavy in those times of trials and suffering and the cruel loss of so many human beings for reasons that remain hard to understand. May their spirits somehow find the peace that did not come to them during their lives on this earth.

PART THREE

LOTUS IN THE LAKE

11

POURING WATER ON A STONE

For a short while, I was detained at Ngachoe monastery with the three other female survivors of Gothang Gyalgo and some sixty to seventy other Tibetan women. While there, I learned that most of the lamas who had been imprisoned there had already passed away. There were new prisoners, and the prison complex had grown in size. We learned that in 1962, Zhang, our former prison supervisor, had been replaced by a new man. During the transfer of the post, the list he received showed there were 2,319 prisoners there at that time. This information was revealed to a prisoner named Tenzin Sangpo, of Lithang, by a Chinese official who was friendly with him. He passed the word to the other prisoners.

A friend managed to obtain an extra chuba for me. Until that point, I hadn't changed my dress in five years. From that time on, I saved the old one for the time of the month when I was menstruating and wore the new clothing the rest of the time. I was very fortunate to get it; my original chuba had been completely reduced to rags.

After a brief regrouping at the monastery-prison in Dartsedo, we were taken to Shimacha Labor Camp in Chethok, near Minyak Ra-nga gang. Minyak Ra-nga gang is one of the five sub-districts, or *qus,* under the Dartsedo administration. That area, now known by the Chinese name Xingduqiao, is about a four-hour drive west of Dartsedo. Gyu la is the main mountain pass between the two regions. Within Minyak Ra-nga khar, there were twenty-one locations that contained prisons and labor camps. Shimacha Labor Camp was located just below the Gyu la, approximately one kilometer east of Minyak. It was on a plain very close to the military airfield that was the last place in Tibet that His Holiness the Dalai Lama had visited on his way to China in 1954. Before the Communist invasion, Tibetans had regarded this region as a happy place. It was often used for picnicking, horse racing, and other such activities during the festivals. Now, lining either side of the highway between the airfield and the junction where the north and south roads branched off toward Karze and Lithang were six labor camps: Shimacha, Nu Fan Dui, Xaya Dui, Wa Da Dui, Mian Fen Chang, and Qen Yu Gai Zo. All were units of Xingduqiao Prison.

When we arrived, there were already about fifty women prisoners in the camp, mainly from Lhasa and Jyekundo, a region in southern Amdo. We immediately noticed the conditions were much better than in Gothang Gyalgo. In Gothang Gyalgo, prisoners had been forced to sleep so close to each other that there was no space to even turn around. If by chance the prisoner one slept next to died during the night, one would have to remain beside the body until the next morning. As the hours passed, one could feel the warmth that the living prisoner had provided slowly ebb away. At least in Shimacha, there was enough space to move in one's sleep.

By this time, almost every prisoner's dress was full of patches of various colors. In Tibetan, we called it *tata*, meaning zebralike. When we were forced to work, our clothes were often torn by thorns; so whenever we happened to see a piece of cloth on a bush, we grabbed it, took it back to the cell, and stitched a patch on our dresses.

Shimacha Labor Camp held about sixty women, including my group of new arrivals, and one hundred men. In our section, there were only women prisoners, a few of whom I already knew. The healthy prisoners were assigned to vegetable gardening. Those who were bedridden due to old age or illness were always kept locked inside their cells; they were assigned to spinning wool into yarn by turning the wool on handheld spindles.

Working in the labor camp were some Guomindang Chinese who were former prisoners. After fulfilling their sentences, they had no place to return to, so they continued on as employees who were free to come and go. One of their jobs was to bring manure from the outside for the labor camp's gardens. When these people came near us, we tried to convince them to help us obtain things from the markets. We asked them to buy us such things as a little piece of butter, some molasses, or perhaps a needle. In exchange, we gave them whatever we had—some clothing or small articles.

My brother Nyima somehow found out about my transfer and brought me a little money. I used one-tenth of this to pay for a needle, which became one of my most valuable possessions.

When we were working in the vegetable garden, we were able to steal some of the vegetables and eat them. We had also managed to stitch unseen pockets inside the lower front portions of our chubas; and when the prison guards weren't looking, we put vegetables inside the pockets. At the end of the work day, the prison guards ran a security check to see if we had stolen any vegetables, but they never noticed the location of the hidden pockets. When we returned to our cells, we gave the vegetables to the prisoners who were bedridden and had no means of sustenance other than the meager prison food.

Before my arrest, I knew very few of the women with whom I was detained; but once we were all together, we realized that we understood each other because we had shared the experiences of many atrocities. We quickly grew in compatibility to the extent that we considered one another sisters.

If one prisoner was feeling ill and was bedridden, while still being forced to spin the woolen threads, she would think, "My friend will bring something for me today." And the women in the vegetable garden who managed to grab something and eat it would be thinking, "My friend is waiting inside the cell; I must bring her something. She is hoping for it, and if I am not able to bring anything, she will feel sad." That is the kind of relationship that existed there.

We women were detained in a building with five cells. Once again, we slept on cold, hard concrete floors. It was here that I was able to begin fashioning a real mattress. Prisoners always walked with their eyes looking toward the ground to see if they might happen upon something useful. Also, when a prisoner died, we shared pieces of the deceased's clothing. During those days, none of us had the time to feel superstitious about such things. The smallest scraps of normally insignificant items became our treasures. Through these means of collecting cloth, I worked on my mattress. From Gothang Gyalgo I'd carried the material that had once lined my chuba. I used whatever scraps of cloth I managed to find, first to extend the cover of my mattress and then to stuff it with the cloth, as well as bits of straw, to give some protection from the hard floor's seeping chill.

I was detained in Shimacha Labor Camp for three years. Unlike Gothang Gyalgo, no prisoners were dying of starvation. In those three years, my health greatly improved because I was able to acquire fresh vegetables.

My Chinese friend Xi was also transferred to Shimacha. Both of us marveled at the fact that we were still alive and that our health was continually improving. Though Xi continued to grumble and complain under her breath at the actions of the Communists, she found more indications that things were changing for the better in our lives. Little by little, I more frequently caught her in a smile, especially when we had fooled the guards with our hidden pockets.

My closest friend there was Yeshi Dolma, and I was also close to a woman named Tsering Yuden. They were entirely trustworthy. We felt totally secure in confiding to each other anything we might do that broke the prison's rules. We were certain that if one or the other were caught, no matter what punishment or torture we went through, the guards would never be able to influence us to speak against each other.

Yeshi Dolma was from a region north of Dartsedo. She was the wife of two brothers who were among the Tibetans who resisted Communist policies between 1955 and 1956, after the destruction of Shapten monastery, the largest in the vicinity of Dartsedo, and the imprisonment of its monks and lamas. Yeshi Dolma's husbands joined other men from the region and took part in fierce and desperate fighting in the mountains. As I and my friends had done, she went up into the forests where they were hiding to give them food and information. She was arrested for these reasons and sentenced to ten years of imprisonment.

Both of Tsering Yuden's parents had died of starvation in prison. One day, shortly after she had been informed of their fate, she was walking alone, herding the family cattle on the edge of a forest. She began to wonder if her cattle would soon be requisitioned by the PLA and realized that none of the family property or possessions would help her to survive, for she had no means of defending her property. Tsering then decided to give the whole herd to the men who were hiding and fighting the Chinese. She made the arrangement with someone who was in contact with the men; and when the cattle were delivered, she felt relief in knowing that at least for a while the men would not be faced with starvation. As soon as the disappearance of her herd was noticed, she came under suspicion. She admitted to her action while under interrogation and was sentenced to nine years of reform through forced labor.

The three of us shared the same cell. Yeshi Dolma was very old, so she was never sent out to work. Throughout the day, while locked inside the cell, she spun wool into yarn while silently repeating the prayer of Chenrezig. Tsering and I were always assigned to work outside in the vegetable gardens.

During the potato planting, we managed to steal one piece of potato for every potato planted. When the potatoes got big, I was able to take a few from every plant, but they were very hard to digest raw. I developed a problem with my kidneys as a result of having eaten the pigs' food at Dartsedo and then these raw vegetables. Whenever I ate food, I always felt a pain inside.

The prisoners were fed some common vegetables such as radish, lettuce, and potato, and one piece of steamed dough. Tsering and I consumed only half of the food because of the availability of the garden crop, and we shared what was left with Yeshi Dolma.

Since there were more than the three of us in the cell, all our interactions were done quietly, for the guards were always pressuring prisoners to overhear what was said in conversations and to report which prisoners were friendly with each other. However, we did sometimes find time to speak of personal things. I always remember how I swore to my friends, "One day, when the time comes, I will speak of everything that we have gone through under the Chinese. When we get out, I promise that somehow I will make these things known."

The improvement of my health, after the terrible years in the prison and two labor camps, was very encouraging. I was now able to easily tie the belt on my chuba. I didn't have to walk with a stick to support myself, and I could easily stand up and sit down. Less than a year before, these things had seemed almost impossible.

◊ ◊ ◊

Sometimes the prison guards and officials got drunk and insulted the prisoners. An official sat on a table, drink in hand, and scolded us. We were never allowed to raise our heads but could only bow as they spoke. Often they singled out the better-looking of the prisoners. These women would be asked to go and take care of the officials' laundry; and, of course, they were manhandled. Two women became pregnant during the first few months I was at Shimacha. After that, it was decided to transfer all male prison guards and officials and replace them with women. From then on, female guards scolded us and stood over us as we worked.

In every prison in which I had been detained, excepting Gothang Gyalgo, the prisoners were made to sing a propaganda song before each meal. One such song was *Shang Shi Li Fu*. Li Fu was the name of a Chinese soldier who had killed many Tibetans during the battles, and we were made to recount his deeds and praise them in song. Another song said, "All people of the world who oppose the Communist Party of China are nothing more than crumbling paper." I was completely against this practice and just murmured when they were singing those dreary songs. Only after the singing were we served our food.

I was always determined to record in my mind as clearly as possible everything I witnessed of the sufferings of the Tibetans under the Chinese. In the light of my many, often unbearable memories, the only possible recourse for me was to go completely against the Chinese, so there was no way that I could participate in the propaganda the prisoners were made to repeat.

In meetings, we were expected to express enthusiasm as we listened to discourses on the meaning of Mao's words about our lives and the future of Tibet. Of course, after the long day's work, our greatest effort was to appear awake and alert and to ignore the stiffness in our muscles and joints, lest shifting our bodies too frequently be taken as disrespect for the evening's message.

◊ ◊ ◊

In 1966, I was transferred—along with Yeshi Dolma and Tsering Yuden—to Nu Fan Dui, the main women's unit of Xingduqiao Labor Camp in Minyak Ra-nga gang. All through my imprisonment, my records from Karze had followed me—to Dartsedo, Gothang Gyalgo, Shimacha, and now to Nu Fan Dui—and so they knew that in each place I had broken the rules. Each time that I was transferred I thought, "Oh, maybe now in this new place, they won't know me." But my records always came to the attention of the authorities, who took it upon themselves to make an example of the uselessness of my crimes. Looking back, it seems that perhaps the constant dredging of these details did serve a positive purpose. Though the difficulties I experienced because of my behavior were meant to serve as a warning to the other prisoners, they instead seemed to strengthen others, giving them a renewed determination to help each other and not be broken by declarations that constantly labeled us inferior beings who deserved to be punished for refusing to accept the Communist ideology.

The unit in Na Fan Dui had eight cells, each holding ten female prisoners. All able prisoners were made to work in the vegetable gardens. The prescribed rule was four hours of work in the morning and four hours after lunch. In the evening, there would be a two-hour meeting. The food situation improved even a bit more than Shimacha: we received a slightly larger piece of steamed dough.

In the mornings, after the staff had taken its time to get up, wash, and eat breakfast, they took us for our first shift in the fields. Beforehand, there was roll call, with all the prisoners standing in line to be counted. Every time we went out, a report was made of how many prisoners went to work and how many armed guards went with us. When we returned, the same roll call and checking was done. In the men's unit, many prisoners had been shot for trying to escape, but no such cases occurred among the women.

After our morning work, we returned for the lunch break, and the prison staff slept for one hour. We used that time to tend to our own work, such as stitching our dresses or mattresses or searching for new straw and cloth bedding. We shared what we had with each other in different ways. Perhaps a patch was given to someone who didn't have any cloth, or elderly people were aided with their needs. During these times, I often visited Yeshi Dolma to see if she needed any assistance.

At two, we again went to the fields. The work was divided into segments: one part of the garden was estimated to require three hours of work, another might need two. However, if for any reason the work in that area was not completed, we were not allowed to leave until it was done.

On Sundays the prison staff went for outings, so we received our meals at ten in the morning and five in the evening. We kept half of our steamed dough to eat in between. Dead prisoners were often found to have these dried pieces of dough in their pockets, and the living hurriedly consumed them.

When we had an opportunity, Yeshi Dolma, Tsering, and I discussed what was happening in the prison. Tsering was a very timid woman. Yeshi Dolma was brave and had taken many risks in her life, but she never spoke out in prison. They both felt I was the only person they could trust. Though they themselves never quarreled with the authorities about injustices in the prison, they always informed me of these incidents.

After the evening's maize gruel, the prisoners were called to meet for two hours of indoctrination. Sometimes the officials castigated me, saying my mind could never be changed and no one would ever like me. Then they told the other prisoners, "But if you people change your minds, you can have a satisfying new life as citizens of Communist China." The two people in charge of the meetings were a senior staff member and a woman named Nu Kasu. They never called us by our names, but referred to us as *niu gui she sheng*, meaning cow demons and snake spirits. In the old Chinese tradition, people used to worship the spirits of creatures that were originally believed to be benign. In later times, this expression came to mean demons who take human form, which, when recognized, revert to their original identities as evil spirits. Mao used the phrase to describe enemies of the People's Republic of China. In Tibet, this term referred to class enemies: former landlords, wealthy peasants, counterrevolutionaries, imperialist enemies such as America, and other bad elements.

We were expected to spend a certain amount of time each day memorizing expressions or proverbs from the "Red Book." Those who were illiterate were made to memorize shorter phrases such as "We are devils," "Mao Zedong is the greatest of the world's leaders," "All the counterrevolutionary elements are nothing more than paper," and "Mao Zedong is our father." We were supposed to be ready to jump up and recite a long list of them. Throughout the years I spent in prison there, I was called hundreds of times to recite, but I always simply said, "I don't know. I don't know how to say these things." Then I was told, "It is inexcusable that you are not able to recite a single verse from the Red Book. This shows us that after all the time you have spent in reeducation, you continue to harbor reactionary thoughts. You have a stone head, because you always think that if you had a knife, you would kill the Chinese."

During the rest times, while the prisoners were supposed to study the contents of the Red Book with a prisoner-teacher, I often spat on it and left it under my hip. One time, when a group of ten prisoners were sitting together, Zhao Shaoyi, a Chinese Guomindang prisoner in her mid-thirties, heard me confide to the other inmates that even if I were to be shot dead, I would not learn to read the Red Book. "What are they going to do to me?" I asked them. "Moreover, how can they have such expectations of one who was never literate?" The next day, Zhao's eyes met mine as I placed the book beneath my hip and closed my eyes to pray. Immediately afterwards, she reported the matter to the authorities. That was when we discovered she was a spy, who were common among the prisoners in Nu Fan Dui.

Three days later, they called a meeting attended by several prison authorities, the other nine prisoners, and myself; I was scolded and made to kneel for two hours. I completely denied having done such a thing and said, "I am not going to accept this. You can ask all the prisoners, and if everyone says that I did what you are accusing me of, then I will acknowledge that I have committed the act. But if only one is saying it, I cannot possibly accept this ridiculous accusation."

Of course, because they all respected me and I was compatible with everyone, none of the other prisoners accused me. Even then, Zhao Shaoyi said, "Adhe dislikes Mao and hates the Chinese." I responded, "I am laughing at Zhao Shaoyi and not at you leaders. I have not made such statements; moreover, all of my inmates further deny such actions on my part."

One woman prison guard was a Tibetan known as Thangu Tuta. Before the Communists had come to her region, she had been very poor, but now she was one of the staff. The Chinese were encouraged to marry Tibetan women, and Thangu had a Chinese husband. Those who agreed to such unions were given special considerations: better food, better housing, raises in pay, and other conveniences. There were several other Tibetan women among the labor camp staff who had married Chinese men, but still they tried to help us and looked the other way when we were stealing vegetables. However, when their superiors were around, they behaved in a very strict manner.

Thangu believed I was innocent of the prisoner's accusation. She questioned the other prisoners and then went to the officials to report that everyone had said they didn't know what the accuser was talking about. Thangu Tuta said, "Since we always heavily condemn Mrs. Adhe, I think this prisoner is lying, especially since Adhe is denying the accusation. I feel that she is just concocting the story in order to get credit with us." Since there was no support for the claim, the charge against me was dropped.

Xao Dolma, a woman who had a Tibetan mother and a Chinese father, was detained for murdering her husband with the help of her new lover. She came to be our most troublesome spy. Whenever she was around, my friends and I were always very careful. She monitored our activities, and even if someone took a small piece of vegetable, she immediately reported it. It was very upsetting to everyone, and since she was given increasing compensations for her deeds, her feeling of power over us expanded to the point where there was not a moment's peace. The prisoners finally devised a plan by which we decided to try to discredit Xao Dolma. A few women managed to convince the authorities that she was living a double life. Then we all got together and said to the officials, "We saw her stealing vegetables," or "We heard her criticizing the Chinese." Afterward, when she tried to say such and such prisoner was saying something that merited investigation, the authorities thought twice about her words. Ultimately, she was no longer able to raise her head. It was unfortunate, but under those conditions life was already very difficult, and a spy who flaunted her authority was unbearable.

Not all of the prison spies were so obvious in their actions. The failure of my Chinese friend Xi to realize this led to her unfortunate end. Xi had befriended two Guomindang prisoners. The three, consumed with hatred for the Communists, used to speak of how, if the opportunity came: "We will someday 'skin out,' like slaughtered animals, the officials who have subjected us to so many tortures and humiliations." They said, "Now that China's relationship with Russia has deteriorated, it is the time for us to somehow take our revenge." Though the probability of doing such a thing was impossible, Xi found some comfort in imagining it and sometimes excitedly and openly discussed the idea. Her words were reported.

As usual, the authorities called a big meeting. Xi was made to kneel with her arms raised. After a while, it became impossible to continue holding her arms up, and when she dropped them, the guards hit her elbows with the butts of their rifles. Xi's arms soon became very weak and started to shake; her face turned an ashen color as tears slowly rolled down her cheeks. She was told, "Tomorrow you will have to explain to us what your plans were, exactly how you were going to skin us out." That night, she committed suicide by hanging herself with a belt. She was around forty years old at the time.

During that period, the beginning of 1966 and at various times throughout the year, we were forced to cover the inner walls of wooden houses with a plaster made of precious Tibetan religious scriptures that were very old and written in inks made of gold and silver. In one of the buildings at the camp was a large room filled with huge piles of scriptures. We were made to tear the scriptures and soak them in water, then mix the paper with mud and straw in large tin containers. This mixture was used to fill in the spaces between the inner planks

of the houses. Though neither Tsering Yuden or I could read, we and
the other prisoners engaged in that work felt a terrible guilt with each
tear of the scriptures. No one could converse normally while the
sound of the ripping paper could be heard as we wondered if such
rare documents could ever be replaced. Tsering said, "I am certain we
are committing a sin. We are casting the holy name of Sangye, the
Buddha, in the mud."

◊ ◊ ◊

One day in 1967, a group of doctors came to the prison and ran a
physical check on the women prisoners. They selected twenty of the
strongest, myself included. We were then taken a distance of about
one kilometer to a building that was part of the hospital for prison
staff and officials. They left us waiting in a large room that had a
powerful heater in its center. Two attendants came in carrying pitchers
and cups, and we were made to drink glass after glass of a sweet drink
containing a lot of sugar. As we waited, we asked each other, "Why
are we here in this comfortable place? It doesn't make sense that the
Chinese should suddenly be so caring." The room was so hot and the
drinks affected us so that our faces began glowing red and the veins
in our arms began protruding. Suddenly, a group of doctors entered
the room and examined our arms. Then they took out packages of
needles and syringes and proceeded to methodically extract a large
amount of blood from each of us. Afterward we were left to rest. No
one could find words to speak of what had happened. We sat numbly
watching shadows on the wall, from time to time looking at our
arms. After a short while, the attendants returned carrying the pitchers and refilled our cups, ordering us to drink more. Within a few
moments, our bodies heated up again. The doctors returned and
again extracted the same amount of blood. A cold wave of anxiety
came into everyone's minds because we could see that we were losing
our blood in a situation when we needed it the most. We were then
taken back to our quarters.

None of the women immediately fell sick or died after the extractions, but after one month we began to notice that all of our faces

were becoming pinched and a strange stiffness was coming into our bodies. Of course, if there had been an adequate diet, perhaps our bodies could have replaced the blood, but our sustenance fell far short of the basic standard of nutrition and in no way compensated by providing the strength needed for recovery.

Slowly, each of us became weaker by the day. One woman from Chatring in Kham named Rinchen Dolma died that very year, as did Yundrung Pelmo of Nyarong. Between the time of the extractions and their respective deaths, the resident physician never treated either woman, or any of the others. Tsering Lhamo, from Karze, died in the second year, as well as a woman from the Tawo region of Kham. One woman named Rekho, from Nyagchuka region of Kham, was always falling, one time badly cutting her head. After the extractions, she was always in a state of giddiness and did not have the strength to work for more than brief periods. From that time until the present, I have had periodic bouts of giddiness and fainting. Fibrillations and cramping of muscles also occur frequently.

One morning, a few months later, the guards came to open our cells. We were called to assemble outside and then were taken to a big hall. Again, I was afraid that they were going to extract our blood. At first I didn't go inside but just stood looking in the door. I saw two prison staffers approaching with scissors, and as they entered the door, they pulled me into the hall. Then they ordered the prisoners to stand in line and proceeded to methodically cut each one's hair, chopping off our long plaits to just below the ears. We were then issued baggy, shapeless blue pants and shirts and blue brimless caps with side flaps and a button in the front. Then they took all our tattered Tibetan clothes to be burned. Unfortunately, that meant that I lost the rosary made from cloth that I'd managed to carry with me since Gothang Gyalgo. Luckily, I had already found a safe place for the picture of His Holiness the Dalai Lama that I had received a few years before embedded in the hat a fellow prisoner gave me—soon after I had arrived at Shimacha, I one day pretended to go outside to urinate and left the photo in a clean place on the mountain where it could not be mishandled by the Chinese.

After that, we were told, "From today onward, none of you are allowed to speak Tibetan. You must always speak in Chinese. From this day, if you utter a Tibetan word or if you murmur a single prayer, you will be prosecuted."

By that time, I'd been in prison for so long that I had picked up Chinese. For the first three or four years after my arrest, I hadn't understood a single word of the language, but gradually, through Xi's help and by always listening and observing, I'd reached the point of being able to follow most of their conversations. However, there were other prisoners who were new, and of course, they couldn't understand Chinese, and there was no way in which to quickly learn. Those people just had to stay mum, unable to utter a single word for several years.

◊ ◊ ◊

In 1968, a decision was made to collect all prisoners who were not physically productive and the difficult prisoners who continued to oppose communism and expose us to an intensive study of the values of its ideology. Tsering Yuden, Yeshi Dolma, and I were among the group transferred to Qen Yu Gai Zo, the twenty-five-years-to-life prison, which was also known as the "Thought Correction. Center" Qen Yu Gai Zo, the most heavily restricted of the five units of Xingduqiao Labor Camp, was also in Minyak Ra-nga gang, on the southern side of the highway near an army headquarters and a hospital.

The very large prison complex was surrounded by high walls with armed guards stationed at intervals. It also served as a labor camp where inmates were assigned to work in various units: carpentry, blacksmithery, tailoring, building construction, and mechanics. In the carpentry section, shelves, boxes, chairs, tables, and beds were made for later sale in China. The Chinese government gave orders for different items needed in Chinese markets.

Most of the women prisoners worked in the vegetable garden, but Yeshi Dolma, Tsering, and I were assigned to the unit that held the heavily condemned political prisoners; and so throughout the year of 1968, we spent most of our time in indoctrination classes. We were indoors almost constantly. Food was brought in from another labor camp. We were unendingly warned that we were not properly reeducating ourselves.

A very unpopular Communist official named Lie Tanda was the main instructor in charge of the classes. During the day we attended three two-hour sessions of Communist propaganda. Individuals were made to stand and make personal references to themselves and their failings. Self-criticism was considered to be a very important factor in reeducation.

I found the entire process to be extremely distasteful. Basically, they were treating adults like naughty children. Prisoners strove to keep a delicate balance between finding something to confess that would be approved as a sincere effort to reform and not saying anything about thoughts that might bring on more trouble if verbalized.

Sometimes our instructors read through the newspapers to inform us of outside occurrences. The articles basically said, "Communist China is superior to every other country in the world. In comparison to us, all other countries are minuscule powers."

The instructors constantly spoke about the strength of the People's Republic of China, which lands they occupied, who were the counterrevolutionaries in the world, how it was only a matter of time before all the "capitalist roaders" would be smashed, and how China had advanced in industry and agriculture. A very bright picture was portrayed of the People's Republic of China being an inimitable world power. They reported how they had progressed here and there in Tibet. They mentioned particular Tibetans who were obstacles to progress and tried to intimidate us by describing the details of how these people had been tortured or executed and showing us photographs of those who had been captured in the forests.

Propaganda posters were displayed all around the room showing smiling industrial workers, farmers, and new tractors, with slogans about production beneath them. And, of course, there was a large portrait of a benevolently smiling Mao Zedong. They told us, "The Dalai Lama is alone and without help in the outside world. He has approached America and other foreign countries—but America is weak and is not respected among the world governments."

Lie Tanda told us: "To believe in help coming from the outside is like an empty dream. I promise you will soon see that communism is a much better system than your old traditions. Then you will be welcomed into the fold of Communist ideology, which will bring happiness in your lives." He also said, "If you still want to believe that there is any value in religion, there is only one way out for you."

Though Lie and the other instructors expended a tremendous amount of time and effort, both theirs and our own, for the purpose of reeducation, their methods simply did not work. When there was a break in the meetings, Yeshi Dolma, Tsering, and I discussed how their approach was like pouring water on a stone: the inside of the stone does not become wet. In a similar fashion, our minds could not be changed by all this tiresome display and could not be made to forget the practice of the Buddhist doctrine. Even if we were made to endure this for more than one lifetime, we said, they would never be successful. Why would we trade our spirit, our culture, our religion, everything that made us what we were, for a tractor, and for crops that would probably be confiscated, or at least heavily taxed?

For a few moments we laughed and joked among ourselves, using the Communists' propaganda as a scapegoat for our humor. In the midst of indoctrination, a sense of humor was an invaluable tool to quickly remind us of our humanity and our individuality. On rainy days, we queried each other as to the fate of the "Paper Tiger," as if he were perhaps being affected by the inclement weather.

Back in the class, Lie told us, "In Tibet, there were no vehicles or airplanes before we came. Today there are roads where they never existed and there are airports. You had never even seen a locomotive before. When we first came to Tibet, you ran away from our vehicles." I could never digest these things, because the purpose of the roads they had made was to plunder the riches of Tibet and expand their military force all the way to the borders of the Himalayan states and India. We'd heard about the road expansion from prisoners taken from U-Tsang. Whenever they touched on this subject, I became agitated and angry and did not listen at all. I'd personally witnessed how they had transported the riches from the monasteries. No matter how important they acted in front of the prisoners, I was never touched by their words, to which were constantly added more and more lies.

Lie often said, "The devil and the deity are the same." He and his assistants referred to us as "black crows" and stressed that "the whole world throws stones at black crows." We were told that our offspring were like wolves in that when they grow up, all wolf cubs will attack other animals. They said that our future generations will have the same mentality against the Chinese, but it will not help them, for no other nation would be willing to oppose China.

Though we never accepted the indoctrination, the words repeated in our heads at night as we tried to sleep. Photographic images of captured Tibetans, statistics, enticing words, belittling comments, and the flat sound of the instructor's voice echoed in our brains. There was no outside stimulus to counteract the relentless drilling that filled the long hours that seemed to have no ending. We had no idea how long the indoctrination process would continue. At night, I tried to counteract the images of the class with prayer.

◊ ◊ ◊

Our program finished in 1969 and we were returned to Nu Fan Dui. It was a tremendous relief to again breathe clean air and to not be forced to listen to someone use all his energy to convince us of something we could never accept, hour after hour, day after day.

Through the years, Thangu Tuta, the Tibetan woman prison guard, had somehow come to respect me and helped me in small ways. She convinced the officials that I was a very clean and efficient worker. She came to me one day and said, "I have arranged for you to work in the prisoners' kitchen as a helper. If you are there, at least you will get enough to eat; and since they have extracted blood from you, you will have an opportunity to regain your strength. Of course, if you try to argue and quarrel with the officials, they will take you out of there and you will lose."

In the kitchen, I had authority over the vegetables. If I was supposed to cook twenty kilos, I managed to cook thirty or forty. The prisoners were to be given half a cup of rations, but I filled their cups.

The prisoners were very happy that I had been given this new employment.

The head cook in the kitchen was a Guomindang Chinese named Lie Hu Yie. Her tendency was to be completely supportive of the Communist officials and to constantly kowtow to them. She was very compatible with Nu Kasu, the head jailer of the women's prison section, for whom eating frequent, well-prepared meals was a favorite pastime. Because Lie Hu Yie always played up to this jailer in many ways, she had been placed in charge of the food supplies.

Lie Hu Yie was always scolding the prisoners. She and the jailer had developed such an unusually close relationship that sometimes it seemed as if they were one person. Lie made no effort to hide certain actions that went against prison rules. When small pieces of meat came for the prisoners' food, she immediately gave part of the ration to Nu Kasu.

One time, the prisoners' kitchen was used to smoke twenty pieces of pork for the prison staff. One day, just before work, Tsering Yuden caught my arm and whispered, "Adhe, I think the cook is trying to steal some of the meat for Nu Kasu. If it is noticed that the pork is missing, the blame will be put on the prisoners." As I entered the kitchen, I saw Lie Hu Yie carrying one of the baskets that women carried on their backs. She looked at my questioning gaze and announced, "What are you looking at? I am going to collect some firewood." She happened to be the only person from the kitchen who had permission to go out to find the wood we needed for the stove. I looked at the basket and saw that it already contained something that was covered with a cloth.

Feeling confident, I lifted the cloth and found the pork contained in the basket. I began fighting with the cook to regain the pork. As she began twisting sharply from side to side in order to turn the basket from my reach, she started shouting, "Help, I need help. Prisoner Adhe is trying to kill me." Tsering Yuden was nearby, and not knowing the truth of the situation, hit me twice on the back worriedly whispering, "Adhe, what have you done? Now you are finished." Guards stationed outside at the four corners of the building heard the commotion and started calling out to the prison staff, and everyone within earshot who had any authority converged on the scene. As the room began to fill, I grabbed the basket from Lie Hu Yie and tenaciously held onto it as the guards pulled us apart.

Nu Kasu arrived and, as usual, she referred to me as "criminal Adhe" and "condemned Adhe." I started quarreling with her, saying, "I may be condemned, but am I the criminal? Lie Hu Yie is stealing the best pork. Tomorrow the blame will be on us; and then perhaps we will be prosecuted, beaten, and thrown into solitary confinement in the small rooms." At that moment, I lifted the cloth and showed the pork to everyone. They were all quite shocked. Afterward, Thangu Tuta told me, "You have done a good thing, but you can't compete with her; and the next time the pork is missing, she may find a way to put the blame on you and the other prisoners." For some time afterward, when Thangu and I were alone, she often suddenly recalled the scene, smiled and broke into laughter as she remembered how embarrassed Nu Kasu had been.

About six months after the pork incident, just before the Tibetan New Year of 1970, all the prisoners were very excited because they had been informed that, finally, this year they would receive a nice meal. There was a section where the confiscated cattle of the nomads, which were being used to feed the prison staff, were kept. A number of yaks were to be slaughtered. It was decided that the prisoners would be allotted some yak meat to celebrate the holiday. The women's section was to receive five yak heads. The prisoners were commenting on their good fortune and were very happy I was going to prepare the yak heads for them.

In preparing yak meat, it must first be burned a little, then cleaned. On the day before Losar (the Tibetan New Year), I had cleaned all five of the heads and left them on the counter. Lie Hu Yie then chopped the head parts. I noticed that after boiling the tongues, she put them to one side. There were other helpers in the kitchen, but though they carefully observed her actions, they were very much intimidated by this woman. We were all wondering what she was planning to do with the tongues, because in Tibet, the tongue of the yak is regarded as a great delicacy, the best part of the meat, and is considered very precious.

I thought, "Oh, she is planning to take the tongues to Nu Kasu," and then I remembered all the prisoners who were anticipating this nice meal. If the tongues were taken from the yak heads, what would be left for the prisoners but skin and bone? I decided to wait and see what the cook planned to do. She wrapped the tongues in a white cloth and put them in a bag. I immediately asked her in Chinese, "What are you doing?" The cook replied "You don't have any right to speak, let alone question me. This is for Nu Kasu." I said, "You can't take these things; they were given to the prisoners for Losar. You know you are not supposed to take them." But the cook coolly walked toward the kitchen door. Once again, I followed Lie Hu Yie and grabbed her. Once again, she started screaming.

This brought the attention of Nu Kasu, who hurried to the kitchen and, in attempting to silence me, threw herself into the fight. As Nu Kasu reached for my mouth, I started yelling at the top of my voice, "These two women are stealing the food meant for the prisoners' celebration. How can this be allowed?" Thangu Tuta came to see what was happening and asked Nu Kasu why she was taking the prisoners' food. "Are you now taking the side of Adhe?" Nu Kasu asked Thangu in an agitated voice. At that moment, I pulled Nu Kasu's hair and then kicked beneath her leg and knocked her to the ground. I was absolutely furious. Other staff members came running into the room and Nu Kasu began wailing, saying that I was beating not only her but also the head cook. In the end, the prisoners got two yak tongues—and I was tied with rope and led past many curious Tibetans to another section of the prison, to one of the small windowless rooms used for solitary confinement.

A few hours later, Thangu came by without anyone noticing, unlocked the door, and entered my room. She stood for a moment looking around and as her eyes adjusted to the light, she saw me and knelt beside me. She whispered, "Adhe, I promise that I will report Nu Kasu had been stealing food from the prisoners for her personal use. I will do whatever I can to help you, but you must realize that now the authorities are very angry."

After three long, uncomfortable days of sitting alone in the windowless cubicle, I was visited by an official who came to question me regarding the incident. I repeated the story, telling him how much that food meant to the prisoners at what should be a happy time of the year for them and how Nu Kasu had never gone without a quantity of good food to eat.

The official pointed out that reporting the theft of the yak tongues was one thing, but I had physically attacked both the jailer and the head cook. He said, "Adhe Tapontsang, in twelve years of detention, you haven't behaved properly once throughout a single day. You'd better be careful and change your attitude. If you touch one more prison staff member, the only way for you will be execution."

When I returned from solitary confinement, I was removed from my kitchen post.

Shortly afterward, our diet improved to the extent that we were sometimes given a small piece of meat in our food. But the head cook continued to make it difficult for prisoners to receive their rightful amount. For example, if five kilos of meat were available for the prisoners, she immediately deducted two kilos for Nu Kasu, quietly put the meat in a bag, and took it to her residence. Some of the women inmates would see this and tell me. I then asked, "Why did you not stop her?" And they said, "You must realize, we are not as strong as you. We simply don't have the courage to do as you have done."

Nu Kasu was a short, heavy-set woman with close-cropped hair. She bore a streak of cruelty that expressed itself in her enjoyment in making our lives miserable by demeaning that which we found most precious. One of her daily assignments was to scold the prisoners by shouting and attempting to humiliate us. Sometimes as she entered the room to commence her daily verbal abuse, she carried a thanka from one of the monasteries, which she then proceeded to use as a cushion for her seat. Being a loyal member of the Communist Party, she completely denied and ridiculed religion. Her personal approach was to consider Tibetans, especially the prisoners, her enemies who must be broken and made to bow their heads.

Thangu Tuta's attitude was a complete contrast. Though she had come from a poor family, she confided to me that she felt more for the Tibetans than the Chinese; and she herself unobtrusively practiced religion. She was a very devout and sensitive woman. She tried all possible means to quietly help the prisoners. She once told me, "No matter what the officials do outwardly, unless you allow it, they cannot enter your heart."

After losing my kitchen job, I was sent to the vegetable garden to work with the other prisoners. The garden was situated quite close to a main road. During the years of the Cultural Revolution, there was nonstop traffic on that highway going in the direction of China. The trucks carried timber, plundered statues and other objects from the monasteries, herbs, wool, and minerals. When the trucks returned to Tibet, they carried the wives, children, fathers, and mothers of the staff members of the prisons and labor camps. In China, not much land is available, whereas in Tibet, land exists in abundance and there are many natural resources to be exploited. The Chinese were receiving allotments of land on which to build houses; and so the traffic continued twenty-four hours a day, carrying civilians who were hoping to make a more comfortable life for themselves. They brought cheap commodities they wanted to sell; and as soon as new truckloads arrived, they took out their wares and arranged them by the roadside. The Chinese always saved their highest-quality commodities for export because they were trying to build up a name for themselves on international markets. The worst quality was sold in Tibet.

There were times during our work when we prisoners witnessed many trucks carrying away larger-than-human-sized statues that had been plundered from the monasteries. I had seen the same thing in Dartsedo, but those had been much smaller statues. Sometimes the trucks briefly halted quite close to where we were working, and we could see what was inside. The statues had been desecrated with ax marks on the heads and sides. The hands were damaged and the faces were completely ruined. Whenever one of us looked up from our work and saw trucks carrying statues, she brought it to the attention of the others. We stood silently in the field with tears falling from our eyes, wondering what had become of the monasteries they had been taken from, watching the precious gold and silver images glittering in the sun as the trucks rolled by to China.

Outside of the camp, we could see male prisoners working on the construction of homes for the Chinese settlers. The former homes of the Tibetans in that area had been requisitioned and demolished. The displaced families received a very small amount of currency in compensation.

Each night during the two-hour evening meetings, Nu Kasu purposely intimidated us and tried to weaken us by attacking us psychologically. On a day when we had seen statues being transported away, she entered the room and, with a bit of a flourish, seated herself on a thanka. Putting her feet up on a small desk, she looked around the room at us. With an expression of satisfaction on her face, she said, "Today you have seen the statues in halves and in damaged forms being taken away. And you have also seen the scriptures being used to plaster the walls. I myself am sitting on this thanka and no harm is coming to me. Your gods cannot protect their images. So from today, you must admit there is no deity and no religion."

After the meeting, some of the inmates, especially my friends Tsering Yuden and Yeshi Dolma, gathered around me. Yeshi Dolma remarked, "Oh Adhe, now we can truly appreciate what it meant for you to fight Nu Kasu, because in listening to her this evening, we have come to fully understand the kind of person our jailer is: so rude and intimidating and purposely making our lives miserable." She and the others thanked me several times in the following week. Sometimes they began to speak and ended up crying in the light of our miserable situation. The prisoners began to refer to Nu Kasu as "the devil-woman."

A few months later, Tsering, who had served a nine-year term, and Yeshi Dolma, who had been detained for ten years, were released. Tsering's whole family—father, mother, and brothers—had been killed by the Communists. As she had no one to live with, she went to a camp where former prisoners without families were staying. Tsering told me, "You should not fight anymore with the staff and Nu Kasu because even when your sentence is finished, they will not release you but will use it as an opportunity to treat you worse. If it is possible Adhe, I will find some means of sending things to you in prison."

Yeshi Dolma still had two children left at home, and so she was able to return there. She also warned me, "It is not possible for us to fight the Chinese with our fists, so please take care of yourself and don't repeat what you have done earlier because I also feel they won't release you after your sentence is completed." She also promised that if her living standard improved, she would send things to the prison for me. It was a very sad time to see my closest, most-trusted friends, who had shared so much with me, leave and go their separate ways. I wondered what they would find in their new lives.

In 1972, I was among a group of men and women prisoners sent to Nyagchuka, on the border of Lithang and Minyak Ra-nga gang. There we were made to cut trees for timber and carry and load logs of inferior quality onto trucks. These logs, which were not acceptable in the market, were used for firewood in the prison. In one area nearby, Tibetans were employed in making charcoal.

Everywhere we looked, there were piles of wood. The entire forest was being cut down. Upon returning to the prison, we had to chop the wood into smaller pieces with an ax and a wedge. The most difficult thing about this work was that my hands immediately began to blister to the point where it was almost unbearable just to hold the ax. Yet, until our quota was finished, we were allowed no breaks. The sores formed abscesses from which liquid flowed, but they were never allowed to heal properly.

While doing this work one day, I noticed that one of the male prisoners was looking at me. It was Aghey, who as a boy had been taken from the battlefield of Bu na thang. He seemed to be in poor health and his clothes were quite dirty, giving him the appearance of a beggar. He was then thirty-one years of age. It was there in the forest region of Minyak that he told me the story of what had happened to his family and about his subsequent arrest. Aghey had been a very sensitive boy and had retained his kindheartedness even through the years of imprisonment. He expressed great compassion toward my situation and the difficulties I had experienced. I felt concern for his health; but he assured me, "You must realize that I have been in prison since I was fifteen years old and have now spent two years longer in imprisonment than all the years I knew in my former life. If I have survived to this point, I am certain that one day we will meet in freedom."

In winter 1974, I was returned to the main section of the women's labor camp. One day, Nu Kasu called me to her office and started scolding me, saying, "So now you have finished your sentence; but unlike other prisoners, you won't be released because when we look at your records, we see that right from Karze up to the women's labor camp, you have always opposed us. Because of that, you will still be kept under detention. Your attitude and behavior have been like throwing a stone on your own feet. All these years, you are the one who has suffered, not the Communist Party. Ultimately, it is you who are at a loss. From now on, if you are not careful, if you don't behave yourself, you will not have any rights. You will have no right to movement. Everybody will be looking at what Mrs. Adhe is doing, what Mrs. Adhe is saying." On the other hand, Thangu Tuta told me, "You are a very determined Tibetan and I support you. The Chinese are always looking for excuses to subject you to different atrocities to make your stay miserable, but you should never be disheartened."

12

REUNIONS

In late spring 1974, I was transferred to Mian Fen Chang, a flour mill located on the same road as the other prisons in Minyak. The morning of my departure, two guards came and took me into the warden's office at Nu Fan Dui, where my papers were stamped and handed over for transfer. We then walked outside to a parked car. One of the men opened the door and directed me to sit in the back. As the driver started the engine, he turned and glanced at me and then pulled the vehicle out of the compound, turning west in the direction of the road to Karze. On the northern side of the road, behind the prison camp, I could see a small river reflecting the sun like a stream of silver. Within a few minutes we passed the army headquarters and the high-security Qen Yu "Thought Correction Center" on the southern side of the road. I pushed my back closer into the seat and closed my eyes, not wanting to remember the year my friends and I had been forced to spend there. Just beyond a military hospital, we pulled off onto the southern side of the road and through the entrance of Mian Fen Chang. The trip had taken no more than fifteen minutes.

After the processing of my arrival, a guard left me alone for a while in my assigned cell. I sat down and remembered the day I received my original sentence of sixteen years. How could so much time have passed? Soon afterward, another guard came to show me my work assignment. As we walked, he explained to me, "This flour mill supplies all twenty-two prisons in the district, meeting the needs of the staffs, the military personnel, the policemen, and the prisoners. The flour is also sent to other regions in Karze Prefecture."

The mill was a huge automated plant. I had never seen such machinery and felt dwarfed by its noise and presence as we walked through the plant's various sections. I was assigned to where the tsampa was being milled. "See," the guard explained, "your work is to take a bag and hold it as flour pours in until it is full, close it, and pile it on one of these shelves." The guard walked away and left me to work alone for a few hours. I could hardly believe my good fortune. From that time on I found myself able to eat tsampa flour all the while I was working. As I would then be full, there was no need to take the regular meals, so I began to give my food coupons to the other prisoners. Due to eating tsampa, my body became quite strong within two weeks.

During one evening meal, a woman who worked in the shipping department noticed me as I sat drinking a cup of tea. "You are a packer. You look better than when you came. It's not so bad here is it? My job is helping to check the tsampa and wheat flour, which is divided into different grades and then assigned to various destinations accordingly. The best quality goes to the staff and the military. The second-best quality goes to civilian Chinese employees in fields like construction, and to the family members of the prison staff. The worst quality, of course, is the wheat used for the steamed dough that all the prisons serve to their prisoners. The remaining chaff is fed to the pigs. So you see, we are very efficient here."

I'd been surprised to notice that there were some major differences in the mill from my previous prisons: there was an absence of armed guards, the cell doors were no longer locked, and it was no longer necessary to relieve oneself inside the cell.

Prisoners at the mill were allowed to earn a livelihood. Each of us was paid twenty-nine yuan a month. Part of that money was spent for ration coupons that were redeemed in the kitchen for meals. If a prisoner was not careful to regulate his or her diet, all the ration coupons would be used up after fifteen days or so. The men had this problem more often than the women; we generally were very regular in our eating. Sometimes we would have coupons left, but the men often went hungry. The remaining yuan had to cover the cost of our clothing and all other basic necessities.

On Sundays, the Chinese prison administrators had meetings with us and asked the prisoners what they had been thinking about during the week. Of course, I had nothing to say and mostly replied, "Today when I worked in the flour mill, I did very good work. In fact, I worked hard all week. I have nothing else to tell you." Then they asked the other prisoners, "How was Mrs. Adhe's behavior? What was she saying to you? What were you discussing?" And they told all the prisoners, "Watch carefully over Mrs. Adhe."

At that time, I never revealed anything personal to any of the prisoners. No one knew what I felt inside. Fortunately, though I had no close friends, none of the inmates said anything against me. Sometimes, just to satisfy the officials, they stood up and said, "Mrs. Adhe did work very hard today."

◊ ◊ ◊

It was a happy surprise to one day discover that Phurba, my sister Sera Ma's husband, was also detained at Mian Fen Chang and was to be assigned work in the same part of the mill. Since my brother-in-law was very old, he was given the job of mending the sacks. Because there were no armed guards, only scattered officials with pistols, we were able to quietly talk during the working hours. Mostly we spoke of the atrocities that had befallen both of us. We talked of other inmates and their prison experiences in order to keep track of what was happening around us. Sometimes we shared reminiscences of our family. As Phurba's detention had been spent mostly with older Tibetans, he had never learned to speak Chinese. If an official shouted at him, poor Phurba became confused and quietly asked me what was said.

One day I was called to the office where an official explained that although I had completed my sixteen years in prison, I had been marked as a "political outcast." As I sat looking at the floor, he continued, "Although you are not a prisoner now, you have not undergone proper mental transformation. You remain hardheaded like a rock. Because you still insist on opposing us, it will not be possible for you to return to your home." I raised my head and looked into his eyes. Then a guard came and escorted me from the room.

◊ ◊ ◊

In 1975, I was ordered to work in the tile-making unit at Wa Da Dui Labor Camp, where I was given the label of "black hat," or *shi lei fen zi*, a designation of four different categories of people: the landowners, the rich, the counterrevolutionaries, and the bad elements. The "capped ones" or "marked ones" were regarded as political and social outcasts. We always had to sit at the end of a row or stand at the end of any line. We were not allowed to look at others above the waist. We were not allowed to socialize with others or attend certain meetings. Black hat prisoners were forced to make weekly reports about their behavior and feelings. At any hour we could be summoned for work.

It seemed that there would be no end to my imprisonment, yet I took some solace in the fact that conditions had markedly improved over the years. I missed the company of my friends and the confidences that we had shared. Yet, I had met a member of my own family in prison. Through all those years, I had learned to live within myself and to keep silent if necessary. I could only continue to pray and see what each coming day would bring. It was comforting to know that Phurba was being transferred to the same place.

◊ ◊ ◊

Wa Da Dui was situated near the place where the northern road along the Sichuan–Lhasa Highway branched toward Karze. That area contained a lot of red clay. One group of prisoners was always engaged in digging the clay. Six harnessed yaks trod the mud as they walked in a circle. The unfortunate prisoner who guided the yaks was made to stand without shoes, even in peak winter.

My first assignment was to join the group of prisoners who were involved in making roof tiles. A prisoner showed me how the mud was placed in a frame made of thin wooden sticks, which held four tiles. As we worked, we sat near a large, round kiln which was heated by a fireplace at the bottom and had a small hole into which the wood that fueled its fire was placed. Prisoners covered the top with a large amount of earth for weight and poured water on the earthen covering to regulate the temperature. As the mud tiles dried, the frames fell off. Tiles were also made in other wooden frames that required them to be pushed out with a piece of wood. After one week of baking in the kiln, the tiles were ready. Most of the tiles were then collected and loaded for transport to China.

The pace of the work was a terrific strain, particularly since we had to spend so much time squatting in one position in order to fill the wooden forms. We were each expected to make twelve hundred tiles a day. In order to accomplish this quota, prisoners had to work from 5 A.M. to 7 P.M. Because we were all concerned about our quotas, we spent most of the long hours working in silence. The only difference in the days seemed apparent in the weather: we moved away from the kiln in the heat of summer, drawing closer as autumn winds tore through our clothing; and finally, the winter made it impossible to properly mix the clay and to keep our hands pliable enough to manage the tiles without breaking them.

The act of working seemed heartless. Living for an uncertain future did not bring comfort. The perishability of our existence was obvious to all the prisoners. As we worked outside, one sound that grew increasingly absent was the formerly reassuring sound of birds. How could one fathom the changes that happened so quickly to wipe out everything formerly familiar, the plan for which our lives in prison were frozen in a single purpose? To survive the hours of pressured monotony, each of us became to some extent numb. However, those times when we did feel the energy to concentrate on something in addition to the task before us, some prisoner quietly began to recite the prayer to Chenrezig and His Holiness, and soon others joined in. I was detained in Wa Da Dui for five years, during which time I dug the earth and made tiles, carried stones, plowed fields, and cut down trees.

Some prisoners were sent to cut trees in the Lho Kho Sung Dhu forest region. We had to walk twenty kilometers, about four hours each way, every day to the logging site on Kushi Lago mountain. At the time, that whole region was being deforested. Prisoners were required to do eight hours of hard work, cutting mostly small trees and branches that would be used to fuel the furnaces back at the mill. A group of guards armed with pistols was sent to accompany the prisoners; and wherever we worked, we were surrounded on four sides. After the wood was cut, it had to be tied into bundles and placed into carts. The prisoners used ropes to pull the carts, which could hold up to five hundred kilos of wood, all the way back to the camp.

Because of my past record, I was usually the only woman they decided to send. I had to use a sickle and had great difficulty in managing it. Although a male prisoner could chop down a tree in three or four swings, no matter how many times I hit the tree, I could not break through the wood. The men sharpened their sickles before using them, but for some time, I could not grasp the technique properly and was not allowed to speak to anyone. Also, I was always slipping and falling. The men knew how to proceed up and down the face of the mountain in a zigzag pattern to aid in their balance as they cut. For some time, being kept a bit separate from them, I didn't realize the benefit of this system and quickly became exhausted trying to climb straight up the mountain.

Before we left for the mountains in the morning, we were given one steamed dough that had to last for the entire day. My elderly brother-in-law, Phurba, was also sent with us. As he wasn't strong enough to cut wood with the younger men, he became the tea maker for the lumber camp and was also in charge of heating up the luncheon meal for the staff.

Every day, each prisoner had to cut six hundred *gyama* of wood, which equals three hundred kilos. Each of us had to pull our own cart, which was very difficult because we had to climb and descend a steep mountain. If you pulled up, the weight would pull you down, so it never felt as if you were getting anywhere. Though it seemed practically impossible, I was made to pull my cart alone after being made to fill it as full as I could and still move it. The guards laughed at me as I struggled and slipped trying to pull the ropes.

When we returned to the labor camp, the wood was weighed. If a prisoner had not fulfilled the quota, during the evening meetings the head jailer asked, "Why haven't you done your share?" Of course, I was usually the person singled out. The jailer said, "In every place that you served a term, you did not perform properly. It is not because you are not capable; you are actually quite hefty"—this was due to my stature—"but it is because you oppose us and you don't want to work."

One thing I can never forget is that, on one hand, the Communists always considered me to be the worst human being on earth, worthy only of being treated like a beast of burden—actually, worse, because at least they would shoot an animal that could no longer work rather than prolong its suffering. However, on the other hand, the inmates considered me to be a most patriotic Tibetan, who was sacrificing her life for our people. Because of this, I was again satisfied in my relationship with my fellow prisoners. There was always someone trying to help me. Somehow, through whatever humiliations I experienced during my imprisonment, something occurred to give me the strength to carry on. At that time, the strength came when I found that Rinchen Samdup, one of my relatives by marriage, was also detained at Wa Da Dui and was assigned to cutting trees for the kiln. Without the guards noticing, Rinchen helped me fill my quota and convinced others to help me, too. With Rinchen and Phurba there with me, I was very happy to once again share trust and companionship.

Sometimes when Rinchen tried to help me with the cart, the guards scolded him, saying, "When she can commit so many crimes, why can't she pull this cart? You are not allowed to pull it for her."

Rinchen quarreled with them: "When she obviously doesn't have the strength to pull it, why are you forcing her? If I don't help, the cart will not move and she won't accomplish her work."

At those times, I said, "You just shoot me here right now. I just can't pull this, so it's better that you kill me rather than waste all this time."

But they wouldn't do it, and they continued to go on like this for two seemingly endless years. I don't know if they were given orders to treat me in that manner; but, frankly, I can't comprehend how they found this type of behavior such a constant source of amusement. Still, one must remember that they had been indoctrinated to believe that I was some vague source of evil, an element that threatened the power and respect the Communist Party had given them. My constant opposition to glorifying the Communist doctrine was a nagging reminder of their own human vulnerability. They were thoroughly convinced that I was one of their worst enemies.

Some of the places we labored were very close to where the public lived, so every day people saw that I was undergoing problems and sufferings. The local people sometimes sent a group of young girls between fifteen and twenty years of age to tease the guards. The girls smiled and played with them while the people hurried to push my cart partway up the mountain. The guards did not notice or at least did not bother to say anything, as they continued smiling and enjoying the girls' attention.

I had tremendous public support from the outside because everyone in the community had heard of me and many had witnessed my difficulties. Sometimes when the girls came to help me, they deftly pushed into my dress some tsampa, bread, or a piece of meat wrapped in cloth as they passed by to talk to the soldiers, who seemed to fully believe that the girls really liked them.

One official named Lho Casu was assigned the role of main lecturer at the evening meetings, and he readily took a dislike to me. Since he began addressing me before he knew me at all, I imagine that he had been delivered some order that encouraged him to give me difficulty. During the meetings, he asked the prisoners, "What has Mrs. Adhe been doing during the week?" He scolded in a manner similar to Nu Kasu and always encouraged the prisoners to report on me. One evening after such a meeting, Rinchen was quite angry. He told me, "When Lho Casu first arrived here, I was sent to pick up his baggage. At that time, Lho Casu had only a face towel in his possession. For that reason we called him a 'true Communist.' I've always wondered how only a few years later he has become a wealthy man."

◊ ◊ ◊

When Rinchen Samdup came to Wa Da Dui in 1974, he was also condemned under the black-hat label. At the age of thirty-three, he had spent nearly half his life under detainment.

Rinchen, Phurba, and I sometimes managed to meet in the evenings after work. During that time we shared some memories of our experiences under occupation. Rinchen told us that when he was sixteen years old, he was invited to join a delegation that was going to visit China for one month. At the time of their visit, "Democratic Reforms" were being implemented in the Chinese society. In an effort to dissolve any remaining notions of class structure, people were not allowed to wear good clothing. A purge of the Guomindang and the wealthy was in progress, and the Communists were executing all leaders above the rank of mayor.

Rinchen recalled, "About three hundred Tibetans from various localities took part in this visit. Because I was young, I could not understand everything that was going on. The elders repeatedly said, 'This does not look good for us.' Though the main points of the tour were the dramatic technological advances made in the factories, the streets of Sichuan were also a form of education. We had seen prisoners being taken away in trucks and were told by passersby that those people were to be executed as enemies of the state."

Although there weren't many occasions when the delegation was allowed to come into direct contact with the general Chinese populace, sometimes they did get a chance to observe how people were faring. Rinchen told us about a visit the group made to a zoo near Chongqing, where lunch had been arranged in a restaurant on its grounds. As they were eating, Rinchen saw an old woman and a child coming toward them. He said, "This was the first time in my life that I saw the effects of severe hunger on a human being. This woman was determined to grab some food, no matter what happened. She picked up a plate and began eating. Some of the people in the restaurant tried to stop her; but no matter what they said or did, she would not put down the food. She ignored them, looking only at the plate and pushing food into her mouth as quickly as she could. The next moment, she was pulled outside by several of the restaurant employees, beaten, and thrown roughly to the ground. The Communist guide told us, 'These people were from the upper class. Now they cannot work, so they don't have food.'"

The group was distracted by what they saw but had to politely finish the meals on their plates. When they went outside, members of the delegation who could speak Chinese asked the woman about her situation. She told them that after the Communists had made purges on the wealthy families, executing most of the men, the other family members had just been wandering around. Their wealth and property had been confiscated and they had nothing left. Many of the older women had difficulty in walking because their feet had been bound in their youth.

Rinchen continued, telling us how the delegation next went to Chengdu, in Sichuan, where they saw long lines of people in the marketplaces wanting to buy one small piece of sweet bread made with walnuts: "The line was so long it seemed it would take hours for people to buy their one allotted piece of bread, and no one knew when the supply would run out. We Tibetans were wearing special tags that enabled us to buy as much as we wanted, so when we arrived, we were served first. Some Chinese came forth and asked members of the delegation to buy for them. The bread cost one yuan, and the Chinese were offering us ten yuan to buy it. We bought some extra bread and gave it to the people behind us in the line without asking for any money."

Rinchen's strongest impression was that it seemed the main concern of the townspeople was to buy food. No one was interested in clothing or anything else. Rinchen and the others wanted to buy some nice articles to bring back home, but they were told that their purchases would only be confiscated by the Communists later.

The marketplaces were all nationalized. The delegation didn't see a single private trader. The older Tibetans said, "Today China is completely different from the years of the Guomindang: we have seen the signs that before long the Chinese will have no freedom. Today the people's faces are loose, but they are beginning to tighten." They compared Chinese Communist policy to fresh leather left in the sun. Initially the leather is very loose and pliable, but in due time, as it dries, it shrinks and tightens. During their visit, none of the Tibetans openly said the Communists were bad, but some of the elders barely ate because they were saddened by thoughts of what might befall our land. The delegation was constantly told, "When you go home, you must explain to the people that Communist China is all powerful. It is like your parent and you must not rebel."

"When we returned home," Rinchen explained, "many from this group were appointed leaders. They were given good pay, but no actual authority, and had no regular contact with the people. Slowly these leaders were made to announce the superiority of the Communist Party, and then they were used to try to convince the people to turn in their weapons."

Rinchen Samdup's oldest brother, a lama, was arrested a few years after the persecutions of the religious communities began. With some friends, Rinchen conceived a plan to free his brother from prison and escape to the mountains. However, the Chinese somehow heard about the plan before it could be carried out. One day in October 1959, eight PLA soldiers and police came to arrest Rinchen at his home. He was handcuffed and taken to the district prison in Dartsedo, a smaller prison than the one in Ngachoe monastery, located in the same town. At the time of his arrest, the prison held about eighty prisoners awaiting sentencing. Rinchen was eighteen years old and was to spend the next twenty-four years in detainment.

After his arrest, he was taken to an office in the prison where he was beaten and interrogated. The officials told him, "If you try to hit an egg on a stone, which will break, the egg or the stone?" He was told that he must try to understand the nature of his crime. "With your mentality and your opposition to us, you are not going on the right path. Ultimately, the wrong path will lead to your death. Compared to big countries like America that are afraid of Communist China, you are just a fraction. Chiang Kai-shek, with three million soldiers, had to run away from China, so what can you do? You are just like a wild rat trying to climb a pillar. Anyone in the world who opposes communism will never be happy. We have so many friends, they can be compared to the raindrops."

Rinchen said, "My inmates and I felt that the recurring references to America were because for us Tibetans, America was the most popular foreign country. Many felt that if the Chinese tried to bully us, America might come to our aid, just as the American government had helped

Chiang Kai-shek. In order to counter that kind of mentality in the Tibetans, the Chinese always referred to America in negative terms."

The officials wanted to know who had been involved in Rinchen's plans, and for that reason he was subjected to many interrogations. He was made to kneel on the floor on the edge of a wooden club, or sometimes on crushed stones. In the winter, he and other prisoners in Dartsedo being tortured were made to stand in cold water and were often asked, "How are you faring now that you have opposed the Communists?" Two other methods of torture were hanging prisoners from the ceiling by their wrists or beating them with clubs.

"For the first three months," Rinchen said, "I was interrogated every day. After it was confirmed my detention would continue, the interrogations occurred once a month." Rinchen Samdup spent one year in Dartsedo prison.

The food at the prison was poor and the servings meager. Before each meal, the prisoners were made to sing a Communist song such as:

> The extent of his crime is so great,
> The sky in comparison is small.
> Every day he tries to destroy the world,
> But the Communist Party is good.
> The Communist Party is good, and remains
> The only salvation of the people.

As was true at other prisons, at evening meetings, prisoners were made to confess their crimes and analyze how evil their actions had been. Those who refused were subjected to thamzing sessions during which almost all prisoners present would be forced to take part under gunpoint.

One of the prison inmates was a woman named Ka Misa whose brother, Padhen, the manager of Gowa Kha monastery in Minyak, had already left for Lhasa. Soon after her arrest, she was stripped of her clothing and tied by her wrists from the ceiling. A small fire, built from below her, scorched her feet. After some time, she collapsed from smoke inhalation and was taken down and immersed in ice-cold water. She did not survive the ordeal. Her fate soon became the talk of the facility.

◊ ◊ ◊

After his year in Dartsedo prison, Rinchen Samdup was sentenced to fifteen years of "Reeducation through Labor" and thus joined the numbers of Tibetans and Chinese caught in the largely unsuccessful experiment to control the nationalistic feelings of individuals through "mind reform," while aiding the Chinese economy through imposed labor. He eventually passed through ten prisons and labor camps, among them, Ghapa Lin Chang, located twenty kilometers east of Minyak Ranga khar. It was the main headquarters for the forest department of a large locality that was being deforested. The Chinese authorities had a labor force of over three thousand Chinese as well as Tibetan prisoners employed in lumbering there. Many of the felled trees were so huge that one log filled a truck.

Rinchen was also detained at Shiwo Rong in Dartsedo under Sateng Qu. There also, a similar number of Chinese took part in deforestation, along with Tibetan prisoners. Before the Communists came, Tibetans had traditionally refrained from hunting and cutting wood in that area because it was considered to be so sacred.

◊ ◊ ◊

Normally, prisoners are free to return to society when their sentences are over, but the Chinese prison system usually finds reasons not to release them. In this way, as we were often told, "The prisoners will never forget who their leaders are." Also, the Communists find it very useful to production to make prisoners work for little or no pay in a system known as Forced Job Placement, which is simply an extension of Reeducation through Labor with no fixed term. There is absolutely no available means of appeal to the Public Security Bureau (the police) or of obtaining legal help from the outside courts, for these institutions actually contribute to the situation. Groups of Forced Job Placement prisoners often continued to work in the same labor camp; or, if the number of those having completed their sentences was small, they might then be transferred to another labor camp where they would be joined by other prisoners with the same designation. Though told that they were now free, they were not allowed to leave; they were forced to continue work according to the labor camp's production schedules and were constantly pressed to prove that they had reformed their counterrevolutionary thought processes.

Some prisoners were kept in detention so that they would not influence those on the outside by either their nationalism or in recounting the extent of the sufferings of the detained. Though Rinchen Samdup's sentence was completed on February 5, 1974, he was told that his release would cause a disturbance in the society and thus it was best for him to remain in detention. Thus, ten days later, he came to Wa Da Dui Labor Camp.

Whenever Rinchen recalled his years of detention, his voice inevitably grew quiet. One evening, after a long day of logging, Rinchen began an old prayer to the mountain deities and then tried to express the contradictions of our past and present. "It was as if someone was forcing you to cut off your own arm, and then those of your friends. My family had lived in the vicinity of the sacred forests. The first trees I ever noticed were the thick grove of white birches that stood in front of our home. My father stood with me in the grove. As he held my hand, I closed my eyes and listened to the wind in the leaves as my father taught me to feel the trees' living presence. As a boy I often lay in the middle of the grove, watching the sun play on the edges of fluttering leaves. The white bark of the trees' trunks and branches seemed to pull the blue right out of the sky, wrapping it around itself like a coat. The dark-rose and coral of winter sunsets were caught and divided into fragments by the spears of bare branches. During the mornings and evenings of festivals, I loved to walk among the trees as heavy, smoky clouds of incense offerings wafted down from the roof and slowly unrolled and stretched between them.

"Now whenever I cut down a birch, it feels as if one more root of my own life intertwined with the essence of our land and its deities is torn and is thrown to fall on the ground with a single thud. I wonder of the dream of my past: everything and everyone I've known has disappeared. There have been so many times I'd have rather died than to be forced every day to take part in something to which my heart was opposed. But of course I realized that my death under these circumstances would have even less meaning than my life."

In listening to Rinchen's account, I was sadly reminded that the life and death of every Tibetan we saw in the camps was a testimony of the bitter result of occupation, a testimony of constant suffering that would most likely never be heard by anyone except fellow prisoners, who were powerless to initiate any change in the future.

◊ ◊ ◊

In Wa Da Dui, prisoners with sentences of two or three years were usually encamped in the mountains cutting down the trees. Prisoners serving more than a ten-year sentence began walking to work from the labor camp around six in the morning. Our average work day was twelve hours. At the time I met Rinchen, we were working in a region known as Gholo Tho.

The forests of different mountains were slotted to be assigned to different groups for cutting: one mountain would be the responsibility of the prisoners, another would be under the jurisdiction of the local authorities. Although most of the wood transported was firewood, a better grade of lumber was taken to the labor camp for use by life prisoners in the carpentry section to make furniture for the camp's administration offices, to construct staff quarters, and to build prison cells.

Prisoners were ordered to fell some larger trees from sections of ancient forests that had never been cut in a place called Ro Xian. The trees were so huge that five men holding hands could just encircle each tree. The prisoners then loaded the trees on military trucks for transport to China.

Funds that came from trading the timber were used by the prison administration for the salaries of prison officials and for construction projects, including new cells. According to the Chinese system, the labor camp had certain financial obligations: with prisoner labor, it had to generate fifty thousand yuan annually for the central government. This obligation had to be fulfilled at any cost.

Nothing was being left on the mountains. Basically, we Tibetan prisoners were all in a state of constant depression. After the Communists had confiscated everything we owned, now they were destroying our land. It seemed that China must not have any of its own wood. We said to each other, "Of course, they can't take the mountains and the land, but otherwise, they are taking everything. If the jewelry of the mountains is not there, it is as if a human being is standing before us without clothing." Many of the elders who had realized the implications had said, "Our land will not be happy for a great many years. There will be many natural calamities, and in time, the harvests will again fail." We prisoners prayed that under the leadership of His Holiness the Dalai Lama, Tibet would be saved. Otherwise, we felt that the Chinese would simply uproot everything and leave our country a wasteland.

In the early 1970s, Tibet was again faced with serious food shortages. By that time, the Chinese had almost totally replaced the traditional cultivation of barley with the propagation of winter wheat, which they preferred. Many of the fields had, through mismanagement, been leached of their original fertility. Tibet experienced its most severe drought in a century and the most severe snowfall in fifty years. In 1972, several regions were beset by severe earthquakes, and crop failures occurred throughout the country. We felt ourselves helpless witnesses to an accounting that would end in sorrow.

During the worst period of food shortages, none of the women in the general public in that area bore children for a period of three years. The Tibetans' diet was so lacking in nutrients that it was not possible for them to conceive.

◊ ◊ ◊

Every Sunday, most prisoners in our camp were allowed to go and do some shopping in the market. Sometimes Phurba would go for me, sometimes Rinchen, for I was never allowed to go out.

During his weekly excursions, Rinchen became friendly with two Chinese prisoners in the camp. Hua Chen, a former engineer, was the acting storekeeper in Wa Da Dui. Before the rise of the Communists, his family had been very wealthy and were senior officials in the Guomindang army. He had received an excellent education. However, in the 1950s the Communists began their purge of the wealthy and Guomindang officials. All people who had held senior positions in the Guomindang were labeled "historical counterrevolutionaries" and faced imprisonment even if they had not actively opposed the Communists.

Hua Chen quickly joined the Communist Party. Due to his abilities as an engineer, he had received special considerations. When the PLA began its invasion of Tibet, he had been put in a position of authority in road construction on the Xikang–Lhasa highway.

But after a few years, he could not bring himself to accept what he was witnessing, and he began to openly oppose his adopted political party. Hua Chen, a Buddhist, always said, "The system is doing everything in the wrong sense, for it is based on robbery and falsehood. They have no worry about these acts and take no heed of the law of cause and effect." This old man openly told the prison staff that he thought the system was no good. During his time in Wa Da Dui, he had often been put in manacles but said to anyone, "I can never accept what the Communists are doing." He told Rinchen that no matter what the cost, it was correct for him to stand up for his beliefs. He said it was true that the Chinese had occupied Tibet, and he was keeping to what he knew.

Hua Chen introduced Rinchen to Li, another Chinese prisoner, also a former Party member. He had been detained in the late 1950s because, at one point, he'd begun to openly oppose the functioning of the Communist system and ideology, and because of his academic background he had been a target of the Anti-Rightist Campaign. Sometimes he shook Rinchen's hand and told him, "In the future, everything will be fine for Tibet. Your leader, the Dalai Lama, has traveled all over the world; and through him Tibetans have come to understand more of the outside world. They have visited different countries and have rapidly acquired knowledge. This is a very good foundation for Tibet's future. The refugees will always defend Tibet's independence because they are becoming qualified and well educated." He also said, "Your leader is safe in India, so do not despair."

Slowly, Li and Rinchen became very close friends. They enjoyed talking whenever the opportunity arose and sharing their meals together. Their closeness came especially out of their shared opposition. Li told Rinchen, "Under communism, there is no freedom for a human being. If there is no freedom, there is no meaning to life." He spoke highly of how much freedom and democracy people have in America, and how several of his friends had studied there in their youth. Rinchen told me of his conversations and what he had heard about the West. We sat together, trying to imagine such a way of life.

It made me quite happy when Rinchen told me about his friends. It was a helpful reminder that our opposition was to a cruel and corrupt political ideology, not to a particular race of human beings. Whenever Rinchen, Phurba, and I talked, we always tried to hearten each other with the hope that somehow the Communists would change and rays of bright sunlight would again shine on Tibet. Of course, we couldn't say these things in front of every prisoner, but if we and perhaps one other compatible inmate were together, we would discuss such matters. Phurba often reminded us, "Because the basic core of the Chinese Communist system is false, its work can have no ultimately worthwhile meaning. If the Party itself is based on the acquisition of power, then ultimately, opposing factions have to develop in the leadership. Eventually, there is no other way but for it to fall. On the other hand, the Tibetan people have such faith in our leader, the Dalai Lama, that even if he asked us to step from the edge of the highest precipice, we would gladly and faithfully do it."

One Sunday, as Rinchen walked through the compound, he looked out on the highway and saw a slowly moving horse cart bringing some new prisoners to Wa Da Dui. He stopped to watch the cart, wondering where this new group was coming from and what news they might have. As it pulled into the camp and the prisoners began to step down, he looked at their tired faces individually.

Suddenly, he saw his older brother, Ngawang Kusho, in the cart—the same brother he had tried to save as a teenager in the attempt that led to his initial imprisonment. As his heart began to pound, he called out his brother's name and raced toward the cart. For a few seconds, they looked into each other's eyes, and then Rinchen grabbed him. Both began crying as they hugged. Rinchen brought Ngawang Kusho to my room, where I was doing some sewing. I looked up to see a tall, very thin man with dark, kind eyes. Looking into them, I felt a calmness come over me, and a sudden concern. It was obvious that he was exhausted. As we made tea, we began to discuss our lives. Ngawang Kusho told us that he had been in the Sha Labor Camp in the region of Garthar, Minyak. He had also done lumbering in Chulo Dzong and Shiwo Rong.

Ngawang Kusho recalled, "Even beyond beatings, starvation, cold, and forced labor, the most difficult thing for me to understand were the public humiliations that people were forced to endure. There were times when female PLA soldiers would try to force me to drink urine. When I refused, it was spilled over my face. We lamas were made to clean fecal matter, which was to be used as fertilizer, out of makeshift toilets. The toilets consisted of a deep hole dug in the ground which was covered with two planks. Quite often, when we climbed down into the holes to clean them out, female PLA soldiers amused the prison staff by purposely urinating from the top so that the urine fell on our faces."

Ngawang Kusho was sentenced to eighteen years of imprisonment but was ultimately detained for twenty. He was very weak at the time we met him, and so Rinchen devoted himself to helping both of us. One Sunday, after returning from the market, Rinchen placed a small package on my bed and sighed, "Adhe-la, for many years I reserved my strength through hatred. I wanted to fight them for taking away my adult life before it had even really begun. When I heard I would not be released after my term of imprisonment expired, a sinking feeling swept over me: that the earth had fallen to the rule of a system that had proved the things we felt gave dignity to the existence of a human being were the illusion, and this, the only stark reality. Lately, I have been feeling differently. I am sorry that you and my brother are imprisoned here. But, if there is no other way, I am glad that I am here with you both, that I can help you in some small ways."

From that moment onward, I saw Rinchen in a different sense. I trusted him completely and came to more fully appreciate what his kindness and his companionship meant to me.

One day, the following year, Ngawang Kusho was called to the office. Rinchen, Phurba, and I wondered what was happening but we weren't able to talk to him until the evening. Looking at the ground and then slowly raising his head and meeting our eyes with his own, he told us, "I can't seem to believe it. I can hardly remember or comprehend the meaning of the words, but this morning they told me that after tomorrow I will be free to leave."

After his release, he became a hermit, devoting most of his time to prayer. He now resides in a rock cave not too far from the village in which he was born, and he occasionally visits a nearby monastery. Sometimes he is visited by the local residents, particularly the children.

◊ ◊ ◊

In Minyak Ra-nga gang region, there is a sacred mountain known as Sha Jera. The mountain itself was traditionally a place of pilgrimage for all festivals and religious occasions. At those times, the people of the region offered prayer and incense ceremonies. In the early 1970s, over three hundred prisoners were employed in mining lead from the mountain. At its base is a small lake. During the summer of 1975, this lake was the site of what was regarded by us Tibetans as a miraculous event. One day, people noticed that an impression of a nomadic tent had manifested beneath the water in the middle of the lake. The Chinese took binoculars up on the mountain to monitor whether the image was moving. They realized that the image was not a natural occurrence, and it frightened them. After a week, the image of the tent began to disappear and a very large green lotus began to physically grow in its place. The flower continued to spread over the lake. The people said that the flower had great significance because of its size and color: green is associated with His Holiness the Dalai Lama, who was born in the year of the Wooden Hog. Green is the color of the wooden element.

Tibetans began to come to the shore in great numbers, carrying khatags. Before long, the Chinese decided to bombard the lake. As a wall of water rose in the lake's center, the people rushed to pick up the pieces of the flower that floated to the shore. Those who managed to preserve the flower's fragments said the petals had the consistency of grass. We Tibetans felt that the apparition and the extraordinarily large growth of the lotus held some kind of promise of better times to come.

One year later, in January 1976, Zhou Enlai, Prime Minister of the People's Republic of China, died. His death was followed in July by that of Zhu De, commander-in-chief of the People's Liberation Army. And on September 9, Mao Zedong took his last earthly breath. The forty-year-long concentration of power was broken. Within a month, the members of the extreme left-wing Gang of Four were arrested at their headquarters by an opposing branch of the PLA; and the Cultural Revolution came to a close. A great earthquake also took place in China. In mid-July 1977, the first indications of a changing policy toward our land were shown, which in turn caused great confusion for the Chinese Communist cadres stationed in Tibet and created a feeling of restless expectation in the hearts of the Tibetan people.

PART IV

An Unstilled Voice

13

LIBERALIZATION

The first wave of freedom began in March 1979 with the announcement that a group of 376 prisoners was to be released. The Chinese called a very big meeting in Lhobasha, and afterward, my brother Nyima came to Wa Da Dui and informed me that they were going to release all the prisoners—except for the ringleaders, which included me. The Chinese had announced: "It was the leaders like Adhe who instigated the Tibetans to go against us. It was not the fault of the ordinary people, so everyone except those leaders will be released." They stated, "In the future, people must not make any attempt to protect Adhe Tapontsang, because she is a woman who has committed a great crime."

We noticed a change of attitude in the labor camp. We were told about Deng Xiaoping's removal of the black-hat designation. They told us, "The people who subjected you to black hat were the Gang of Four. From today, you are not snake spirits or devils, but you are real human beings. From now on, you can wear proper clean clothes, you can raise your heads, and you can have freedom of movement. You will no longer be subjected to thamzing."

The Chinese government agreed to a request by the Dalai Lama to allow an official fact-finding delegation of the exiled government to enter Tibet. The purpose of the delegation was to reestablish a relationship with their countrymen, who had had no contact with the outside world in twenty years.

Earlier, there had been no proper amenities for washing one's clothes or one's body, even a little bit. Anyone who tried to wash would be asked by officials, "Why did you wash your hair today? Why are you looking clean today? What is your plan?" But in 1979 we were told, "Now you have to clean your clothes. You have to wash your hair and dress properly because the delegation of the Dalai Lama is arriving this year."

They announced to the public: "You must have smiling faces and carry the prayer wheel here, the rosary there." There were no monks left in the area; but they asked if anyone had any clothing left by the monks, and they started making monks' robes. To give an appearance that conditions were normal, they ordered some people to don the robes and walk up and down the highway to be seen.

During the first half of 1979, Tibetans were forced to take part in the rapid renovation of the monasteries that were visible from the highways, while monasteries in more isolated regions were ignored. Sometimes a small chapel would be constructed on the former site of a large monastery. To replace the gold and silver statues that had been looted, new ones were sculpted of clay. The walls were painted in the traditional manner, and paintings of the Tibetan deities were hung on the walls. But there were no rinpoches left to consecrate the chapels, and there was no one left alive who remembered the scriptures. The site of these lifeless restorations brought tears to the eyes of the Tibetan people.

Lobsang Sampten, one of the Dalai Lama's brothers, was a member of that first delegation. Although freedom of assembly had been banned for more than twenty years, thousands of people lined the roadsides to get a glimpse of the group, especially of Lobsang Sampten. Now we knew we had not been forgotten, and outside of the labor camps, there was nothing the Chinese could do to discourage the people.

On the day of the delegation's arrival at our camp, the prisoners were called to a meeting in a big hall and were locked inside. As soon as the meeting was announced, I returned to my room and declared myself to be sick. I sent one of the inmates for Rinchen Samdup. I asked him to report that I was unable to leave my bed and was thus requesting permission to not attend the meeting. Rinchen Samdup and Phurba went to the officials and said, "Adhe is not well. She is very weak and unable to come to the hall." The officials said, "If she is sick, we'd better lock the door. We can't allow her to go outside."

Meanwhile, I had covered my face and walked out onto the highway. My intention was that if I happened to meet anyone, even if I just had a moment to say a few words, I would try something. Lobsang Sampten arrived in a convoy of about twenty cars. I saw him waving to the people, and I tried my utter best to reach the car in which he was riding. Perhaps he could see that I wanted to tell him something, but there was no time—all the cars kept moving, so I had no opportunity to speak. Although it was disappointing, the very fact that such an event had occurred was remarkable, and even if I could not reach him, perhaps someone else would be able to. Even if we could not speak directly to the delegation's members, we knew that they would see enough to realize how our land had changed. They would see the ruins of the monasteries and the rags we wore for clothing. They would at least see the people's faces; somehow the evidence of our suffering was sure to be recognized.

After the visit, we prisoners discussed how the times were changing. Daring to hope the situation would improve, we ventured that perhaps a day would come when His Holiness the Dalai Lama would himself visit Tibet and come to our own regions.

After the label of black hat was removed, I was allowed to make a fifteen-day visit to my native town. Phurba and Rinchen were kept in the camp to assure my return. I was given a document to be shown to the local authorities upon my arrival home. The journey took a day and a half. As the bus approached Karze, I felt a cold numbness come over me. From a distance, I could see the places where I had spent so much time in my youth. Other memories also came to me: the memory of my arrest, of being dragged to the monastery, of my son crying and calling to me.

Was it really twenty-one years ago? Had my son grown up? Would I meet him in just a few hours? As the bus pulled into the Karze station, I was amazed to see how many Chinese were in the streets. It seemed that all the signs were in Chinese. What had happened to the Karze I had known? So many of the buildings associated with my life there were in ruins. Everything looked different. I wanted to see my mother. My mind could not absorb the shock. It all seemed unreal.

When I reached Lhobasha, I learned that our home and its entire contents and all our land had been confiscated after my arrest and had never been returned. I was directed to the place where my brother Nyima was living. As I approached the house, Nyima opened the door and looked into my eyes as he took my hand. We stood for a moment, and then he led me inside. I asked him, "Where is Mother?" He told me, "Adhe, our mother has already passed away." "What happened to her?" He said, "Shortly after your arrest, they confiscated everything. Not even a bowl was left to us. One by one, all our family members were arrested, except for Mother, who was so old, and Bhumo, who was ill. I was taken for forced labor in a commune. From that time on, Mother was left with nothing. It was a period in Karze when there was a tremendous shortage of food. Friends tried to help, but no one had much to share, and Mother no longer had a reason to live and did not want to deprive the younger people of food on her behalf. She grew very weak, and before long, her face grew pinched. She slowly died of starvation in 1968."

I next wanted to know the fate of my son. Nyima told me, "Adhe, Chimi is no more." I immediately asked, "Was my son taken by the Chinese? What happened to him?" My brother swore that Chimi had not been taken by the Chinese but had fallen into the river and drowned. But somehow I felt that was not the whole truth. So, a few words were to be my only answer to twenty-one years of waiting in fear and hope. Just like that, in a few words that disappeared into the air, my waiting was over, and there was nothing.

My elder mother had died during the first famine. Chale and Aso, the second and third oldest sons of my elder mother, Bochungma had died from beatings inflicted during thamzing sessions in Karze. My brother Ochoe passed away from starvation some time in 1961 while still under house arrest in Karze. Shortly after my arrest, Ahtra, my brother Jughuma's wife, had been charged with not handing over all the valuables and jewelry that belonged to our family. Through thamzing and threats of death, she had been coerced into revealing the hiding places of our remaining valuables. Ahtra is a very timid woman, and the situation left her in a constant state of fear and great distress. Later, she had been labeled an outcast under the black-hat designation, which was removed just shortly before my return. One of her two children, her daughter, Lhakyi, had survived. Lhakyi has a son, Jughuma's only grandchild. My daughter, Tashi Khando, and my brother Nyima were the only family members remaining at home.

My dear sister Bhumo, the wife of Pema Gyaltsen, had gone mad shortly after Pema's death and died in misery. Sera Ma had been taken to work in the communes. Because she was weak and had difficulty with her legs, she was given the assignments of making tea and babysitting for the children of those who worked in the fields. She suffered years of deprivation, but thankfully, some of her children had remained near her in the same commune and had helped her whenever they could, and thus she was still alive. Upon seeing each other, we fell into each other's arms and cried. Sera Ma had been certain that we would never meet again. By that time, she was quite old and had great difficulty standing. She told me how sorry she was that she and the rest of the family had been unable to help and protect me.

My nieces and nephews had been children when I was arrested. Now they were grown. Only six of my childhood friends, including our former servant, Choenyi Dolma, remained alive in Karze. My friends and remaining family told me that they were waiting for me to come back, that they would take care of me. They brought their sons before me and made them promise that if anything happened to their mothers, they themselves would gladly take over the responsibility of my care. As is traditional in Kham when making a promise, they each held my hand in turn.

Shortly afterward, my daughter appeared in the doorway. She had been one year old when I was arrested; now she was twenty-two. We didn't recognize each other. Nyima took her hand and said, "Adhe, this is your daughter, Tashi Khando." I was surprised to find a grown woman standing before me, and she was equally surprised to find a mother. At first we felt quite shy and awkward. Then slowly she came to my side and touched my hand as we searched each other's eyes, and in the next moment we were both in tears.

The river looked the same to me. It was the only thing that seemed familiar. Among the people, there was hardly anyone that I knew from my time. All the most learned and capable people of the society had already perished, having been among the first to die. Kharnang and Karze Day-tshal monasteries and the temple of De Gonpo, so active during my youth, were completely destroyed and plundered. Wild shrubs grew where Karze Day-tshal monastery had once stood. The lamas and rinpoches of my youth were all gone.

Sometime during the Cultural Revolution, Karze monastery— including the magnificent Dugkar thanka—had been destroyed, with the exception of one small building. Before this happened, the Chinese seized and imprisoned its caretaker, Chagrong Sonam Tobchen. After the demolition of the monastery, he was paraded with both his hands and legs in chains before an enforced public gathering where he was denounced as a leader of the reactionaries. He was then shot. In order to intimidate the general public, a proclamation was issued announcing that no one would be allowed to take delivery of his body. The chains had been used to bind his hands and legs for such a long time that they had cut through the flesh and had exposed his bones. Those who had witnessed the state of his body told me that they had spontaneously burst into tears of despair.

Fortunately, two of the incarnate lamas of Karze monastery, Lamdark Rinpoche and Sigyab Tulku, had managed to escape to India. Lamdark Rinpoche then lived in Switzerland for some time and returned to Tibet years later. However, two other lamas, Saraha Rinpoche and Lhodrang Namkha Gyaltsen, perished.

Even looking into the forest and the hills, one could see that the herbs and flowers had been exploited to the extent that the hills were completely barren. I was overwhelmed by the devastation. How could such a complete lack of reverence for life ever be explained? How could one rationalize the enslavement of the Tibetans as "freeing" us from a system that, though imperfect, was our chosen way of life? They took away our families, homes, possessions, land, religion, culture, and the right to speak our thoughts publicly. They destroyed our forests, animals, and flowers. They tried to convince us that we were evil, that we were less than human beings, and subjected us to violence and humiliations that could not have been imagined before their arrival. They seemed a people enslaved to a system that had no soul—a system of plunder and destruction, hatred, and lies.

◊ ◊ ◊

Initially, I sent my brother, Nyima, to take my papers to the authorities in Karze, but they demanded that I appear in person. When I entered the Public Security Building, I was directed to an office where a Chinese official was sitting behind a desk smoking a cigarette. I handed him my papers and he looked through them. He then warned me, "You must not talk to anyone in the society and be very careful not to mention anything that might spark a demonstration against the Chinese in Karze by the younger generation. If a demonstration or any sort of uprising arises, you will be held personally responsible. Is that understood?" I slowly nodded my head, and he told me, "If you behave yourself, you will be allowed to stay for the full fifteen days; but if you stir up any problems, you will have to return before that time is over."

Because my surviving friends were still afraid of being seen with me, they came to see me in the night. We informed each other of everything that had occurred in our lives in the past twenty-one years. With sadness, they told me of the fates that had befallen most of the women who had worked with me in the resistance. I had known some of them from my childhood, when we had lived in freedom, and they had been among the bravest and most trustworthy of my friends. Now they were dead. As we discussed these things, those listening cried until their eyes were red and swollen.

One friend told me how she and other women in the resistance had often said how grateful they were that I had never given their names to the Chinese. They had always been expecting that today, tomorrow, or the day after tomorrow, their turn would come. They had spoken of me as having taken on their deeds as my own and suffering for their sake. But, of course, it could not have been any other way, for we had been "friends among friends." In the end, despite having kept silent regarding their identities, I could not save most of them. So many people were brutalized and destroyed, often for petty reasons, or for no reason.

I was told that in many cases our friends who suffered and perished had even told their children how I'd worked for the Tibetan cause and fought the Chinese. They had mentioned how they wanted their gratitude and respect for me to continue in our native land.

◊ ◊ ◊

We couldn't go to the graveyard in the daytime because of the police, so one night under the cover of darkness, I took one of my nephews and a few other family members to the place where my family is buried. As is traditional, I brought various foodstuffs to offer to their departed spirits. I lit a small fire and started talking to the deceased, telling them what had happened in my life and recalling their lives and the times that I had spent with them. I spoke to them of the oppression we had all suffered, telling them everything that was in my heart. I don't know how long I sat speaking to their graves in the night, hoping that somehow they could feel my love for them.

Nyima began to fear for my well-being and tried to convince me to leave, saying, "You must not dwell on these things, Adhe. You must learn to live in the present." After some time, all my family members became very nervous and suggested that we should get going. After a few more minutes, I felt I'd had a satisfactory visit, and we left.

◊ ◊ ◊

I made one of my friends swear to tell me the truth of what had happened to my son. I told her, "I have been to the cemetery and have seen the graves of my mothers, my father, my brother Ochoe, my brother Aso, my brother Chale, Pema Gyaltsen, and my sister Bhumo. All of my immediate family members who have perished are buried close by each other in one section of ground, but there is no sign of my son. Tonight you must tell me what has happened to him."

I swore that I would not cry, and so my friend confided, "After your arrest, your son became mad. He started constantly running up and down calling for you and wouldn't let anyone touch him. He just stayed alone crying and screaming. When people tried to stop him, he bit their hands and broke away. Once when this was happening, he ran and lost his balance on the river's edge. When he fell in, no one was able to save him. By the time we reached him, it was too late."

No one at that time knew what had become of my favorite brother, Jughuma. The only thing that I'd heard in all those years was that he was free. How strange it was to return to our home without him. I remembered all the happy times we'd spent together, and how we had tried to find a means by which we could always be together in our home. I remembered his smile, his patience, and the love he had constantly showered on me. I wondered if we would ever see each other again in this life. It didn't seem as though it would be possible.

I learned of the great kindness that Tsola, a nomadic woman who was one of my childhood friends, had done for my family. After my arrest, Tsola took my daughter and brought her up. She had a baby of her own at that time, and so she breastfed both of the children together. All of my surviving friends went quietly to Tsola and donated such food as butter, milk, and cheese, saying, "Please take care that Adhe's child survives with you."

I also learned that my daughter's marriage had recently been arranged with the son of someone that I knew. Of course, I would not be able to attend her wedding. I tried not to tell her too much of what I had been through and assured her that now everything was all right. I wanted her to have a happy life and did not tell her about the cloud of sorrow that covered my heart. Though my daughter and I felt a close bond, we had never really known each other. I wanted her to have as normal a life as possible and not be consumed with hatred for those who occupied the land in which she lived. I feared this would happen if she learned too much of my past and that she might endanger herself if she rose in opposition to the Chinese. Anyway, Tsola was her mother now.

Sadly, I began to prepare for my return to Wa Da Dui. On the bus again, as I passed Karze, I could only think, "There is nothing left." All the pain, separation, and loss of those twenty-one years seemed to well up in my heart. It had been unbearable—and now, there was nothing.

Back in Wa Da Dui, Rinchen and Phurba were anxious to hear news of home. Because of Phurba's advanced age, I was as evasive as possible. Because everything that I had striven to live for all these years was gone, I saw no reason to carry on. I just sat dumbly on my bed. Lho Casu ordered the other prisoners to drag me to work, but they stood by helplessly.

Lho Casu walked into my room and stood before me. Looking up from my bed, I quietly told him, "Please shoot me. It doesn't matter." I couldn't stop thinking of the fact that my family and friends were gone, of how they had all suffered, and how everything was over. There was nothing left. All these years I had been living for nothing, and now I didn't have to try any more. I started to laugh uncontrollably; sometimes I sang and sometimes I cried. A terrible restlessness came over me, and I began to wander around muttering to myself, totally unaware of my immediate surroundings. I never wanted to sit down—I just wanted to keep moving, pacing, seeing nothing, until the time came when I could walk no more. This made the Tibetans who had known me in the labor camp very sad.

One day, Phurba and Rinchen took me to a lama who was imprisoned there. He was a very compassionate man who had received some training in Tibetan medicine. He performed moxibustion (burning a certain aromatic plant over many points on my body) and prayed for me. A short while later, for what reason I am not sure, I slowly began to come out of that state. My mind again began to register my surroundings, and I could feel the terrible aimless agitation wearing off. I began to remember what it was like to sit and relax and to exist in the present.

◊ ◊ ◊

At Wa Da Dui, there was a respected lama among the prisoners whose name was Aso. One morning, he came to me saying, "Hello Adhe, I must tell you that last night I had an interesting dream." He continued, "You must know the *kalsang* flower. It has always been my favorite because of its beautiful fragrance. In my dream, I was walking past your cell and found one such flower growing close by it. This gave me the idea that something good is to happen in your life." At that time, I couldn't even imagine that the flower signified my freedom, but now I feel that this was what the dream meant.

I felt some inspiration when my friend, Sonam Dolma, was released from Wa Da Dui in late 1979. Although I shuddered to think of what she might find in returning to her native land of Golok, at least she had survived her twenty-four years of imprisonment and had managed to retain her strength and dignity. When we were imprisoned together at Nu Fan Dui, we were among the five strongest women working in the fields. For that reason, we had often been used to pull ropes attached to plows. It was terribly tiring work and we often fell, especially when the soil was wet. Yet, each had constantly encouraged the other to carry on. Sonam was an extremely religious woman and very strong; she was never willing to say a word renouncing her people during the reeducation meetings. In the evenings after those long and exhausting hours we often spoke quietly together. During our conversations she sometimes recounted the story of the 1956 massacre at the mountain known as the Abode of the Golden Dragon in Setha. The lifeless body of her husband, Washul Tolho, was dragged before her as the Chinese warned her that this would be the fate of those who opposed them. She always cried when speaking of those sad and unfortunate events. It seemed that part of her was left behind on that mountain, and since that time, she never fully adjusted to the present.

Upon leaving Wa Da Dui, she looked long into my eyes. We both realized that her land was far from my own and we would probably never meet again. She told me, "I am certain you will be free one day, and I don't feel that you will live quietly. Please remember what I have told you: I am certain that you will be free, even if the entire world forgets you."

◊ ◊ ◊

One evening after work, when we were sitting together, my brother-in-law Phurba turned to Rinchen and said, "I have a request to make of you. I am hoping that you will be willing to live with Adhe in the future." Extremely embarrassed, I told Phurba, "It really doesn't matter, because I have already gone through so much, I am certain that I can manage somehow. Moreover, because Rinchen is ten years younger than me, I would find it embarrassing in the society." But Phurba was one of the few remaining elders in the family, and he was adamant that I should be taken care of. He told me, "Rinchen-la is a good-hearted man, and he will be able as a younger brother to take care of you in times of need."

Later that year, Phurba and most of the other prisoners were released. I was to be detained for five more years.

In the evening meetings, the same people who had enforced the old rules declared, "Deng Xiaoping has a good policy now." It was no longer necessary to make the weekly report, and the officials ceased to harass us. The situation was more relaxed. My family knew where I was, and I had tremendous public support. The local people continued to find ways to bring me butter, cheese, meat, and tsampa. My detention remained my only serious problem.

In 1980, I was given work herding twelve yaks. In the morning, while the yaks were used to stamp out wet clay to make a proper consistency for bricks, I cleaned out the cattle shed and put out the fodder they ate in the evening. Around noontime, several of us prisoners would take them up on the hill to graze. I spent most of that time praying to Dolma and thanking her for saving me and praying for those who had not survived. By that point, I had gone through the worst and was now hoping that one day I would be free.

It was sad to be in the mountains. All around us were the signs of destruction and deforestation: only tree trunks were left on the hills. Older people herding cattle said, "Before the invasion of the Communists, the forests were so thick we could hardly walk into them for fear of tigers, leopards, or bears. But now, look at what they have done." They spoke of how all the wildlife in this area had become extinct.

◊ ◊ ◊

I was finally released, largely due to the efforts of my brother Jughuma. Our family had learned that he was living in Nepal, and one of my nephews went to Kathmandu to find him. A Tibetan who traveled with my nephew suggested that my brother write to the highest authorities in Dartsedo asking why I was still being detained when everyone else had been released. Jughuma wrote them and said that if I were released, he would come to Tibet to meet me. Soon after the letter arrived in district headquarters in Dartsedo, it was brought to me. When I finished reading it, the official asked, "What are you thinking?" I could only look straight ahead, then questioningly at him. He said, "Your brother now wants to return to his native land, so you had better prepare to come out."

Jughuma was alive. How long had it been? I finally knew—*almost* for certain—that we would meet again. Suddenly, I felt very weary; yet, at the same time, I began to perceive a subtly rising sense of elation. So many years had passed. I had long ago given up hope of ever again being with him. Now his face came to mind so quickly that I felt he had always somehow been with me. Even if I tried to explain, how could that prison official possibly understand what it meant to know that Jughuma, my dear brother, had somehow found me. I lowered my head until I was excused.

Before my release, a top official at Wa Da Dui named Tsu Suje warned me, "You must be very careful not to reveal anything to the public about your experiences and the Chinese methods of labor through reeducation. If you should decide to say anything about the starvation of prisoners or what happened to your relatives, it will be regarded as a crime." He continued, "If you do speak of these things and we find out, you will once again be detained."

I was released along with Rinchen one winter day just after the Tibetan New Year in 1985.

Many prisoners came to say good-bye. They gave me whatever they could spare to help me in the future. I had three bags containing the small mattress I had started making in Gothang Gyalgo, a newer mattress that someone had given me, a quilt, a cup, and a few articles of clothing. One woman gave me a chuba in fairly good condition. No monetary form of dispensation was given on my release, just some papers that had to be presented to the police in Karze.

One of my nephews came to collect me at the prison. We took a bus to Karze. The ride was depressing, for we kept passing so many recent ruins of Tibetan monasteries, forts, and other historical sites. The normal sights of a Tibetan locality—prayer flags and *mani* shrines, small stones with inscribed prayers—were not in evidence. The environment was desolate. Even as I looked around me on the bus or at the people we passed along the way, it was distressing to note that they were all dressed in Chinese clothing and there was no glow of happiness on their faces. All along the route to Karze, we weaved through a steady stream of trucks full of logs and many Chinese military vehicles.

I mentioned to my nephew that it was alarming to see the greatly increased presence of civilian Chinese and the diminished number of Tibetans. I asked him, "Why are Tibetans wearing Chinese clothes?"

He explained, "For quite some time, the Chinese did not permit us to wear our native dress. The price of wool is very high and many people can't afford it. Nowadays, these Chinese uniforms are more readily available than Tibetan clothing and cheaper to buy. They have also begun selling some clothing of poor quality made in the Western style, but it is expensive. They have built textile factories in Tibet that produce cloth of four different qualities; the first three qualities are sent to China and the poorest is sold in Tibet. Also for years they forced us to cut our hair because they say that long hair is reactionary and dirty." He added, "I can't remember when things have been any different."

I asked him, "Why don't we see any prayer flags and mani temples?" He told me that nothing was being done for the restoration of the small monasteries in the region. Monasteries being rebuilt in eastern Tibet receive attention only when the abbots agree to the conditions laid down by the authorities.

My region had been a land of pristine beauty, a place of great religious sanctity. I remember standing in front of my house on countless early mornings waiting for the rising sun. As it rose, it touched the golden roofs of Karze monastery in the distance, causing them to glitter brightly in the pink morning light. I watched with delight as the sun's rays hit the rocky, snowcapped mountains and the forest below. But now, the mountains around Lhobasha were barren: there were no forests left.

As we stepped down from the bus in Karze, we heard the blaring of Chinese music over the loudspeakers. Every morning at 7:30, the noise began with a constant barrage of Chinese news, programs, and music; and it continued throughout the day. No programs of Tibetan language or music were ever heard. The ticket booth of the bus stand was staffed by Chinese soldiers. All signs and tickets were printed in Chinese. All negotiations had to be done in the Chinese language, which was very difficult, since most Tibetans do not speak Chinese and almost all the Chinese people never learned to speak Tibetan.

As I walked around town, I found that the slates and rocks on which Tibetans had carved mani inscriptions had been used in the road pavements. This gave Tibetans a lost feeling: if we looked to the left or the right, there would be a stone with a sacred prayer at our feet, and it was sacrilegious to walk on them.

Choenyi Dolma, my family's former servant, was the first to come and meet me after my release in 1985. She told me how she had spent years praying for my safety in the labor camps and how the stories she had heard from my brother had frightened her. Her life had not improved as a "liberated citizen" of the Communist Chinese. She had spent years of starvation and hard work in a commune.

One day as I was walking down a street in Lhobasha, I encountered two men and a woman who seemed familiar. We stopped to look at each other, and suddenly I realized they were Bhombi and Sonam Gyurme, the servants from my in-laws' home, and Tenzin Ngodup, an elderly nomad who had been a close friend of my brother Jughuma. Bhombi, by that time, was also very old. She came forward and touched my hand, saying, "Is this Adhe? I am so happy to see you again. I was worried that you might have died in the prison. You have undergone so much suffering." Sonam Gyurme reminded me that he had sent a lump of butter when my brother Nyima had visited Gothang Gyalgo. He told me it was impossible for him to forget what the Chinese authorities had done to my life: "Before those years, we had so much freedom. I have many fond memories of days spent with your husband, your brother, and their friends, riding through the hills, drinking chang, camping together, and dancing beneath the stars. Your brother Jughuma was one of the finest marksmen I have ever seen. Your husband was a fine man, Adhe, a fine young man."

Taking my hand, Tenzin Ngodup told me, "Nowadays, those of us who remain here are but slaves, allowed to reside in a home that was once our own; and after years of hardship, we are now permitted a few comforts: a few modern inventions and toys to make us forget the meaning of what it is to be a Tibetan. However, our memories of better days remain with us, and the hope that somehow a brighter day is yet to come."

I have not seen my sister-in-law Riga since the day of my arrest. I have heard that she is alive and is living somewhere in Amdo, but we do not not know if her husband, Pema Wangchuk, has survived and is with her.

◊ ◊ ◊

The Communists were now trying to create an impression of religious tolerance, and thus Tibetans were allowed to begin rebuilding Karze monastery in earnest in 1983. Anyone from the region who looked upon the site was both gladdened by the progress of the building and deeply dismayed by the memory of the long and distinguished history of the original structure and the religious freedom we had once known.

Due to the strong propaganda against me, there was hardly anyone in my region who hadn't heard of me. Even the children quietly came around and said, "That is Adhe. That is the lady." Everyone was very supportive and did whatever they could to help me. I told my friends and relatives, "I have now spent twenty-seven years in someone else's land, and only in 1985 am I able to return to my own native land and be with my daughter."

Sometimes when we were in our beds, my daughter called out, "Mother, is this a dream or are we really together?" This made me feel quite happy; but at the same time, I thought it was not important that I be happy. My most cherished possession at that time was the mattress I'd started piecing together in Gothang Gyalgo. So many of the small pieces of cloth had come from the clothing of dead prisoners, some of whom had been my friends. Aside from the scars of my physical injuries and the hat that was given to me in Gothang Gyalgo, the mattress was the only physical reminder of my imprisonment that I could carry with me. My daughter used to beg me to get rid of it, saying, "I can't stand it. Please throw it in the river." But somehow I couldn't. It is with me even today.

◊ ◊ ◊

One day, I borrowed a friend's horse and rode to the site of the home that I had shared with my husband and family. Although I felt it was necessary to return there, I dared not think of what I would find. I spent most of the ride just looking at what was before and around me, praying for all who were lost in suffering, praying for light to come into the consciousness of men, and bowing in my heart to the deities of the mountains whose majesty had been abused. As I stood in the field that surrounded what had once been my home, a wind was blowing. It seemed a desolate place.

When at odd moments the wind suddenly stopped, silence seemed to fill all that I could perceive. I looked upon a broken shell of barren walls. A passing stranger would never know that this had been a place of happiness. Within those walls a young mother had borne her first child. He had been a beautiful child.

◊ ◊ ◊

The focus of Chinese policies had outwardly changed from concentrated attempts at completely destroying all vestiges of Tibetan culture to starting programs to extract Tibet's natural resources. The authorities now strove to accommodate the ever-increasing population of Chinese settlers and to promote stability in the region. For this purpose, there is an increasing number of military facilities under construction in Karze Prefecture.

In carrying out these policies, the Chinese administration gave Tibetans a certain amount of freedom to rebuild their lives to the point of being somewhat self-sufficient. The commune system had been a complete failure and was abandoned in the early 1980s. Tibetans were allowed to return to their traditional farming methods. Some were once again allowed to have herds of yak or sheep and thus were able to reach some level of prosperity. Sometimes when we met with friends in the community, we prepared a large amount of food and shared meals. But I told those present, "As we share this food, I immediately think of my companions in prison and everything becomes black in my heart." Many times those recollections killed my desire to eat. Now and then, I pressed them to understand that it was not my time to be happy again because most of my friends, inmates, and family had died and were buried all over eastern Tibet.

A thought began to grow in me: "I must go to India to inform His Holiness and everyone in the world, whomever I meet, about how my people perished from the Chinese atrocities." It seemed that unless I could find people to tell the story to, I could never be satisfied. In me, there was no feeling of "living" in Tibet.

I was never again able to meet my fellow inmate, Tsering Yuden, because the place in which she had settled was a great distance from Karze. But one day, Yeshi Dolma arrived at my door in Lhobasha. Before either of us could utter a word, we were embracing and crying. She said, "Oh Adhe, I am delighted. I thought I would never see you again because I'd felt that something bad might have happened to you." She was thoroughly impressed to see me standing outside of a prison.

She and her family had just barely enough to eat. She told me, "My children have grown up, and we are just learning to know each other all over again. Sometimes I feel that I am living with kindly strangers to whom I cannot fully express the details of much of what has made me the person I am today, and why it is so hard to adjust to this new way of life." It was awkward for both of us to communicate with our children. I was glad to realize someone could understand my difficulty. I told her, "I also don't know how much of the past to share with Tashi Khando. It worries me." Yeshi then made a point of taking some butter and tsampa from her bag and saying, "See, I promised to help take care of you and I am doing it. For the moment let us tend to the present." Taking my hand, she quietly remarked, "Only with time Adhe, everything is so different. I know it is hard to adjust." We spent three days together. There were so many things to discuss. In the nights we slept together, and as soon as morning came, we would be talking again. There were times when we could not help but cry as we recollected what we had gone through. When she was leaving, she begged me not to further oppose the Chinese because she feared that they might again detain me. She said, "It is best now if we just bow our heads and live quietly."

◊ ◊ ◊

In 1986, it was announced that the Panchen Lama was going to make a visit to Karze. On the day of his arrival, people lined both sides of the road waiting with khatags in their hands. He arrived in a motorcade of twenty cars and waved to everyone from an open vehicle as he rode by. People ten to twenty years older than me were crying and praying that in the future they would welcome His Holiness the Dalai Lama and the exiled Tibetans in the same manner. I tried to make my way as near as possible to the dais from which he later spoke.

The central component of his speech was, "You are all Tibetans. Tibetans should wear Tibetan dress. You should read and write the Tibetan language, and you should never forget the practice of religion." I am sure that all the Tibetans who were present remember those words very well. Of course, he couldn't go beyond this limit because he was heavily guarded and his every word was monitored. Still, these three points carried a weight of importance for us.

The location chosen for the Panchen Lama to address the people of Karze happened to be the same place in which the Communists had held their first meetings, during which they had promised they had only our best interests at heart and would soon be leaving. It was also the place where, eight years later, Pema Gyaltsen was executed and I received the sentence of my imprisonment. Standing in the large crowd before the Panchen Lama, I was reminded of that terrible day so long ago and was amazed that somehow, after all those years of hardship, I was still alive. I prayed for Pema Gyaltsen, as every detail of his execution played in my mind. The huge field was called Do go thang, in what we knew as the Gyanka section of Karze. I do not know what the Chinese call the field today.

As I stood recalling those events, painfully feeling the disappearance of the years in between, I began to feel weak and overwhelmed. I tried to stand very still in an effort to control the tears that silently began to fall on my face when, suddenly, a friend tapped me on the shoulder. It was Aghey, who had been arrested as a boy after the battle of Bu na thang and had been released in 1979 after twenty years of imprisonment. He took my hand and smiled, saying, "So, somehow we have both survived reeducation under Chinese communism. How fortunate we are in being together here today to see Panchen Rinpoche." He told me that he was now living a very simple nomadic life in an area of Nyarong. I had always been struck by a certain sweetness and quiet simplicity in Aghey's character. Though he'd been imprisoned since he was a child, the experience had somehow not hardened him. Knowing that he was free, I felt a few moments of peace.

Before the Panchen Lama's appearance, the Chinese had announced that no Tibetan home could have a portrait of His Holiness the Dalai Lama. The Tibetans were very annoyed and began speaking of boycotting the speech. One Tibetan said, "If we cannot have a portrait of His Holiness in our homes, I will not go for Panchen Rinpoche's teaching." And the next Tibetan said the same until, finally, it was a unanimous decision. We had been allowed to keep His Holiness's portrait for some time, and no one was willing to accept a return to the infringement of a right we considered as basic. Tibetans who worked for the Chinese were discouraged against keeping photographs of the Dalai Lama, but even many of them had family photographs in a frame with a portrait of His Holiness hidden behind them.

When the Panchen Lama spoke to the people, he said, "Perhaps it was a misinterpretation of something that you have heard. There is no way that the Chinese will not allow you to have a portrait of His Holiness." He told us, "Compared to His Holiness, I am nothing. There is a vast difference. It is like comparing the thumb of a hand and the little finger." He said that he had no authority to be above His Holiness. His words reassured the people and we began to attend the teachings.

The Chinese officials did not like his statement. Afterward, several Tibetan staff heard one of them telling him, "You should have just said that they will be allowed to keep the portraits. Also, why should you say that there is a vast difference between you and the Dalai Lama?"

◊ ◊ ◊

There is a region outside of Karze where the Chinese had been interested in setting up a hydroelectric power station. When they began digging in the earth, large deposits of gold were discovered. My daughter now lives in that region. A family that is related to her husband ran a water mill there, and ten of their family members were involved in the work.

They told Rinchen and me that since we both had suffered so much and now had nothing, maybe we could extract some gold to start our new life. There was a lot of debate with the Chinese staff as to whether we should be allowed to do that, but somehow they finally relented. We mined gold for four months. We dug up the earth and put it into a sieve, then, as soon as we went to clean the gold in the water, someone appeared and stood very close by to watch and weigh what was found. Whatever amount was extracted, the office gave us half of its value. I managed to find sixty-five grams and Rinchen collected seventy. We eventually took three thousand yuan away with us. During that time, we had worked very hard and my strength finally failed. For some time afterward, it was difficult for me to move or carry out simple actions, but Rinchen encouraged me, saying, "Now we are so close. Just rest for a while and realize that the time is coming for which you have waited so long."

One day, a letter came from my brother in Nepal, saying, "You should come to Kathmandu to meet me. You can go on a pilgrimage to Lhasa and various religious sites in Nepal, and then we can return to Karze together." I gave this letter to the police at the Public Security Office in Karze. The authorities told me, "Now, you'd better rest and live quietly with your daughter. You can send one of your nephews to meet him." I ignored what they were trying to tell me and said, "It will be no use sending one of my nephews, because unless my brother sees me, he won't come."

In the minds of the Chinese, my brother was returning to the "motherland" and turning away from the Tibetans in exile. The staff officials had a meeting to discuss whether they should allow me to go. The Chinese leaders were against my going, and they said, "It will be a great disadvantage and a great setback if we let her leave Karze. It is better to send one of her nephews." The Tibetan staff reminded them, "Before her brother went to Lhasa, he was a member of an important political committee that had been set up in Karze Prefecture." They stressed the propaganda importance of his return.

After a few days, I was called to the police office and told that permission had been granted for my visit to Nepal, but it was important that my brother and I return very quickly. The police tried to convince me how well they would look after Jughuma and me when we returned. They said, "How futile it is to die outside one's native land, to leave one's bones in a foreign place after death." They said, "If you come back, we will appoint you to a special political consultative committee that is being organized in Karze Prefecture; it is a hand-picked group." Though I did not believe that such a committee would actually have any power, I pretended to agree with whatever they said and told them, "It is very important that my brother return home. As a former committee leader, he will be remembered by many people and will have their respect. I feel that he will be able to make a great contribution to a unified motherland."

One official said, "Meanwhile, you must remember that Tibet is the land of the Communist Chinese. Internal affairs should be kept within our own country." In other words, he was indirectly telling me that I should not speak about the battles that had been fought in Tibet, about the executions, the starvation, the prison atrocities, and all the destruction suffered by the Tibetan people.

Rinchen and I traveled by bus for seven days to Lhasa. One very striking thing we encountered during the journey was the sight of hundreds and hundreds of trucks carrying wool, leather, and timber in the opposite direction. As each truck went by, we looked carefully to see what was inside. The pieces of leather were dried and set in huge piles. Logs reached to the tops of the trucks.

Most of the beautiful and easily accessible regions of Tibet were now full of concrete Chinese structures that looked like so many boxes. Hundreds of Chinese settlers were visible. Most of the small Tibetan communities were up in the mountains, and the houses were tiny dilapidated dwellings. Our "liberators" had obviously taken the best that the land had to offer for themselves.

This was my first visit to the holy city of Lhasa—the pilgrimage I had dreamed of throughout my childhood. Immediately upon our arrival, without even stopping to find a place to stay, we went to the Jokhang and Ramoche shrines to receive the blessings of the thirteen-hundred-year-old statues of the Crown Buddha Shakyamuni and the Jowo Mikyoe Dorje. The life-size statues represent, respectively, the Buddha at the ages of eight and twelve. It is believed that these are the two remaining of four original statues of the Buddha that were made in India during his lifetime and had received his personal blessing. These two have been considered the most sacred of Tibet's religious treasures ever since they arrived in our land in the seventh century.

The Jokhang's setting now seemed odd. We walked across a wide, paved square toward it, but instead of being surrounded by Tibetan buildings, we saw only newly built, square concrete houses and two large modern buildings which to us looked very ugly. Approaching the shrine, we prostrated on the flagstones of the courtyard, worn smooth by generations of pilgrims, and gave thanks for our safe arrival. As we went to buy offertory khatags in the courtyard outside the Jokhang, we saw a line of vendors—all dressed in Chinese clothing. As we drew closer, it became apparent that all the vendors selling articles for religious offering were Chinese.

We rejoined the pilgrims and walked toward the large, white incense burners in the courtyard. On the roof above the main entrance of the red and white building, the sun shone brightly on a gilded image of the symbol of Buddhism, the *ridag choekhor*, the eight-pointed wheel of Dharma flanked by a tender fawn on either side. Turning the great prayer wheel, we prayed for the protection of our faith and entered the shrine, walking slowly past the stone statues of the deities that guard the four directions.

It seemed as if I were dreaming, so unlikely it had been that I would ever make this pilgrimage. At that moment, my whole life seemed a dream. It was wonderful to witness the reverence of the Tibetans in that holy shrine. Although most of them were ragged-looking, their eyes shone with devotion and faith.

The Jokhang had not escaped the ravages of the Cultural Revolution. In 1975, many of its statues were destroyed and the frescoes on its walls defaced. Many of its monks were killed or badly beaten and imprisoned. The courtyard was turned into a pigsty. Even in 1987, many of its chapels were closed. The only statue in the shrine to escape destruction or desecration during the Cultural Revolution was the Jowo Shakyamuni: some of the monks had managed to hide it.

When we were visiting the shrine of the Jokhang, we wanted to pray before the Jowo Shakyamuni, but no time was allowed for reflection and prayer. Everyone had to keep in line and upon reaching the shrine would immediately be told, "Keep moving!" One day, Rinchen found this very unsettling and spontaneously began to loudly shout, "May His Holiness return to the Potala! May Tibet regain its independence and have a time of happiness!" The caretaker became very nervous and began saying, "Okay, okay, please...."

It was with great sadness that I heard the story of how the Jowo Mikyoe Dorje statue of the Ramoche shrine had been desecrated. In order to facilitate its transportation, the heavy statue had been cut in half. The lower half was discarded in Lhasa, though it was later hidden by monks, who kept it safe. The upper half of the statue had been taken to China, where the gems and gold leaf that covered it were removed. What remained was then discarded in an enormous heap of damaged statues in a storehouse on the outskirts of Beijing.

In 1981, Tibetan delegates traveled to Beijing to attend a meeting on religious affairs. Among the delegates was Ribhur Trulku, a lama of Sera monastery, who pleaded for the return of what remained of Tibet's religious treasures plundered during the Cultural Revolution. The delegation's requests were denied. However, throughout that year, the Beijing government received further requests from the Panchen Lama and several other high lamas from Amdo. Finally, as the matter came to be viewed as a challenge to Beijing's new policy of liberalization and religious freedom, the decision was made to allow Ribhur Trulku and a small group of Tibetans to visit China, where they discovered the upper half of the sacred Jowo lying in that dusty heap. They arranged for the return of tons of statues to our land.

Back in Tibet, the Jowo Mikyoe Dorje was restored. By 1985, repairs of the damage the Ramoche had suffered during the Cultural Revolution were nearly completed and the beloved Jowo was returned to its pedestal. The other statues in the Ramoche were newly made replicas of the originals. These did not contain the precious religious relics that are customarily placed inside the images and were but empty shells.

As Rinchen and I discussed the fate of the Jowo Mikyoe Dorje, I closed my eyes, remembering a day when the sun had shone hot on my shoulders, and kneeling on the ground, I had glanced around to make sure no one was watching as I tried to remove the soil encrusting a small potato by wiping it on the skirt of my chuba. One more glance around and I bit into the potato, feeling the remaining grit mix in my mouth with the potato's bland, starchy flavor. Suddenly, out on the road, a line of trucks were approaching, their contents glittering brightly in the sun.

Rinchen and I also went to the Potala palace. Very few of its hundreds of rooms were open to the public. It was quite a sad moment for us, knowing that His Holiness was not there. His throne was empty and there was a khatag on the table beside it. I found old Tibetans crying as they prayed for Tibetan independence and for His Holiness to return. I listened to two old women, with tears streaming down their faces, cry out, "It is impossible for us to die without seeing the return of His Holiness." The feeling in the summer palace, Norbulinka, was just as sad.

We had brought a huge lump of the finest dri butter from our region, which we used to make butter-lamp offerings in the Jokhang, the Ramoche, the Potala, and other shrines in Lhasa. We prayed for all the inmates who had lost their lives under the Communist occupation that their spirits might rest in peace. Mentally, I spoke to them, telling them that I was still on the earth and that I was in Lhasa making these offerings on their behalf. Being able to make such a large number of offerings in these sanctified places gave me a certain satisfaction, although I knew that somehow I must do more.

Rinchen and I discussed how the hands of the Communists had even reached this far. They had managed to make the holiest of our religious sites Chinese; and as we walked through the streets, we heard Chinese music, and a great variety of Chinese goods were being traded in the market. After looking down at the contents of a vending stall, Rinchen turned to me and said, "What can we do? Everything is in their control."

During our stay in Lhasa, we were fortunate to meet Tibetans who were very helpful to us. One family knew of my long experience and did not take any fee for our lodging. They told us the best places to walk and which streets were not safe. They told us of the three main prison complexes outside of Lhasa—Drapchi, Sangyip, and Gutsa— and warned us not to try to communicate with foreigners while we were in the city or do anything else that would draw attention to us. They also warned Rinchen not to wear his dagger because, most likely, it would be confiscated. They spoke of how fortunate we were to be going to India where we could see His Holiness.

We began to feel happy because now we were one step closer to reaching India and achieving our goal. On the other hand, the memories of our companions in prison who had starved, who had been tortured and executed, were constantly in our minds. The only way we could manage to not dwell in constant misery was to pray and make offerings. But every time I began to walk into a temple, one of the inmates' faces came to mind.

One day, we went to a small lake below the Potala, where we fed the fish. A Chinese man hurried over to us. "How would you like a photograph? You see it is good quality, like this." And so we had our picture taken beside the lake. We later learned that this artificial lake had been constructed in the late 1960s by the forced labor of Tibetan children. These were the children of people who fell under the higher strata of "class distinction": those who had worked for the Tibetan government, the ruling families, lamas or monastic personnel, landowners, military people, businessmen, artists, writers, and scholars. Most of the residents of Lhasa were in one of those categories. For almost twenty years, the children were not allowed to attend school but were sent to work on road construction in different parts of Tibet. In Lhasa, this lake is regarded by the Tibetans as "a memorial to the children's suffering."

When I showed my pass to leave Tibet to the police in Lhasa, I told them that I was going to bring my brother back from Nepal because I didn't want him to die in a foreign land. They were delighted to hear that. But it was very difficult for me to get a Nepalese visa. Even after a four-month wait in Karze, they hadn't issued it.

In Lhasa I went to a lama for divination. He told me, "I feel that if you join with a group of people who are leaving Tibet, you will be able to reach Nepal, even without the visa." He also warned me of the possibility of upcoming protests in Lhasa. The next morning, we left for Kathmandu.

14

FREEDOM

The road east of Lhasa goes over the Kamba Pass. It is traditional in Tibet for high passes to have a mani shrine made of a pile of stones. It is adorned with prayer flags by those who have successfully negotiated the mountain's height. Any traveler who reaches that point adds a stone as a token of respect and piety to the mountain deities. Rinchen and I were relieved to see that a mani shrine still existed on Kamba Pass, and we earnestly prayed there for a safe journey through Nepal to India and that we might return one day with His Holiness to an independent Tibet. We each added a stone to the pile and tied a khatag to the line of rope. Then we carried on with our journey.

Descending from the pass, we could see Yamdrok, the turquoise lake, the largest in Tibet. It was certainly the largest lake I had ever seen. It extended far into the distance, meeting the mountains on the far horizon. Despite its size, its surface was calm and silent. Its beautiful color shone light blue in the sun.

Our group traveled on to Shigatze, the town in which Tashilunpo, the Panchen Lama's monastery, is located. Unfortunately, we arrived in the night and didn't have any time to go on pilgrimage. We spent one night there and one in Yenum, a trading town.

Finally, we arrived in Dram, the last exit point from Tibet on the western border. The customs authorities wanted to look through our bags. They asked where we were going and I replied, "We are going to bring my brother back to Tibet." "Oh, very good," said the guards, and we were allowed to go without any further trouble, even though neither of us had the necessary Nepalese visa.

Dram is on a hill. To enter Nepal, you must descend approximately five miles and then cross a bridge in the center of which is a line of demarcation. Before I left Tibetan land to enter Nepal, I prayed to

Dolma to protect us and to ensure that we had a safe passage all the way to India.

On the other side of the line, the side that was Nepal, there was a Tibetan standing alone. As we crossed the bridge, he approached us and touched my hand, asking, "Are you Adhe?" I asked him to introduce himself. He said that although he didn't know me, my face very much resembled that of my brother, who had sent him.

The entire trip from Lhasa had taken five days. Suddenly, we were free. We had left Tibet for the first time and possibly the last. Upon our arrival, we felt a sense of rising emotion and were a bit stunned. We could only force ourselves to look ahead to the many possibilities we would now encounter; to think of an iron door closing behind us would have been unbearable. After another ten hours of travel, we reached my brother's home in Kathmandu.

Jughuma had to be awakened from sleep when we arrived. As we looked at each other for the first time in thirty-three years, we realized how much we had both aged. My brother had become an old man with white hair and a lean, wrinkled face. I thought, "Poor man," and took his hand, touched his hair, and hugged him. Then we began to speak of the long years since we had laughed and raced our horses through the meadows, the years since we had sat together and looked at the stars in the night sky. We spoke until dawn, when we heard the crowing of a bird, and Jughuma said, "We'd better sleep."

Jughuma had told me that before his escape from Tibet in 1959, he had been one of the Khampa guards protecting the Dalai Lama at the Norbulinka Palace during the events that ultimately led to His Holiness's exile from Tibet. He explained how the Chinese had approached His Holiness during the *Monlam Chenmo*, the great prayer festival celebrated fifteen days after the Tibetan New Year, and had requested that he attend a dramatic performance at the Chinese camp. His Holiness hesitated, for the invitation had come at a most inconvenient time: aside from his duties in presiding over the festival, he was studying for the exams for which he'd spent much of his life preparing, which would result in him receiving his geshe degree.

A few days later, during the procession in which His Holiness traveled to the summer palace, Tibetans noticed an unusual occurrence: for the first time since the occupation of Lhasa, no Chinese were in the crowds that lined the roads to bid him their respect.

Soon afterward, Kusung Depon, the commander of the Dalai Lama's bodyguard, was summoned to the Chinese camp. He was told by General Dan Guansen that His Holiness must agree to a date, preferably March 10. The general said that the usual retinue that accompanied the Dalai Lama, including his chamberlain who traveled everywhere with him, would not be allowed to attend; no armed Tibetan guards were to line the road that led to the camp, and no Tibetans were to be allowed within a certain distance of the camp. He also insisted that all preparations were to be kept in strict secrecy.

Kusung Depon was greatly alarmed by the unusual orders and the unrelenting attitude of the Chinese general. He knew that it was impossible to keep His Holiness's actions a secret, particularly during this time when the festivals filled the streets of Lhasa with one hundred thousand pilgrims. There were many Khampas in Lhasa at that time, and the Chinese had started a campaign of propaganda describing the Khampas as "evil reactionaries" who were the "pawns of the American imperialists."

Four high lamas from various regions in eastern Tibet had been invited to such theatrical performances and had never returned; three had been murdered and one sentenced to imprisonment. Further adding to the people's mounting fear, an announcement had recently been made over Chinese radio that the Dalai Lama would soon be visiting China, although he had never agreed to such a trip.

The day before the proposed performance, the people of Lhasa took it upon themselves to protect the Dalai Lama: an estimated thirty thousand people surrounded the Norbulinka, refusing to allow him to leave. The crowd chanted slogans demanding an end to Chinese occupation and Chinese interference in the Dalai Lama's rule. The situation grew increasingly tense as the day progressed.

Five groups of men from Karze were in Lhasa at that time, and they all said they would gladly risk their own lives to protect the religious government. The monasteries were sympathetic to the Khampas situation, but they were soon seized and lost all power to help them. Shortly after the monasteries were taken over, Phuntsog Gyatso, a leader from Karze, was arrested by the Chinese. Some Khampas, along with certain members of the Mimang Tsongdu (People's Assembly)—the first major Tibetan resistance group, organized in reaction to Tibet's first famine—wanted to attempt a rebellion against the Chinese, beginning with the capturing of the Chinese leaders. A movement of additional Chinese troops and military equipment was entering the city.

A volunteer army was formed. Some left to regroup on the outskirts of Lhasa. Those who remained attempted to secure horses, mules, and ammunition. It was decided to send some men with money and ammunition to inform the main camp of the Volunteer Freedom Fighters (VFF) in Lhoka, a region south of Lhasa. The rest would remain in Lhasa to protect the people, watch the roads, and if necessary, resort to guerrilla tactics.

Agony at the thought of His Holiness facing danger drew together the fighters. The leaders of the Mimang Tsongdu united with the Khampas and Amdowas, and they decided to meet with the Kashag, the Tibetan Ministry. Pema Namgyal, one of the men from Karze, was the highest-ranking member of the military group. He and some of his men approached the ministers, and the Kashag promised that His Holiness would not attempt to meet with the Chinese in the Chinese camp. My brother was among the ninety-seven armed soldiers who joined Pema Namgyal in the responsibility of protecting the main entrance to the Norbulinka Palace. A committee of sixty or seventy leaders was elected; they vowed to barricade the palace so that His Holiness could not be taken. Another seventy-six men volunteered to defend the Jokhang and other important revered sites.

On March 16, the Dalai Lama received a message from the Chinese requesting him to make known the exact building he would be inhabiting in order to ensure his safety. He did not send details of his position, perhaps believing that if the Chinese did not know where he was, they would refrain from using heavy artillery. At 4 P.M., two heavy mortar shells were fired from a Chinese camp, landing in a marsh outside the Norbulinka's northern gate.

At that point, there was no question that the time had come to make preparations for the Dalai Lama's escape. Under the cover of darkness, one hundred soldiers of the Tibetan army were sent to guard a shallow crossing of the Kyi River southeast of the Potala. During the night, the Dalai Lama's mother, sister, and younger brother were spirited from the palace. His Holiness followed soon afterward disguised as a soldier.

At that time, there were between thirty thousand and fifty thousand Chinese troops in Lhasa. The city was surrounded with the heavy artillery of seventeen modern howitzer cannons. The Chinese had not yet discovered that the Dalai Lama had left the city; and while thousands of Tibetans still surrounded the palace, the shelling of Norbulinka began at 2 A.M. on the morning of March 20. It continued throughout the day; and then the Chinese turned their artillery on the rest of Lhasa, including the Potala, the Jokhang, and neighboring monasteries. There were many casualties among both military and lay Tibetans. The famous Tibetan medical college, the Chakpori, was almost completely destroyed; by the following day, all those who had stood in its defense were killed.

The great monasteries of Sera and Drepung were severely damaged. Priceless treasures and manuscripts contained within their walls were destroyed. Ganden monastery suffered less damage. Thousands of monks from these monasteries were either killed or taken as prisoners. The Norbulinka and the people remaining inside were hit by eight hundred shells; thousands of bodies lay on the ground inside and outside it. At the end of the first day, the Chinese entered the Norbulinka and began turning over the bodies of the dead, searching for that of the Dalai Lama. They had decided to attack regardless of the possibility that he might be killed, and his apparent escape infuriated them. They claimed that he had been "kidnapped by reactionary rebels."

The fighting continued for three days. On March 28, China announced the dissolution of the Tibetan government.

Jughuma continued, "During the bombardment, the walls of many buildings became hollowed archways, and trees were easily uprooted by bombs. We had never seen anything like this occur in Lhasa, such wild and immediate destruction, and had never even realized such devastation was possible." At this point, Rinchen Samdup brought us each a cup of tea. Thanking him, Jughuma took a sip and told us, "During the bombing, I and a group of Khampas escaped from the Norbulinka and went to an ammunition storage room in the Potala. The caretaker was so terrified, he could barely move. We took his key and opened the door. Each of us took two or three rifles, filled our chubas with bullets, and then reentered the battle. Six of my friends were killed shortly thereafter. The remaining men headed on foot in the direction of Nepal. We joined more Khampas on foot who were traveling with a heavy gun. Just before we reached the border, we found ourselves under the surveillance of Chinese airplanes. We managed with great difficulty to shoot down one low-flying plane. It made the Chinese pilots realize that armed people were hiding in the mountains, and they raised their planes' altitude.

"During this time, my friends and I witnessed the bombardment of many Tibetans on the plain below. Using binoculars from our vantage point on the mountainside, we saw Tibetans who were out in the open running in fear from the planes, but there was no place to hide."

Jughuma then said that when he first entered India, he was sent to a place in Assam known as Missamari. The first to arrive there were monks and Khampas who had engaged in the fighting. In those first few weeks, the people suffered terribly. They were totally unaccustomed to the food that was available, the water supply became contaminated, and many people contracted fatal amoebic dysentery. At night, the air was filled with the buzzing of mosquitoes. The climate was such a drastic change that many Tibetans succumbed to the heat alone. For a while, it seemed that at least one person was dying every day.

"With the grace of His Holiness, no one troubled us. No one said we were not allowed to go here or there, or that we were not allowed to trade." From that time on, Jughuma spent his life in an atmosphere of freedom. He worked for several years as a porter in the mountains, then sometimes on road construction, until he had finally earned enough to settle in Nepal and start a small trading business in Kathmandu. Through all those years, he remained alone, haunted by the memory of his wife and two children who had been left behind in Karze.

At the time we were reunited, he was eighty-two years old. He had become a spiritual practitioner, keeping a butter lamp continuously lit and spending most of his time sitting and turning his large prayer wheel while praying that somehow the beings of the world might be uplifted to a consciousness beyond greed and misery.

In the Mount Kailash region of northwestern Tibet, there is a shrine known as the Purang Khorchag Jowo. It is said that at one time many years back, a sack of silver appeared inside in front of the statue during the night, even though the doors had been locked. When the people found the silver, they became convinced that it had not been delivered by human hands, and so it was used to coat the statue. The remaining silver was used to make water-offering bowls and butter lamps.

Some friends of Jughuma's who were blacksmiths were present when the Chinese, pointing guns at Tibetans' heads, forced the local people to destroy the shrine and desecrate it by urinating on the temple. After the demolition, some Nepalese porters took a chance and stole one of the shrine's butter lamps. Jughuma bought the butter lamp from the porters—the same lamp he keeps lit to this day. Even when he didn't have enough to eat, he sacrificed to keep butter in the lamp. At the age of fifty, he decided to devote his life completely to spiritual practice. While in Nepal, he accumulated one hundred thousand turnings of the mani wheel. He told us that in his younger days he committed many sins, and now only sincere penance and interest in spiritual understanding were left for him.

Due to his age, Jughuma was having a lot of difficulty living alone; and at that time, he was suffering from dysentery. We got him a good bed and bought him clean clothes. Then he told me, "Before you take care of me, you must first go and see His Holiness. I can never be satisfied until I know that you have done this."

And so one morning we boarded a bus for a land that we had

never seen, so different from anything we had known. Traveling along dusty roads and looking out the window, we were amazed by the difference in the style of clothing in India. We noticed that although there were many poor people in India, they were free to move about and go wherever they wanted. This comparison with my country made me feel quite sad. Still, it was exciting to have arrived in a country in which the atmosphere was one of freedom. Soon we would see His Holiness! The joy in my mind felt as if the weight of a mountain that had long been pressing on my heart had suddenly been lifted and the ponderous burden had disappeared.

I was left only with the anticipation you might feel approaching the village of your childhood, knowing that you are expected, knowing that you will be welcomed by friends who had been a part of your life for many years. Although separated by a great distance and many obstacles, their memory has been carried in your heart and the ravages and tests of time had somehow not been able to discourage the destiny of this reunion. Soon, very soon, it would happen.

Along the way we ate bread and dal. I had never seen oranges before and found them to be quite good. Rinchen was a little less adventurous and at first hesitated to taste something that looked so odd. Everything was so different and, compared to Tibet, so prosperous.

We traveled directly to Varanasi, where His Holiness was giving teachings to a large public audience that was mostly Tibetan. Afterward, I heard a woman say to some people, "Oh, now I am very satisfied for having received the blessing of the Dalai Lama," and they walked away happily. But I was not satisfied with seeing His Holiness from a distance and felt this was not achieving what I had come to India to do. Rinchen and I decided to just stay and wait. Soon afterward, the guards told us that we must leave.

Of course, neither of us could speak Hindi or English, but we decided to try to find our way by bus to the residence of His Holiness. At the bus stations, we kept repeating those two words "Dharamsala" and "Dalai Lama." We rode on several buses, just hoping that they were taking us to the right place. I prayed to the guardian deities of Tibet for protection, as I had done throughout the journey from

Nepal. The second night after leaving Varanasi, we arrived at a bus stand long after darkness had fallen. Some Indian men were walking around the station, and Rinchen approached one of them to inquire in Tibetan the name of the bus station. It seemed the man did not follow the question. We could not understand his response, and we were too tired to think of another way to make ourselves understood. Deciding that more people would come around in the morning and we would then probably find someone who could help us, we settled into waiting throughout the cold night, trying to rest on benches in the open air. Finally, we managed a few hours of sleep.

In the morning, sounds of traffic and movement began to stir, and soon we were surrounded by the sounds of people speaking loudly and rapidly to each other in Hindi. We sat up in a rather confused state, but then I saw a Tibetan woman and asked her, "What is this place called?" The woman answered, "You are in Dharamsala." I was delighted and called to Rinchen: "Rinchen la, we have arrived in Dharamsala! You don't have to worry about anything."

We were guided to a guest house, where we rested for a while, and then we walked down a mountain road to Namgyal monastery, the monastery of His Holiness, to offer thanks for our safe arrival. At the guest house we were assured that His Holiness would be informed that we had arrived.

Upper Dharamsala was inhabited by Tibetans and some Indians. There were shops and restaurants with Tibetan names. There were many Tibetans, most of the women wearing traditional dress, and quite a few Westerners in odd, colorful shoes and clothing. We saw laughing Tibetan children and small barking Apso terriers running in the streets. In the center of the town was a small temple with brass prayer wheels which people turned as they walked by. There were also other refugees like us—people who had lost everything, who had just arrived and were trying to adjust to living in an atmosphere of freedom.

After a few days, we were taken for an audience with His Holiness the Dalai Lama. The moment we were ushered into the audience room and I saw His Holiness, the cries of my inmates who had prayed to him as they were dying of starvation came into my mind. Everything blackened in my heart and I became very emotional; but then I immediately realized, "This is no time for emotion, because I won't be able to fulfill my responsibility." His Holiness was waiting and looking at us. Approaching the man I had waited my entire life to see, it seemed I also felt the yearning of those many who had died with his name upon their lips. I was so moved that I even forgot to prostrate: bending my head, I just quickly sat down some distance from him as I continued to try to control my emotions. His Holiness called to us, "Come forward." He had to repeat his request three times until we moved a little closer. I was worried about getting too near him with the filth in our clothes that we had carried with us from the labor camps and our trip. But mostly, I had an inner sense of defilement from the brutality of my experiences. I reported everything with my head down so as not to take a chance of sending a bad smell from my mouth toward His Holiness. I proceeded to inform him of how the religious community had perished, how so many Tibetans were killed. Fortunately, I found that I remembered everything I had been waiting all those years to tell him.

When I told him of the fate of the lamas at Ngachoe monastery prison, he was sad and moved, and he prayed in silence for them. His face was cold and still as I gave details of the state of the prisoners and the conditions in the labor camps.

His Holiness asked if I wanted to go back to Tibet or stay in India. I told him, "I am not going back." He advised me to be calm and told me that now I shouldn't feel bad about what I suffered, that now I should be strong. He sat quietly for some time and then softly asked us how the Chinese could have perpetrated such inhuman treatment against fellow human beings.

His Holiness took my hand and told me, "You have suffered so much. You should now record your experiences in a book for the sake of the dead and the living." His eyes were filled with compassion, and his presence filled my heart with the realization that our journey had not been in vain. Silence enveloped the room as His Holiness lowered his head in prayer.

Then Rinchen informed him of his own experiences. I think the entire audience took around two hours. When we left, we felt deeply fulfilled.

During later audiences, His Holiness inquired about the arrangements for my story to be written and stressed that I must somehow find a way to work on this project even if I could only talk into a tape recorder. However, due to my illiteracy, it was not until spring 1990 that I found a way in which to begin.

When we returned to Nepal, Jughuma was very happy. Soon afterward, I began to feel, "Now that I have informed His Holiness the Dalai Lama, it is time to inform the world." Of course, I didn't know much at all about the world outside Tibet. Because of Chinese propaganda and the fact that they had always pushed the word "America" so strongly on the prisoners, we thought at that time that every Westerner was an American.

One day as I was cutting some vegetables, someone knocked at the door. I opened it to find Dechen Wangmo Shivatsang. The meeting was a great surprise, for we had both been beautiful young girls when we had said good-bye in late 1956. I hadn't imagined we would meet again, and now we hardly recognized each other. As a young girl, I had worn a necklace of four Zi stones and used imported lotions for my complexion; now I wore an old, ill-fitting chuba and my face was lined with sorrow. Dechen Wangmo thought I gave an appearance of someone who had undergone great hardship, while I observed in amazement how much she herself had aged.

Dechen Wangmo was now poor and hadn't even earrings to wear; she had sold her jewelry to help her family. She told me that when the Shivatsang family reached Lhasa, they had stayed in a rest house at the invitation of the Dalai Lama. Upon leaving Tibet, they had stayed for some time in Kalimpong, in northern India; and in 1962 they had journeyed to a refugee camp in south India known as Byllakuppe. She told me of the tremendous hardships Tibetans suffered in the beginning from the intense heat and the wild jungle inhabited by elephants and other dangerous animals, which had to be cleared before they were able to build houses and plow fields for cultivation. The refugees had suffered ill health, many crop failures, and various other setbacks but, finally, over a period of years, succeeded in creating a successful community. As we spoke of our life experiences, there were many occasions when both of us could not help but be overtaken with emotion. We lapsed into long silences as memories—too dear and fragile to say aloud—awoke and emerged as living things would from their places of rest.

15

"TESTIMONY FOR THE DEAD AND THE LIVING"

Around January 1989, I received a visit from Michelle Bohana, of the International Campaign for Tibet, a human rights organization based in Washington, D.C. Michelle was the first Westerner I ever spoke with. It had been about a year since our audience with His Holiness; and, since returning to Nepal, I had not spoken to anyone about my experiences. I was happy to meet Michelle, yet at the same time, I was fearful of what the Chinese might do to my relatives. When she asked my name, I lied and said, "I am Dechen Lhamo." At some point during our conversation, I finally decided to tell her about my life experience. Afterward, Michelle told me, "It is very important the world be made aware of these things so that more understanding and support will be forthcoming for Tibet." She informed His Holiness, and the Tibetan government was informed that I had an active case. Shortly thereafter, I was invited to attend the first international hearing concerning Tibet, which was to be held in Bonn, Germany, in April 1989. Before the hearing, we learned that on March 5, martial law was declared in Lhasa after ten thousand Tibetans marched through the streets in enraged protest over conditions prevailing there.

As we were driving into Bonn from the airport, I saw that everything was very clean and it looked like a happy country. What struck me the most were the undisturbed meadows and grasslands inhabited by farm animals. When I saw those cattle and horses playing and moving freely with an abundance of grass to eat, I realized how much freedom these animals of the West had—more freedom than many humans who live in Tibet and other places in the world. I started to cry and then struggled to regain my composure in order to properly face whatever would be expected of us when we reached Bonn.

In addition to Rinchen Samdup and myself, another recent refugee from Tibet had been invited to attend the hearing—Lobsang

Jinpa, a young monk who had escaped from Lhasa in 1987.

The hearing had come about largely because of the initiative of Petra Kelly and Gert Bastian. At one point, Petra threatened to resign from the Green Party, which she had co-founded, if the hearing was not given proper attention. From early in her career, Petra had devoted herself to human rights issues, alternatives to war, and the protection of the environment. After the founding of the Green Party and her election to Parliament, she immediately began raising the painful questions of people who are oppressed for the monetary profit of other nations.

Gert Bastian was a general in the German army until 1982, when he quit to protest nuclear proliferation. He joined the Green Party and was elected to Parliament, where he served until 1987. When we first met Petra and Gert in Bonn, we did not realize who they were because of the language barrier and the confusing presence of so many people. Once we knew, the three of us decided to offer khatags to them, which symbolized the purity of the Tibetan cause. Petra and Gert were naturally reserved and polite people. We were impressed with their blue eyes, the first we had seen of that color, and the sincere concern we saw in their faces. As we placed the khatags around their necks, they murmured embarrassed thank-yous. But within seconds, they broke into friendly smiles, and I was grateful to realize we had these friends who before that day we had never met. "Friends," Petra said as she took my hand, "we are so glad that you come here to speak for your people."

Everything about Germany was new to us. We spent three days in a hotel operated by the German government. Our room was on the thirty-ninth floor. We found so many things surprising. We could not understand who was opening the automatic sliding-glass doors. When we walked into the elevator, we thought we were entering a windowless bus. It moved so quickly that I covered my head in fear. It took a while for us to realize we had gone straight up and that we were at the top of the building!

Rinchen and I were confused about dining. He told me, "We'd better watch very carefully how people in the Western world eat—

how they use a fork, how to hold the knife." In Tibet, forks had been unknown to us. We always followed the movements of the people surrounding us during lunch and dinner. At the same time, we pretended to be accustomed to these situations. Until we actually learned how to eat according to the Western custom, I mostly just ate bread. After three days, we left the hotel, for we had been invited to stay with a Tibetan family.

Rinchen and I had many things we wanted to talk about at the hearing. Although we had practiced speaking in Dharamsala, we still were not certain how to express what we wanted to say in our brief allotment of time. While we were waiting to deliver our speeches, the bright lights of the meeting room bothered my eyes; finally, someone gave me a pair of sunglasses to wear. At times while waiting, I felt overwhelmed with emotion, realizing, "This is the day. This is the hour for which I have waited more than thirty years." Our nervousness was overcome by a feeling of thankfulness for the opportunity we had been given to inform everyone there of what we had experienced and witnessed in our lives.

Four people from the Chinese media were present in the hall. Of course, in Tibet, there is no way that a Tibetan could speak of these things openly without being immediately arrested and detained. During the hearing, we found ourselves amazed at the contrast in freedom between our past and the present.

While waiting, I kept reviewing the most important aspects of my detainment. But when the moment finally came, it was not necessary to think at all, for what I was speaking of was a part of me; it was inside me, and every detail of the suffering of my fellow human beings was as clear as the days on which those events had happened. After a short while, I noticed that most of the delegates in the audience seemed to be crying. I also noticed that the Chinese media representatives appeared angry and uncomfortable. At the end of the hearing, a document known as the "Declaration of Bonn" was unanimously adopted by the participants.

During our visit to Bonn, we participated in a small demonstration in front of the Chinese embassy with Petra, Gert, and others. I was given the opportunity to help in holding a large Tibetan flag—a moment I couldn't have imagined being a part of in my own country, where the display of our flag is a criminal offense. It gave me one of my sharpest moments of realization that Rinchen and I were indeed free human beings.

One day, while we were walking with our friends, Rinchen noticed a small wild plant growing along the side of the road. He pointed it out and said, "Many Tibetans, including ourselves, ate this plant during the years of starvation. In the prison camps, we searched for it in moments when the guards turned their heads." Gert told us that during the difficult years of World War II and its aftermath, many Germans searched for the same small plant to ease their hunger. Petra told us, "Germany was a venue for so much destruction and horror during the Second World War. Perhaps now, with this hearing, we Germans can in some way finally serve as a venue for peace."

The small Tibetan community in Germany all gathered to meet us when we arrived. They were delighted to encounter Tibetans who had recently been in Tibet and to share our experiences. There was a great feeling of solidarity, and of course, there were some sad moments when we all cried.

During our stay, an influential German citizen showed us great kindness by offering us permanent residence in his country. He told us, "You have both suffered very much in your lives, but now you can live here. You won't have to worry about your livelihood. You will be taken care of." We were grateful for the remarkably generous offer but replied that my brother was in Nepal with no one to take care of him; and as for ourselves, our personal comfort and well-being were not particularly important when most of the Tibetan population was suffering.

When we bid good-bye to Petra and Gert, we experienced a feeling of great closeness and thankfulness to them for being so expressive in their support of His Holiness and the cause of Tibet. A feeling of kinship will always remain with us. I told Petra how, when the goal of freedom for our people is achieved, we will introduce all our friends from different countries who have helped the people of Tibet to those who have remained inside our land.

◊ ◊ ◊

I returned to Kathmandu and concentrated my attention on caring for my brother. We stayed in a small community located on the hill below the Swayambhunath temple, a two-thousand-year-old site of a great chorten and many shrines. I climbed the hill to do kora around the temple in the morning and evening. Although I'd made some good friends, I needed to spend a certain amount of time alone each day to pray and be with my own thoughts. Climbing the hill to the temple, I saw slopes planted with medicinal trees and hillsides covered with the yellow flowers of mustard plants and other crops. In the early morning, when I stopped to look below, the entire valley would be filled with mist, giving it the appearance of a great lake. In those moments, my heart was quiet and I prayed to the deities for direction.

One day, as I was sitting in the house spinning wool, Tenzing Atisha, an official of the Tibetan government-in-exile, came to the door. He told me that I had been invited to another hearing that would take place in the country of Denmark. After I made arrangements for Jughuma's care, we left together for Dharamsala to make the preparations.

While there, I visited all the temples of Dharamsala to pay my respects and to receive the blessings of our protective deities for a fruitful visit. The day we left, we were bid farewell by four Tibetans who, with great difficulty, had recently escaped from our country. They came over to us and placed khatags around our necks. With tears in their eyes, they said, "Ama, you are doing a great thing. You are going not just to tell your own story, but you are bringing the message of the sufferings of all of Tibet to the attention of the outside world."

We arrived in Copenhagen early in the morning of November 18, 1989. Within one hour, I was being interviewed for a television program.

We had been invited to stay in the home of Lhaka Rinpoche, the most important incarnate lama of Bathang, who had been born in Markham. That night, I experienced a terrible pain in my knee, and I walked back and forth in my room trying to find some way to ease it.

Tenzing Atisha saw the light beneath the door and came to ask why I wasn't sleeping. He was quite worried because the hearing was to be held the following morning, and he feared that since I was to be a featured speaker, the date of the enormous undertaking might have to be changed. He began to speak of contacting a doctor, but I couldn't bear the idea of all that complication. Then he happened to recall that he had in his possession some precious pills that had been blessed by the Dalai Lama. He offered them to me and shortly afterward, I was able to drift into a peaceful rest.

The hearing had been organized by the Tibet Support Group of Denmark and the Tibetan Cultural Center. Despite local elections being held at that time, there was a large attendance of approximately five hundred people. When my turn came to speak, I stood up, unfolded a khatag, and offered it to the audience on my extended arms, saying, "I greet you on behalf of my Tibetan people, who have endured so much suffering." They seemed to appreciate my gesture. Again, it did not seem possible to encapsulate the tragedy of the Tibetan people in such a short space of time—only twenty-five minutes. Although the audience seemed to respond positively, I was not sure how far my message would be heard. At the close of the hearing, the speakers adopted a resolution calling on the Danish government to officially receive His Holiness the Dalai Lama on the occasion of his next visit.

That evening, Danish television gave very good coverage of the hearing, including my interview. Seeing my image on the television, I felt satisfied at being able to do some small share of work for my country. We were happy to see that the national newspapers also covered the event.

The following day, we decided to try some shopping. Of course, since we had come from India, we did not have much money, and so we decided to go to a secondhand shop. The woman who worked in the shop was very kind. As soon as she saw me, she said, "Oh, I saw you on television. I am so very sorry about what has happened in your life. Please, if you are looking for some clothing, take whatever you want." I felt quite shy and took a coat and two small items.

Tenzing Atisha assured me that it would be all right to take a coat for Rinchen, also. Then, very gratefully, we left the shop.

During our stay, we visited the Danish Parliament, where we met Viggo Fischer, chairman for the Committee of Foreign Affairs, which initiated the hearing. He was truly supportive of the Tibetan cause and told us that the government of Denmark was prepared to do anything to aid the people of Tibet, provided that other countries join in the initiative. Since Denmark is a small country, it must join with others in order to create an impact on the world community.

These beginnings gladden my heart, yet, through many years of disappointment, I have come to learn that the most noble of causes is not always enough to motivate a world whose leaders do not consider the rights of human beings their main concern.

EPILOGUE

THE WHEEL OF TIME

In 1989, Rinchen and I moved to Dharamsala, for we felt living there would provide a greater opportunity to speak with the many foreign journalists now expressing interest in interviewing me. Unfortunately, at that time we could not convince Jughuma to join us, and we made temporary arrangements for his care. We were given a room in a large building that houses many other refugees. Although we do not have many physical comforts, they are not necessary. It is a blessed experience to live in a place where one can say and do what one wants, free of fear and suspicion.

After moving to Dharamsala, I felt great concern for my brother's welfare and was constantly frustrated by the distance between us. It is not easy to make a journey to Nepal by bus, and so it was not possible to visit him often. In summer 1990, I heard that he was not well and that he requested me to come to Kathmandu. I stayed with him for several months and during that time was able to convince him to come and stay with Rinchen and me in Dharamsala.

While we were still in Kathmandu, friends began telling us that some strangers had come to them asking questions about me and asking where I might be found. These people seemed rather suspicious, so my friends told them that I had already left. Shortly thereafter, we did leave Nepal and traveled to Sarnath in India, where His Holiness was to give the Kalachakra initiation in December 1990. To receive this spiritual initiation was Jughuma's last major desire, and I was very happy that we could be together in an atmosphere of freedom to appreciate the heritage of our religion. Especially for Tibetans who experienced the severe persecution of our religion in Tibet, to receive these teachings from His Holiness is an immeasurable gift worth any risk or discomfort.

Sarnath is the site of the first teaching of the Lord Buddha. There is a beautiful temple, which contains a relic of the Buddha, surrounded by the archeological ruins of a large Buddhist monastery that was destroyed by the Moguls in the ninth century. The only building left standing from that time is a great chorten.

Because Jughuma and I had left Nepal early to evade the strangers who were searching for me, we arrived in Sarnath nearly two months before the Kalachakra was to begin. We stayed in a tent on the grounds of the local Tibetan monastery and were later joined by Rinchen Samdup. Though Jughuma was still weak and required much care, sharing that time with my brother was tremendously rewarding for me.

In mid-December, more pilgrims began to arrive, their numbers multiplying every day. An estimated 150,000 attended the Kalachakra teachings: Tibetans from our homeland, exiled Tibetans from India, Nepal, the United States, and Europe. There were also Ladakhis, Nepalese, and people native to Western countries and other parts of Asia. Tents sprang up all over the area.

Every day and evening during the Kalachakra, a tightly packed shuffling crowd circumambulated the chorten, walking three times around the path at its base. Most of the people prayed aloud—OM MANI PADME HUM and other prayers—each adding a particular rhythm to the chorus. Just beyond the chorten and down a flight of stone steps was the excavation of the ancient monastic ruins, where, as night fell, thousands of butter lamps and candles were offered by the pilgrims. At that time, one could study the exhilarated expressions of Tibetans who had just come from our land: some very old, some young, some of the men from Kham dressed in traditional clothing with threads of red silk tied into their hair, and young women who reminded me of the friends of my youth. Many were refugees like myself. Each face stood out for a moment, illumined by the light of the burning lamps and candles, and surrounded by smoky waves of heat, as prayers were offered to the Lord Buddha, the deities, and His Holiness the Dalai Lama for freedom to come to our land and for an end to humanity's suffering. During this time, and all during the teachings of His Holiness, I continued to pray for the prisoners who had died at Gothang Gyalgo and for others I had known.

The Chinese government did not want Tibetans to attend the Kalachakra because of the possible exchange of political information. Still, many took great risks to attend. The Communists did not seem to realize that, by causing great difficulty for the people who wanted to go to Sarnath, they were helping to bring about the creation of exactly what they feared. Many Tibetans, some from my region, found their way to my tent and informed me of recent cases of persecution. Many did not dare attempt to return to their homes.

Many different kinds of people who write about Tibet are considered authorities on the subject. But I feel that, next to His Holiness the Dalai Lama, the most knowledgeable people concerning our country are its elders. They have directly experienced the introduction of communism to our land and can remember what happened in the towns and villages: the suffering, deprivation, and insane cruelty that began to surface as soon as the people resisted being slaves to the Communist system and having their entire culture erased. Yet, the elders have no voice. I have spoken to many of those who endured years of Chinese rule, and their view of the matter is unified: they abhor the Chinese occupation and rule. Even today, the first thing the elders do in the morning and the last thing they do at night is pray for the independence of Tibet and the return of the Dalai Lama. If someone from their region goes to India, upon his or her return, the elders bring that person presents and ask, "What is the news? Have we come any closer to achieving our goal?"

The elders' resentment of the occupation is even greater today than when it started, because they see the imminent threat to the Tibetan race itself through the massive movement of Chinese citizens into Tibet and the controls put on the birth rate of the Tibetan population. Under such circumstances, the resistance of a people will naturally be far greater.

We Tibetans believe in the identity of our own race. For more than a thousand years, the people of our land have considered themselves

to be a separate race and culture from the Chinese. We want future
generations to have that feeling, that same sense of identity. When
the elders pass away, their prayers are directed to His Holiness the
Dalai Lama in exile and the Tibetans abroad for a brighter future for
Tibet. Tibetans believe, "Unlike grass, which can be wiped out in a
strong wind, we are as the earth."

The Tibetan people are waiting for the day when our land will
once again be our own sovereign nation. We consider the Chinese
policy for our country to be ultimately futile, because the earth will
remain. No matter how many problems we are facing or what sacri-
fices we have to make, we do not give up hope.

We know that our life in Tibet under Chinese control has no
future. But no matter what the Chinese do to eliminate the feeling of
nationalism in Tibet, it remains very strong. Tibetans believe, as do
most people in the world, that life is most precious. Still, against overwhelming odds, they join in the demonstrations, willing to sacrifice
their lives in the belief that it will help realize Tibetan independence.

◊ ◊ ◊

My whole life's happy and miserable times are recorded here. I am
now sixty-four years old. I am a poor, illiterate woman, and in the
ways of knowledge, a fool. Yet, I am blessed to be living now in exile
under the leadership of His Holiness the Dalai Lama, without the
difficulties of confrontation with people who would like to destroy
all that I am and believe in. I can finally live without labels being
applied to my existence. At last a free citizen, I do not feel preoccu-
pied with my own happiness and livelihood; and I can endure the
sadness I feel at times at being separated from my native land, family,
and friends.

But mine is just one story. We meet so many other Tibetans who
have suffered, who have lost everything, including their families. My
heart also aches for those who remain in the prisons of Tibet.
Between 1987 and 1993, there have been at least one hundred
demonstrations, large and small, demanding freedom for my country.
A few have taken place in the prisons themselves.

China has now chosen to implement what may prove to be the greatest of the trials the people of my land have endured: in announcing an economic opening of Tibet, preparations are being made for a mass migration of Chinese settlers far beyond anything that has been attempted so far. Recalling how drastically changed my region appeared after my release from prison in 1985, my heart grows increasingly sorrowful to think of a Tibet nearly unrecognizable to its native people.

◊ ◊ ◊

This book was prepared over many long interviews with an American woman whom I have come to consider as a daughter and to whom I have given a Tibetan name. I want the book to endure as a living testimony for this world so that even tomorrow when I am gone, people can read it and know the times of independent Tibet and the times of occupied Tibet. Tomorrow, when Tibet is free, the exact details can be pinpointed: where the labor camps were, where the prisoners are buried. The evidence remains in the mass graves and the sites of tremendous suffering.

What I have found over the years is that all my recollections remain intact. They are forever imprinted in the depths of my heart. For me, this book is a living testimony on behalf of Tibetans who have lost their lives under Chinese rule. It is the voice that remembers the many I have known who did not survive. I feel that with its completion, my responsibility is to some extent fulfilled. I pray that the world will be freed from such atrocities and miseries as I and other Tibetan people have suffered.

May the necessity of peace in this world be realized, and may people come to understand that conflicts cannot possibly be resolved by force. I hope that readers of this book will come to the aid of the Tibetan people, for all who live on this small planet are interrelated, and the suffering of one is, on some level, the suffering of many.

I have full faith that there is nothing on this earth more powerful than the truth. Sooner or later, truth must be recognized.

APPENDIX

HISTORICAL SUMMARY

Tibet is a region the size of Western Europe perched at the center of Asia's highest mountain ranges. China and Tibet have a long history of political, spiritual, and cultural relationships with each other; throughout the centuries, the nature of those bonds has shifted time and time again. In the seventh and eighth centuries, Tibet's independent empire reached parts of China, Central Asia, and India. In the early thirteenth century, Tibet came under the influence of the Mongolians, before they seized power in China and declared themselves emperors of that land. The nature of Tibet's relationship to these Mongolian rulers was ambiguous, and according to some definitions it might be construed as a form of vassalage. It is on the dubious basis of this relationship with the Mongolian rulers of China that contemporary China claims sovereignty over Tibet, despite much evidence for the independence of Tibet from early times until the twentieth century.

The story related in this book takes place in the eastern Tibetan region of Kham, which, although culturally Tibetan and connected with the central Tibetan government in Lhasa, traditionally maintained a high degree of autonomy under the rule of local chieftains up until the Chinese invasion in 1950. The history of Kham and its relationship with its Chinese neighbors is both colorful and complex. Here, we shall return only to the mid-eighteenth century, in order to understand some of the forces that led to the tragic events of Ama Adhe's life.

In the epoch of the Qing Dynasty, which was the Manchurian outgrowth of the former Mongolian empire in China, the Manchurian rulers of China claimed suzerainty over central Tibet and jurisdiction of the indigenous Tibetan territories of Kham that lay east of the Bum La pass, between Bathang and Chamdo. In 1835,

Gonpo Namgyal, a ruthless and powerful chieftain from Ama Adhe's natal region of Nyarong, began a campaign to subjugate and unify neighboring tribes, reclaiming from the Manchurian rulers areas of Kham that extended to the kingdoms of Beri and Chagla on the traditional Chinese frontier.

In 1896, the Manchu Army again mounted a brief incursion into Kham. In 1904, the British Younghusband expedition arrived in Lhasa, where British representatives signed a new convention with the Tibetans that denied Chinese authority in central and eastern Tibet. This action alarmed the Manchurian rulers of China, who were concerned that an alliance between the Tibetans and the British might bring an armed force of imperialists to the formerly well-protected southwestern frontier of their empire.

In response to the situation, the Assistant Chinese Resident in Lhasa, Feng Chuan, was sent by the Qing court to Bathang, the area of Kham in which Chinese influence was the strongest. His orders were to make plans for agricultural development in this fertile and temperate region. Although the monasteries in the area strongly opposed his plans, Feng Chuan made no pretense of his utter disdain for their authority. He received instructions to gradually reduce the native rulers' power and to bring the region under more effective control of the Qing government. A program was then established to bring one hundred Chinese settlers to the region.

The situation in Bathang deteriorated quickly. In April of 1905, the Tibetans revolted; and Feng and his followers were killed in a narrow gorge not far from Bathang. This event, overshadowed by the greater concern of British imperialist incursion, was followed by a major invasion by the Chinese General Zhao Erfeng in 1905. The general sought to transform Kham into a thoroughly Sinocized region in which only Chinese temples would be built, Chinese words spoken, and Chinese dress worn.

Parts of Kham were again invaded by Zhao Erfeng's Sichuan Army in 1912–13, and again in 1917. At that time, the Tibetans managed to drive the Chinese almost completely beyond Tibet's original borders. Eric Teichman, the British Consular General stationed in

Dartsedo, intervened to convince the Tibetans that they could not hold areas so close to Chinese population centers. The Tibetans agreed, and an armistice between the Tibetans and Chinese was signed at Rongbatsa township, near Karze.

Zhao Erfeng's achievements in the province collapsed in the decades following the dissolution of the Manchurian Imperial Dynasty in 1911. In the disruptive years that followed, Sichuan, Yunnan, and eastern Kham fell to the control of powerful Chinese warlords who set up their own semifeudal alliances, refusing to join under the leadership of Chinag Kai-shek, the military leader of the Nationalist Guomindang. The warlords' armies controlled large areas of Sichuan, extorting taxes from the peasantry and profiting from the opium trade. The warlord Liu Wenhui had troops stationed in several garrisons in Kham, such as Karze, Bathang, and Nyarong. In 1939, the Guomindang declared the incorporation of eastern Kham as Xikang Province.

After the 1931 Japanese invasion of Manchuria and China, the Guomindang and the Communists realized that they had to unite to drive out the aggressors, who had relentlessly bombed their cities and committed atrocities against their people. But the tenuous trust between the two Chinese factions dissolved even before the Japanese were finally forced out of their Manchurian stronghold in the spring of 1946. Soon afterward, the Chinese resumed their civil war. Though the United States had come to the aid of Chiang Kai-shek, by late 1948 the Guomindang were thoroughly defeated by the Communists under the leadership of Mao Zedong. Chiang and many of his followers fled to Taiwan, and the remnants of his army scattered in panic.

On October 1, 1949, Mao Zedong addressed the citizens of Beijing from the terrace of the Gate of Heavenly Peace, one of the entrances to the Forbidden City, the traditional residence of China's rulers since the Mongolian Yuan Dynasty. He proclaimed the birth of the People's Republic of China and formally declared his position as its leader. Referring to the previous century of heavy-handed European presence, he stated, "The Chinese people will never again be enslaved," and told the immense audience that the time had now come when China would rule its own land; indeed, the time had come for its influence to rise and its rule to spread throughout the East.

In late 1949, upon the arrival of the Communist army in Dartsedo, a Tibetan town on the traditional border between Tibet and China's Sichuan province, the Guamindang leader Liu Wenhui immediately surrendered all the territories under his jurisdiction. Soon after the Communists gained control of the city, Liu's son was shot. Liu's properties were confiscated, and he was assigned a figurehead position on a Communist committee.

On November 24, 1950, the Chinese government announced that the "Tibetan Autonomous Region Government in Xikang" had been created. This region, formally known as Dartsedo Autonomous Prefecture, was comprised of twenty-two districts, including Karze, Nyarong, Trango, Derge, Tawo, and Lithang.

After consolidating their power in the early 1950s, the leaders of the new China instituted the "Five-Year Plan" of 1953–57. Wishing to rapidly advance the development of heavy industry, they dramatically increased the production of items such as planes, ships, trucks, steel, and heavy machinery. During those years, 56 percent of national investment was allocated to the importation and production of such interests.

Meanwhile, partly due to Chinese reliance on Soviet aid, agricultural production fell sharply. In the aftermath of two successively poor harvests in 1953–54, the importance of agriculture as both a means to finance industrialization through exports and to provide nourishment for China's dramatically increasing population became apparent.

Deng Xiaoping, who as chief political commissar of the South-West Military Region had been one of the major leaders to organize the invasion of Tibet, now strove to convince Mao Zedong that the accelerated communalization of the "minority regions" was a means to quickly install Communist-trained cadres in those areas. Deng argued that increased agricultural production under the commune system would help right the increasing imbalance toward industry in China's economy.

Although the more moderate Prime Minister Zhou Enlai and Chairman Liu Shaoqi advocated a more gradual shift towards communalization, known as "Peaceful Methods and the Gentle Path," Mao followed Deng's advice and quickly implemented the policy of "Peaceful Methods and the Militant Path," which allowed no other option for those regions that Mao chose as the locations for the first experimental communes. Kham was one of those regions, and the first major step in setting up the new social system there was a concentrated attempt to disarm the populace. At the same time, Tibetans like Ama Adhe, who refused to cooperate with the new policies, were captured, detained, tortured, and imprisoned. Tensions between the Tibetan people and the Chinese occupiers increased dramatically throughout all the regions of Tibet. In March 1959, the Dalai Lama left Tibet for India, where he has remained in exile ever since.

The ongoing stress of steel production during the Five Year Plan and the ensuing Great Leap Forward left agriculture neglected in most of rural China. In 1959, a clash of ideologies resulted in a schism in relations between China and the Soviet Union. The Soviet Union cut off its grain shipments, and China faced the first year of a three-year famine that resulted in the death of millions from starvation.

The Chinese government saw the newly communalized Tibetan agricultural system as an answer to the problem of feeding the Chinese populace. Tibet's harvests were increased by sowing multiple crops, and the yield was immediately requisitioned for use by the People's Liberation Army or for shipment to the Chinese heartland. Tibetans themselves were reduced to foraging for wild plants, worms, insects, and refuse from Chinese compounds. Throughout Tibet, the basic commodities of meat, butter, and vegetables were not available. In the famine years of 1959 to 1962, tens of thousands of Tibetans perished.

Between 1962 and 1966, the situation slowly began to improve, principally due to the modifying influences of Liu Shaoqi, Chairman of the People's Republic of China, and, to a lesser extent, Deng Xiaoping, the Communist Party's secretary general. A few years earlier Deng had played a very different role as one of the strongest advocates of the socialist reforms that had led to total social upheaval in

Kham and the destruction of many of Tibet's most esteemed monasteries during that period.

In 1960, Liu Shaoqi was one of the most distinguished members
of the Communist Party, second only to Mao in authority. Then,
Mao stepped down as Chairman of the Republic, accepting Liu as his
successor. Liu approached the country's deteriorating economy with
new and effective economic policies: allotting private plots of land to
peasants, a partial return to agricultural free-market exchange for city
dwellers, and a raise in pay for the working class. The resulting success of the policies caused his rapid gain in popularity among the
people and created increasing distrust and fear in Mao's mind.

By 1966, Mao Zedong, believing that his authority was being
undermined by the rise of "capitalist roaders," appealed to the youth
of China to throw aside all due process and social norms to destroy
his opponents. Liu Shaoqi and Deng Xiaoping were among the
countless individuals who faced the purges of the new reform, known
as the Cultural Revolution.

The Cultural Revolution was carried out under the direction of the
so-called Gang of Four, which included Jiang Qing, Mao's third wife.
Jiang Qing oversaw the actions of the Red Guard, which was comprised
of Chinese youth who were catapulted into positions of authority.
Under their direction, China's social structure was overturned.
Scientists, educators, writers, artists, actors, anyone who had had contact with the West, old enemies, and those who simply disagreed with
the actions of the Red Guard were in danger of imprisonment or death.
Confessions extracted through torture were the order of the day. The
result was that fourteen years after the establishment of the People's
Republic of China, class warfare still raged in the streets.

By August 1966, the anarchy of the Cultural Revolution reached
Tibet. Established Chinese officials were forced to leave Lhasa.
Portraits of Mao were hung from the walls of every building and gate
in Lhasa, and the Red Guard set out to establish the total destruction
of Tibetan culture. They inaugurated their drive by attacking the
Jokhang shrine in Lhasa. Mobs poured into the shrine to deface statues, destroy priceless frescoes, and set fire to thousands of pages of

ancient scriptures. During the next ten years, untold thousands of Tibetans died brutal deaths, while much of the remaining Tibetan populace was subjected to degradation, humiliation, starvation, and extreme physical abuse. Before long, the Red Guard turned on itself and split into various warring factions.

The ideology of the Cultural Revolution called for the destruction of the "Four Olds." In Tibet, the Communists now strove to completely eradicate: Old Thoughts, any signs of Tibetan nationalism; Old Culture, the traditional Tibetan religion; Old Customs, whatever remnants still existed of the Tibetan social structure; and Old Practices, which meant any practices that were recognized as Tibetan, including speaking the Tibetan language.

Within two years after the fall of the Gang of Four and the death of Mao Zedong in 1976, Deng Xiaoping, who had emerged as the head of the military and the leader of the Party moderates, came into power in China. In 1978, he contacted Gyalo Thondup, one of the Dalai Lama's brothers, and informed him that he wanted to establish contact with the Dalai Lama. Deng invited Gyalo Thondup to visit Beijing to discuss the Tibetan situation. During several meetings, Deng admitted that many mistakes had been made in Tibet, and he expressed concern for the future. Deng told Gyalo Thondup that he felt the country would be best served by the Dalai Lama's return. He realized that twenty-eight years of Communist rule had not changed the defiance of the Tibetans, who still recognized the Dalai Lama as their only rightful leader. After the excesses of the Cultural Revolution, China saw a pressing need to concentrate efforts in building up its economy. The new leaders realized the necessity of convincing foreign powers that China's internal policies had undergone significant change. They also realized that the only hope of reunification with Taiwan existed in convincing its leaders that a new era of cooperation was under way in the motherland. Through compromise, Deng hoped to ease the situation in Tibet, where there were still scattered violent revolts by Tibetans. He and his associates set about to blame all excesses that had occurred in Tibet during the Communist occupation on the actions of the Gang of Four.

Unfortunately, these apparently encouraging overtures to the Dalai Lama and the Tibetan people were soon denounced by other leading members of the Communist Party in Beijing. Despite improvements in some areas of Tibetan life, underlying conditions for Tibetans living in Tibet remained grim. The conditions for the Dalai Lama's return never materialized. On January 1, 1979, the People's Republic of China was granted official recognition by the United States, and the issue of the Chinese occupation of Tibet soon became a Chinese "internal affair."

Although Chinese policies in both China and Tibet were greatly liberalized in the early 1980s, 1989 saw an intense crackdown against political protesters in Lhasa, paralleling the infamous crackdown against the Tienamen Square democracy protesters in Beijing that same year. Around the same time, the campaign for Tibetan independence picked up momentum outside of Tibet when the Dalai Lama was awarded the Nobel Peace Prize for his ongoing nonviolent campaign for Tibetan independence, and, when the first international human rights hearing regarding the Tibetan situation convened in April 1989 in Bonn, Germany.

Since that time, Tibet has gained increasing attention on the international political scene, as Chinese policies within Tibet itself ebb and flow from the more liberal to the more repressive and back again. Readers who wish to obtain current information on the situation in Tibet and/or want to contribute their efforts to the Tibetan cause should turn to the "Resources on Tibet" section at the end of this book.

GLOSSARY OF NAMES, PLACES, AND TERMS

KEY TIBETAN PROPER NAMES

Ahtra. Jughuma's wife; Adhe's sister-in-law.

Aso. Third son of Bochungma, Adhe's elder mother.

Bhumo. Adhe's sister, five years Adhe's senior.

Bochungma. Dorje Rapten's first wife; Adhe's elder mother.

Chale. Second son of Bochungma, Adhe's elder mother.

Chimi Wangyal. Adhe and Sangdhu's son.

Chomphel Gyamtso. A lama of the Nyingma sect of Tibetan Buddhism; root guru of Jughuma and Dorje Rapten.

Dalai Lama. Reincarnate lama who serves as the spiritual and temporal leader of Tibet. Belonging to the Gelugpa lineage of Tibetan Buddhism, the Dalai Lama is considered to be the manifestation of Chenrezig, the buddha of compassion. Tenzin Gyatso, the Fourteenth Dalai Lama, fled Tibet in 1959 and established the Tibetan Government-in-Exile in Dharamsala, India.

Dechen Wangmo Shivatsang. Adhe's childhood friend; daughter of Wangchuk Dorje and sister of Pema Wangmo Shivatsang.

Dolma Lhakyi. Adhe's oldest sister, also known as Sera Ma.

Dorje Rapten. Adhe's father, *trimpon* of Nyarong district.

Gyari Dorje Namgyal. Leader of the Gyaritsang clan during Adhe's childhood.

Gyari Nyima. Son of Gyari Dorje Namgyal; chief administrator of district during the early stages of the Communist occupation.

Gyaritsang family. Ruling clan in Nyarong district prior to the Communist occupation.

Jamyang Samphel Shivatsang. Highly respected chieftain in the Karze region; his son, Wangchuk Dorje, married into the Gyaritsang clan.

Jughuma. Adhe's older brother; he escapes to Nepal during the resistance in Kham.

Karmapa. Head of the Karma Kagyu lineage of Tibetan Buddhism.

Kharnang Kusho. The Tapontsangs' family lama.

Lhakyi. Jughuma and Ahtra's daughter.

Ngawang Kusho. Rinchen Samdup's older brother; sentenced to eighteen years of imprisonment and hard labor for his participation in the Khampa resistance.

Nyima. Adhe's younger brother.

Ochoe. Adhe's brother; compelled to serve on the Communist political committee in the early days of the occupation.

Paljor. Jughuma's assistant.

Panchen Lama. Reincarnate lama second only to the Dalai Lama in Tibet's spiritual and political hierarchy. While the Dalai Lama fled Tibet in 1959, the Tenth Panchen Lama remained inside the country and became deeply involved in Chinese intrigue. The Tenth Panchen Lama died in 1989, and his reincarnation has been in detention since 1995.

Pema Gyaltsen. Bhumo's husband; tried along with Adhe for his role as a resistance leader, and eventually executed.

Pema Wangchuk. Riga's husband; Adhe's brother-in-law.

Pema Wangmo Shivatsang. Adhe's childhood friend; daughter of Wangchuk Dorje and sister of Dechen Wangmo Shivatsang.

Phurba. Dolma Lhakyi's husband; he is eventually detained with Adhe at Mian Fen Chang and Wa Da Dui.

Riga. Sangdhu's elder sister; wife of Pema Wangchuk.

Rinchen Samdup. Relative of Adhe's by marriage; spent twenty-four years in detainment, ultimately with Adhe at Wa Da Dui.

Sampten Dolma. Sangdhu's mother; also known as Ma Sampten.

Sangdhu Pachen. Adhe's husband; dies from food poisoning early in the Communist occupation.

Sonam Dolma. Adhe's mother; Dorje Rapten's second wife.

Shivatsang family. Ruling clan in the Karze area; united with the Gyaritsang family through Wangchuk Dorje Shivatsang's marriage into the Gyaritsang clan.

Tapontsang family. Adhe's family; literally meaning "Commander of Horses."

Tashi Khando. Adhe and Sangdhu's daughter; raised by a nomadic woman, Tsola, in Adhe's absence.

Tsola. A nomadic woman and close childhood friend of Adhe's; raises Adhe's daughter Tashi Khando during Adhe's imprisonment.

KEY CHINESE PROPER NAMES

Chiang Kai-shek. Guomindang leader, defeated by Mao Zedong's Communists in 1949.

Deng Xiaoping. Communist Party secretary general during much of Mao's tenure.

Liu Shaoqi. Chairman of the People's Republic of China.

Liu Wenhui. Chinese warlord who controlled the Nyarong district prior to the Communist invasion.

Mao Zedong. Chairman of the Chinese Communist Party.

Tien Bao. Tibetan collaborator with the Chinese; originally known as Sangye Yeshi.

Wu Shizang. Commander of the Chinese Army division that first entered Karze.

Xi. Chinese prisoner who befriends Adhe at Gothang Gyalgo.

Zhou Enlai. Prime Minister of the People's Republic of China.

Zhu De. Commander in Chief of the People's Liberation Army.

PLACE NAMES

Amdo. Area of eastern Tibet that borders Kham.

Bathang. Region of Kham that neighbors Adhe's regions of Nyarong and Karze.

Bu na thang. Open plain on which a large battle between the Khampa fighters and the Chinese occured in 1956.

Chagla. Independent feudatory state in pre-invasion Kham. Known as the "Native Tibetan State of Chagla."

Chamdo. Administrative center southwest of Karze; site of early Chinese garrisons.

Dartsedo. Town on the traditional border between Kham and the Chinese region of Sichuan; eventually incorporated as the seat of the Dartsedo Autonomous Prefecture under Chinese governance.

Derge. Region to the west of Karze.

Dharamsala. Settlement in the northern Indian state of Himachal Pradesh; home to the Dalai Lama's Tibetan Government-in-Exile and a large Tibetan refugee community

Dram. Exit point from Tibet from which Adhe and Jughuma enter Nepal.

Drapchi. Large prison complex outside of Lhasa.

Drepung. One of Tibet's three major monasteries. The others are Ganden and Sera. All were destroyed within Tibet and have now been reestablished in exile in India.

Dza Chu. Major river running through Adhe's village of Lhobasha and on to Nyarong.

Ganden. One of Tibet's three largest monasteries.

Gholo Tho. Region in which Wa Da Dui Labor Camp is located

Gothang Gyalgo. Labor camp at which Adhe is detained between 1960 and 1963.

Gutsa. Major prison complex outside of Lhasa.

Jokhang. Central temple complex in Lhasa that houses what may be the oldest statue of Shakyamuni Buddha in Tibet. Every Tibetan attempts to make a pilgrimage there at least once in a lifetime.

Karze. District headquarters in Adhe's immediate region. Also referred to as Karze Autonomous Prefecture, Karze District, Karze Region. At least two monasteries that Adhe discusses share the region's name: Karze Day-tshal monastery and Karze monastery.

Kathmandu. Capital of Nepal, where Adhe and Jughuma initially arrived after fleeing Tibet.

Kawalori Massif. Group of mountain peaks visible from Adhe's childhood home in Nyarong region.

Kham. Region in eastern Tibet where the majority of Adhe's story takes place; center of the Tibetan resistance to the Chinese invasion throughout the 1950s.

Lhamo Lhatso. Sacred lake east of Lhasa; site of the vision that indicated where the fourteenth incarnation of the Dalai Lama would be found.

Lhasa. Capital of Tibet; the political, spiritual, and cultural center of the Tibetan cultural world.

Lhobasha. Village in Karze where Adhe moves in late childhood and lives until her arrest in 1958.

Lithang. Region to the southwest of Karze.

Markham. Town south of Lithang.

Minyak Ra-nga gang. One of the five subdistricts, or *qus,* under the Dartsedo administration; region adjacent to Lithang.

Mount Kailash. Sacred mountain located in Western Tibet; one of the primary pilgrimage sites for Tibetan Buddhists.

Nyagchuka. Area on the border between Lithang and Minyak Ra-nga gang.

Namgyal monastery. His Holiness the Dalai Lama's monastery, now located in exile in Dharamsala.

Norbulinka. His Holiness the Dalai Lama's summer palace in Lhasa.

Nu Fan Dui. Women's unit of Xingduqiao Labor Camp in Minyak Ra-nga gang; Adhe is transferred there in 1966.

Nyagto. Northern area of Nyarong district ruled by the Gyaritsang family prior to the invasion; Adhe's childhood village is located in this area.

Nyarong. Adhe's native region; the family leaves it to move to Karze to escape the fallout of a bitter feud within the ruling Gyaritsang family.

Potala Palace. The Dalai Lama's primary residence in Lhasa.

Qen Yu Gai Zo. "Thought Correction Center" within the Xingduqiao prison; Adhe is transferred there in 1968.

Ramoche. Major shrine in Lhasa that houses the Jowo Mikyoe Dorje statue of the Buddha; along with the Jokhang, this is one of the most important pilgrimage sites for Tibetans.

Sangyip. One of the three major prison complexes near Lhasa, along with Drapchi and Gutsa.

Sera. One of Tibet's three largest monasteries, located outside of Lhasa.

Sergyi Drongri Mukpo (Abode of the Golden Yak). Sacred mountain located in the region of Setha; the mountain served as the site of a major battle between the Chinese and the Khampa guerrillas in 1957.

Sha Jera. Sacred mountain located in Minyak Ra-nga gang; the site of a miraculous event in 1975, when a huge green lotus grew in the middle of a lake at the mountain's base, giving Tibetans in the area a sign of hope.

Shigatze. Tibet's second largest city, located to the west of Lhasa; Adhe and Jughuma pass through the city on their journey to India via Nepal.

Shimacha Labor Camp. Located in Minyak Ra-nga gang, Adhe is detained at this work camp from 1963 to 1966 with the other survivors of Gothang Gyalgo.

Swayambunath. Located on the northwestern outskirts of Kathmandu, Swayambunath is one of the largest and most sacred Buddhist *stupas* (reliquaries) in the world. It is also one of the centers of the Tibetan exile community in Nepal; Adhe stops here on her way to Dharamsala.

Tashilunpo. The Panchen Lama's monastery, located in the city of Shigatse.

Tawo. Region on the eastern border of Kham; one of the five regions that comprised the Dartsedo Autonomous Prefecture.

U-Tsang. Central Tibetan province in which the city of Lhasa is located.

Wa Da Dui. Labor camp within the Xingduqiao prison complex; along with her relatives Rinchen Samdup and Phurba, Adhe is employed here in a deforestation campaign from 1975 to 1979.

Xikang. Town in China's Sichuan province from which the Chinese governed Adhe's region of eastern Tibet; also the endpoint of the Xikang–Lhasa highway constructed during the early years of the Chinese occupation.

Xingduqiao. Large prison complex in Minyak Ra-nga gang, which includes the individual labor camps of Shimacha, Nu Fan Dui, Xaya Dui, Wa Da Dui, Mian Fen Chang, and Qen Yu Gai Zo. Adhe served time in many of these.

GENERAL TERMS

Unless otherwise noted, glossary terms are phonetically rendered Tibetan terms.

ama. Mother.

Amdowa. Person from the region of Amdo.

bodhisattva. A Sanskrit word meaning a highly developed spiritual being who is committed to attaining enlightenment in order to help other sentient beings.

chagtsel. Religious prostrations—a movement in which the hands are pressed together and raised above the head, moved down to the throat, then to the chest. The prostrator then kneels on the ground and may stretch out full length. Prostrations are often done in groups of three.

cham. Monastic dances performed during calendrical ceremonies; they often involve richly colored costumes and masks.

chang. Homebrewed barley beer enjoyed by Tibetans.

Chenrezig. Known as Avalokiteshvara in Sanskrit, Chenrezig is the bodhisattva of compassion and the patron deity of Tibet. The Dalai Lama is considered to be the human incarnation of this deity.

chorten. A religious reliquary that can range from very small to quite large in size. Chortens are often found on mountain trails, as well as within religious shrines.

chuba. Traditional wraparound Tibetan dress, worn by both men and women.

Cultural Revolution. Social and political upheaval instituted throughout China by the Gang of Four and carried out by the Red Guard between 1966 and 1977. During this time, much of Tibetan culture was irreparably destroyed.

dayan. Big silver coins issued by the Chinese.

Democratic Reforms. Reforms under which Tibetan lands and properties were communalized, beginning in 1956.

Dharma. Truth.

Dolma. Known as Tara in Sanskrit, Tara is a female Buddha or bodhisattva who is known to protect those who seek refuge in her.

dri. Female yak.

drogpa. Tibetan nomad.

droma. Root vegetable.

drong. Wild yak.

Dugkar. Fierce female deity who holds a white umbrella and appears on the gigantic thanka unfurled at the Karze monastery's yearly festivals.

dzo. Crossbreed between a yak and a cow.

dzong. Fort or district headquarters.

Eightfold Path. The means of attaining enlightenment according to Buddhism.

Gang of Four. Group of extreme leftist Chinese leaders, led by Mao Zedong's wife, Jiang Qing; this group orchestrated the Cultural Revolution.

Gelug sect. The newest of the four sects of Tibetan Buddhism, and the one to which the Dalai Lama belongs.

Gesar epic. Traditional Tibetan epic passed down in oral form between generations; it tells the story of Gesar, an early warrior king of Tibet.

geshe. Highest degree attainable within the Tibetan monastic educational system.

Gong An Ju. Chinese term referring to the police force deployed throughout Tibet.

Great Leap Forward. Rapid advance in heavy industry instituted by Mao in the late 1950s.

Guomindang. Nationalist rulers of China led by Chiang Kai-shek; they were defeated by the Communists in late 1949 and fled to Taiwan.

gyama. Measure of weight.

Gya mi. Tibetan term for the Chinese.

hurtson chenpo. Diligent workers; Tibetan term used by the Chinese Communists to refer to those Tibetans who supported their policies.

Jampelyang. Known as Manjushri in Sanskrit, Jampelyang is the bodhisattva of wisdom.

Jowo Mikyoe Dorje, Jowo Shakyamuni. Large statues of the Buddha housed respectively in the Ramoche and Jokhang shrines in Lhasa; these life-size statues represent the Buddha at the ages of eight and twelve. It is believed that these are the two remaining of four original statues of the Buddha that were made in India during his lifetime and had received his personal blessing. Both were damaged by the Chinese, but they were later found in a Chinese trash heap and returned to their original location in Lhasa.

Kagyu sect. One of the four sects of Tibetan Buddhism; headed by the Karmapa, the Kagyu lineage is known for its emphasis on meditation rather than intellectual study.

Kalachakra initiation. One of the highest tantric initiations within Tibetan Buddhism; the Dalai Lama bestows it periodically in different locations.

kalsang. A particular kind of flower popular in Kham.

kashag. The cabinet of ministers within the Tibetan Government-in-Exile.

Kham. The eastern part of historical Tibet. Kham is traditionally considered to be one of three major divisions of Tibet; the other two regions are U-Tsang and Amdo.

Khampa. An individual from Kham.

khatag. Ceremonial white scarf presented as an offering to lamas or to family and friends on special occasions.

kora. Circumambulation around a religious shrine or chorten.

lhamo. Tibetan folk opera, performed in villages and at monasteries during special festivals.

Long March. Six-thousand-mile trek across China undertaken by several columns of the Communist Army during 1934–1936 as they fled Guomindang troops; the March passed through areas of Kham.

Losar. The Tibetan New Year; based on a lunar calendar, Losar usually occurs around the month of February, and is the occasion for great celebrations throughout the Tibetan world.

lungta. Literally "wind horse," this word is used to refer to prayer flags strung between buildings and on mountain passes to release prayers into the world.

ma. Mother.

Mahakala. Sanskrit term for a fierce deity popular within the Tibetan pantheon.

mandala. A Sanskrit term meaning a celestial palace of a Buddha.

mani. The short form of OM MANI PADME HUM, this term is used to refer to anything with this prayer inscribed on it; i.e., stones (mani walls) or prayer wheels (mani wheels).

mantze. Chinese word meaning "wild barbarians"; used by the Chinese soldiers to refer to the local Tibetans.

Metog Yul. Literally "Land of Flowers"; a nickname for Adhe's childhood region of Nyarong.

Mimang Tsongdu. Literally "People's Assembly"; a group that agitated for rebellion in central Tibet in reaction to the first Tibetan famine in the late 1950s.

Monlam Chenmo. Great prayer festival held in Lhasa yearly.

mudra. A Sanskrit term denoting hand postures used in religious ceremonies; also sacred symbols.

niu gui she sheng. Chinese term meaning "cow demons and snake spirits," used to refer to Tibetans who did not comply with Chinese demands.

Nyingma sect. The oldest of the four sects of Tibetan Buddhism.

OM MANI PADME HUM. Often translated as "Hail to the Jewel in the Lotus," this is the mantra of Chenrezig, the bodhisattva of compassion.

Padmasambhava. Also known as Guru Rinpoche, Padmasambhava was the Indian saint credited with bringing Buddhism from India to Tibet in the seventh century.

People's Liberation Army (PLA). The military wing of the Chinese Communist Party.

pon. District commissioners within the traditional Tibetan system.

puja. Offering ritual—a word used commonly in Hindu contexts and within Tibetan communities now residing in South Asia.

Red Book. Book of proverbs and sayings attributed to Mao Zedong; required reading for all prisoners during the Cultural Revolution.

ridag choekhor. Literally "deer dharma wheel," this Tibetan Buddhist symbol consists of the eight-pointed wheel of dharma flanked with a deer on either side, and is often found adorning monastery rooftops.

rinpoche. High lama.

samsara. Sanskrit word for the beginningless cycle of death and rebirth which is of the nature of suffering.

Sangye. Tibetan word for "Buddha."

shi lei fen zi. Chinese term meaning "black hat"; applied to a particularly unruly group of Tibetan prisoners, including Adhe Tapontsang.

Sichuan Army. The division of the People's Liberation Army that eventually invaded Kham.

thamzing. Struggle sessions conducted within Tibetan communities by the People's Liberation Army and the Gong An Ju police.

thanka. Religious painting.

Three Jewels. The central components of Buddhist faith: the Buddha, the Dharma, and the Sangha (community of believers).

trimpon. Judge, or counsel of the law; position held by Adhe's father, Dorje Rapten.

tru-zo. Part of the local marriage ceremony that Adhe goes through.

tsampa. Roasted barley flour; this serves as the staple food of most Tibetans.

tulku. Incarnate lama.

yuan. Chinese paper currency.

Zi stones. Rare patterned stones popular in Tibet.

BIBLIOGRAPHY

Ackerly, John. "The Long March: A Report Prepared by the International Campaign for Tibet." Washington, DC: International Campaign for Tibet, 1991.

Andrutsang, Gompo Tashi. *Four Rivers, Six Ranges: A True Account of Khampa Resistance in Tibet.* Dharamsala, India: Dept. of Information and International Relations, 1973.

Avedon, John. *In Exile from the Land of the Snows.* New York: Random House, 1986.

Barnett, Robert and Shirin Akiner, eds. *Resistance and Reform in Tibet.* London: Hearst, 1994.

Bruger, Bill. *China: Liberation and Transformation, 1942 1962.* London: Croom Helm Ltd. 1981.

Cheng, Nien. *Massacre In Beijing: China's Struggle for Democracy.* New York: Time Books, 1989.

Chesneaux, Jean. *China: The People's Republic, 1949–1976.* New York: Random House, 1979.

Dalai Lama, the Fourteenth. *My Land and My People.* New York: McGraw Hill, 1962.

Ginsburgs, George, and Michael Mathos. *Communist China and Tibet.* The Hague: Martinus Nijhoff, 1974.

Goldstein, Melvin. *A History of Modern Tibet.* Berkeley: University of California Press, 1989.

International Commission of Jurists. *The Question of Tibet and the Rule of Law.* Geneva, 1959.

Kapp, Robert. *Szechuan and the Chinese Republic, 1911–1938.* New Haven: Yale University Press, 1973.

Moraes, Frank. *The Revolt in Tibet.* New Delhi: Sterling Publishers, 1966.

Norbu, Jamyang. *Warriors of Tibet.* London: Wisdom Publications, 1986. First published as *Horseman in the Snow*, by the Dept. of Information and International Relations, Dharamsala, 1979.

Norbu, Jamyang. *Illusion and Reality.* Dharamsala: TYC Books, 1989.

Patterson, George. *Tibet in Revolt.* London: Faber and Faber, 1960.

Richardson, H.E. *Tibet and Its History.* London: Oxford University Press, 1972.

Select Work of Tibetan Historical Sources, Vol. 3: The 18th Army Receives the Mission to March into Tibet. Lhasa: Tibet People's Publishing House,1985.

Select Work of Tibetan Historical Sources, Vol. 4. Lhasa: Tibet People's Publishing House, 1985.

Shakabpa, Tsepon W. D. *Tibet: A Political History.* New Haven: Yale University Press, 1967.

Smith, Warren, ed. *China's Tibet: Chinese Press Articles and Policy Statements on Tibet 1950–1959.* Cambridge, Massachusetts: Cultural Survival, 1989.

Smith, Warren. "The Nationalities Policy of the Chinese Communist Party and the Socialist Transformation of Tibet." *Resistance and Reform in Tibet.* Robert Barnett and Shirin Akiner, eds. London: Hearst, 1991.

Sperling, Eliot. "The Chinese Venture in K'am 1904–1911, and the Role of Chao Erh-feng." *The Tibet Journal.* Dharamsala:1979.

Teichmann, Eric. *Travels of a British Consular Officer in Eastern Tibet.* Cambridge: The University at Cambridge Press, 1922.

Thomas, Lowell. *The Silent War in Tibet.* Garden City, New York: Doubleday, 1959.

Tibet: 1950–67. Hong Kong: Union Research Institute, 1968.

Tibet Under Chinese Communist Rule. Dharamsala: Dept. of Information and International Relations, 1976.

Tsondru, Yeshe. *The Essence of Nectar.* Dharamsala: Library of Tibetan Works and Archives, 1979.

Wangchuk, Tseten. "Major Political Events of Tibet 1949–1990." Unpublished paper, 1992.

Yin, John. *Government of Socialist China.* Lanham ,Maryland: University of America Press, 1984.

RESOURCES ON TIBET

There are many organizations around the world that work in as many ways to aid the Tibetan people, both inside and outside of Tibet. A comprehensive listing here would be impossible, but we hope that inspired readers will contact one of the organizations listed below to receive more detailed information on current issues and campaigns within the larger Tibetan political cause and cultural world.

THE OFFICE OF TIBET (New York)
241 East 32nd Street
New York, NY 10016
phone: (212) 213-5010; fax: (212) 779-9245
e-mail: otny@igc.apc.org
http://www.magicoftibet.com/tibetny

THE INTERNATIONAL CAMPAIGN FOR TIBET
1825 K Street, NW
Suite 520
Washington, DC 20006
phone: (202) 785-1515
fax: (202) 785-4343
e-mail: ict@igc.apc.org
http://www.peacenet.org/ict

STUDENTS FOR A FREE TIBET
241 East 32nd Street
New York, NY 10016
phone: (212) 481-3569
e-mail: ustcsft@igc.apc.org
http://www.tibet.org/SFT/

THE TIBETAN RIGHTS CAMPAIGN
Seattle, WA
phone: (206) 547-1015; fax: (206) 547-3758
e-mail: trcseattle@igc.apc.org
http://members.aol.com/Tibetan/

THE MILAREPA FUND
443 Tehama St. 3rd Floor
San Francisco, CA 94103
phone: (415) 278-9889
fax: (415) 278-9876
e-mail: milarepa@milarepa.org
http://www.milarepa.org

WISDOM PUBLICATIONS, a not-for-profit publisher, is dedicated to making available authentic Buddhist works for the benefit of all. We publish translations of the sutras and tantras, commentaries and teachings of past and contemporary Buddhist masters, and original works by the world's leading Buddhist scholars. We publish our titles with the appreciation of Buddhism as a living philosophy and with the special commitment to preserve and transmit important works from all the major Buddhist traditions. If you would like more information or a copy of our mail-order catalog, please contact us at:

199 Elm Street, Somerville, Massachusetts 02144 USA
Tel. (617) 776-7416 • Fax (617) 776-7841
http://www.wisdompubs.org

THE WISDOM TRUST
As a not-for-profit publisher, Wisdom Publications is dedicated to the publication of fine Dharma books for the benefit of all sentient beings and is dependent upon the kindness and generosity of sponsors in order to do so. If you would like to make a donation to Wisdom or receive more information on book sponsorship, please contact our office.

Wisdom Publications is a non-profit, charitable 501(c)(3) organization and a part of the Foundation for the Preservation of the Mahayana Tradition (FPMT).